Tempest-Tost

Tempest-Tost

Race, Immigration, and the Dilemmas of Diversity

Peter I. Rose

New York   Oxford
OXFORD UNIVERSITY PRESS
1997

Oxford University Press

Oxford   New York
Athens   Auckland   Bangkok   Bogotá   Bombay
Buenos Aires   Calcutta   Cape Town   Dar es Salaam
Delhi   Florence   Hong Kong   Istanbul   Karachi
Kuala Lumpur   Madras   Madrid   Melbourne
Mexico City   Nairobi   Paris   Singapore
Taipei   Tokyo   Toronto

and associated companies in
Berlin   Ibadan

Copyright © 1997 by Peter I. Rose

Published by Oxford University Press, Inc.,
198 Madison Avenue, New York, New York 10016

Oxford is a registered trademark of Oxford University Press

Library of Congress Cataloging-in Publication Data
Rose, Peter Isaac, 1933–
Tempest-tost : race, immigration, and the dilemmas
of diversity / Peter I. Rose
p.   cm.
ISBN 0-19-510070-0
1. Refugees—United States. 2. Minorities—United States.
3. Pluralism (Social sciences)—United States. 4. United States—
Emigration and immigration. 5. United States—Ethnic relations.
6. United States—Race relations. I. Title.
E184.A1R719   1997   305.8'00973—DC20   96–38822

Permission to reprint lyrics from the following is gratefully acknowledged:
"The House I Live In." Words by Lewis Allan. Music by Earl Robinson.
Copyright © 1942 by Lewis Allan and Earl Robinson (Renewed).
All rights administered by Chappell & Co.
All Rights Reserved. Used by Permission.

1 3 5 7 9 8 6 4 2
Printed in the United States of America
on acid-free paper

For my grandsons, Jordy and Robert

The legacy of slavery will perpetually haunt the imagination of Americans like a painful dream.

ALEXIS DE TOCQUEVILLE

Send these, the homeless, tempest-tost, to me.

EMMA LAZARUS

Of every hue and caste am I, of every rank and religion. I resist anything better than my own diversity.

WALT WHITMAN

Contents

Preface

I

For the past forty years the study of minority groups in America and their relations with one another and with those in the majority has been the main subject of my research, teaching, and writing. Late in the 1970s I began to explore a related field: international migration and, especially, the flight and resettlement of refugees. This newer involvement was manifest in a variety of activities: field research in government offices, refugee camps, resettlement centers, and inner-city neighborhoods in this country and abroad; the development of new courses at Smith College and a seminar at Harvard on immigration and refugee policy; a series of journal articles and commentaries and an edited volume, *Working with Refugees*, published in 1985. That small book summarized the proceedings of a symposium to which I had brought together a cross-section of those I had interviewed in various parts of the world. Included in that meeting, the first of several, were the former Deputy High Commissioner for Refugees at the UN and several other international civil servants, U.S. diplomats and government officials, heads of voluntary agencies, case managers, resettlement officers, and foot soldiers engaged in rescue, relief, and resettlement, representatives of refugee communities, and several scholars who long had been engaged in the topic that, in a formal way, was still relatively new to me.

The fact is that my own personal involvement in the subject long predates my professional one. It goes back to two critical periods in my life: the first was nearly six decades ago when escapees from Nazi-dominated Germany began arriving at our door in Syracuse, New York. Alma and Max Einstein and Walter Leipzig lived with us a long time; so did Michael Weingott, evacuated from London after the Blitz. Many others came, too, though they stayed only long enough for my mother and father to help them find new homes. I grew up hearing stories of persecution, escape, long periods of anxious waiting, then hurried movement, often into the unknown. From my foster aunts and uncles—and one foster brother—and from other refugees who were friends of my parents and, later, from teachers of mine, I came to have some understanding of what it meant to be to be stigmatized, labeled, then forced to flee; the importance of others in the process of providing protection, aid, comfort, and welcome to the uprooted. I learned something of the dependency of the dispossessed, too.

In 1953 I met my future wife, Hedy Cohen, a young Dutch emigrée who, from the ages of six to ten, was hidden in an Amsterdam cellar by a courageous friend. Hedy and her sister, Betsy, the only survivors in their family, had come to America in 1947 with the help of the American Jewish Joint Distribution Committee. (Years later the JDC would be one of a number of refugee agencies I would be studying.)

I have no doubt that, although it was secondhand and thus vicarious, the refugee experiences of those to whom I was closest helped shape my own *Weltanschauung*. Yet, despite my involvement in the study of race and ethnicity, and, more specifically, marginality and problems of insiders and outsiders, I never thought of studying or writing about refugees or refugee policy until 1979.

The exodus of "boat people" from Vietnam several years after the end of a war I had vehemently opposed, the horrors of the Cambodian genocide, and the call to assist those who straggled across the Thai border escaping from Pol Pot's maniacal cadres, turned my highly personalized empathy to active research into the meaning of exile, the particular experiences of Asian Americans—and, later, of others—and the more general matter of the making and implementing of America's immigration and refugee policies.

Through interviews with numerous resettled refugees and those who assisted them and many others in their host societies, I also became more and more aware of the tensions their presence created or exacerbated with those already here. Time and again my attention would be drawn to the fact that, as many newcomers undergo the transition from the status of "refugee" to that of "immigrant" and then "ethnic," they recapitulated a familiar story. They became new minorities only to find themselves resented by the old ones. Observing and sometimes recording the competition between the groups, one of the clearly continuing challenges of life in this multicultural society, was to lead me back to the broader subject of intergroup relations in the United States as will become evident in the pages that follow.

II

My thoughts on refugees, race, and the dilemmas of diversity are most fully developed in the title essay of this book and in "From Pariahs to Paragons" and "Of Every Hue and Caste," three of the five that appear in Part I of *Tempest-Tost*. Two other essays address the changing nature of commitment in the realm of civil rights and an essay on the politics of resentment, a case study zeroing in on encounters between some African Americans and some Jewish Americans.

Part II is a potpourri of interviews with some of the key players in the overall drama such as then-Prince, now-King Sihanouk of Cambodia and eight of the most powerful leaders of the principal refugee agencies, commentaries on the sociology of exile, the politics of rescue, the psychology of altruism, and the results of a survey of the opinions and recommendations of a cross-section of those in "the business of caring." Some of the chapters in this section, such as "Caretakers, Gatekeepers, Guides, and Go-Betweens" and "Long Night's Journey," are straightforward reportage based on experiences in field offices, refugee camps, and neighborhoods of newcomers; others—for example, "In Whom They Trust"—are more analytical. While many are specifically related to various aspects of responses to the victims of the war in Indochina, all are attempts to convey to the reader a sense of refugee work not only as a complex activity but as a fascinating case study in the professionalization of volunteerism.

Part III consists of a selection of reviews and review essays of books by some of those who also write about refugees and refugee policy, and on race and ethnicity, many of whose ideas have often helped to shape my own. There are also commentaries on recent writings about the African-American experience, immigration—especially from Europe and Asia— and on American Jews, members of a cohort still seen by some as the quintessential successful "model minority" and by others as successful-but-hardly-secure, classic "marginal men."

While the essays I have chosen to include in all three sections of the book vary somewhat in format, style, and length, they have two common if somewhat contradictory features. Each is informed by a sociological perspective, reflecting my training and still-preferred orientation; but none can be said to be entirely "value-free." These are personal analyses, accounts, assessments, and critiques.

Readers will quickly note that many of the views, reviews, and interviews seem to be period pieces. They are. Save for making minor emendations, all previously published papers included here appear very much as they did originally. Although tempted to do so, I refrained from going back and adding corroborating evidence to support a point made a year, a decade, or even longer ago, for that matter, amending what I now realize was a somewhat oversimplified explanation for a complex social relationship.

III

If greater awareness of the "tempest-tost" and attempts to address their needs are the guiding spirit of this book, there is also a subtext. It has to do with the continuing matter of interminority conflict mentioned above.

The connection is made clear when one reflects on a response made in 1970 by the French observor Raymond Aron to a question about how he saw the progress of American integration. "You [meaning America] did very well in assimilating national minorities," he said, "but not nearly as well with racial minorities." The latter, he said, is "a permanently un-integrated fringe, consisting chiefly of blacks and Puerto Ricans."

At the time Aron offered his remarks the major concern was resolving America's classic and persisting dilemma, what Winthrop Jordan simply labeled "White Over Black." Little was being said about non-black non-whites.

With the unanticipated influx of many new immigrants and refugees from Asia and Latin America in recent years, society has become more heterogeneous, more multicultural. Yet, with rare exceptions, many of those long on the bottom (Aron's "un-integrated fringe" which others call "the ghetto underclass") are still on the bottom. As a society, we continue to do quite well in assimilating or at least accommodating and then acculturating "national minorities," now including many Mexicans, Koreans, Vietnamese, Indians, and others Aron might have called "racial," too.

Even today, with the considerable backlash against immigration, especially in the key states of California, Texas, Florida, New York, New Jersey, and Illinois, few would gainsay that the considerable racial tension that exists in such places is not so much between whites and non-whites as between blacks and non-blacks. In spite of considerable advances in civil rights legislation and policies, Americans with roots in Africa (which includes most Puerto Ricans) remain the odd ones out. Most are understandably outraged and many are increasingly embittered at their continued relegation to subordinate status by the discriminatory attitudes and practices—both subtle and direct. Many have also come to resent the new Americans, whether immigrants and refugees, who are perceived as interlopers, unfair competitors in the factory and farm and on the campus, and, in many cases, members of a new class of oppressors. Moreover, because—like Jews—the new immigrants often remain distinctive, the poorest as well as the seemingly privileged are ready scapegoats and targets for the release of pent-up frustrations not only of traditional nativists but also of those other very old Americans who, on this issue, have sometimes become their unlikely bedfellows.

The tempests that stir passion and fear, altruism and resentment are not only off-shore.

P.I.R.

Stanford, California
April 1996

Acknowledgments

S HELDON MEYER of Oxford University Press encouraged me to put this volume together, and waited patiently while I kept being distracted by other commitments; now, with production editor Joellyn Ausanka, he will finally see it through the stages of publication. It is the third book we have done together. I take this opportunity to thank him for his warm friendship, his consummate editorial skills, and his incredible equanimity. And I thank Joellyn, too.

I am also grateful to the original publishers of my views, inteviews, and reviews who gave permission to me and to Oxford to allow them to be reprinted here.

Much of the field work discussed in Part II could not have been done without the support for travel and research I received from the Weatherhead Foundation, the Exxon Educational Foundation, and the Rockefeller Foundation. The Rockefeller Foundation was helpful in another way. I was privileged to be a Resident Scholar at the Foundation's Study Center at the Villa Serbelloni in Bellagio, Italy, for five wonderful weeks in the mid-1980s. While I was there the title essay was first drafted and the seed for what became this book was germinated. The assistance of each of the previously named foundations, Smith College's fund for faculty research, and Harvard University's Kennedy School (where I spent a year as a visiting scholar and edited many of my field notes), is gratefully acknowledged.

The yeomans' (yeopersons') services David van der Wal and Stella Wong provided in helping to prepare the manuscript for final editing is also most appreciated.

The pulling together of all the pieces and the fine-tuning of the manuscript was done at Stanford University, where I have been a Visiting Scholar at the Hoover Institution. I came here in early February 1996, to complete the essay "In Whom They Trust," to finish the editing of the rest of the manuscript, and to dig into the Institution's superb archives in preparation for my next one, a study of the early days of the International Rescue Committee. The Institution's library is a treasure trove of papers of many refugees and refugee workers, including Herbert Hoover himself (who led relief efforts in Belgium and in the Crimea after World War I) and of the several major agencies in which I am interested.

After several months of working here and interacting with my new colleagues, I, an old-fashioned liberal, must report that I sometimes feel like a refugee tossed onto a strange shore myself. But, like the best of the refugee workers I met in dusty camps in Southeast Asia and Central Europe and in resettlement centers throughout this country, my hosts provided me with solace and comfort and asked for nothing in return—not even a change in my political orientation! Now that I am about to leave, I want to thank everyone affiliated with the Hoover Institution as well as those in Stanford's Department of History and the members of the Seminar in Comparative Ethnic Studies for the kind hospitality and support extended to me.

VIEWS

From Pariahs to Paragons

C HINESE exchange students. Japanese salesmen. Korean greengrocers. Recent immigrants from Hong Kong and the Philippines. Thousands upon thousands of refugees from Vietnam, Laos, and Cambodia. Asians are everywhere. Some say they are taking over but, more often than not, the comment is made only in mock horror.

Although "takeover" is a far from accurate image, in recent years the United States has become a magnet for any number of people from Asia. While many have come to study or to ply their wares, many more have come to stay. Between 1970 and 1980 the number of persons who specified Asian or Pacific Island ancestry to United States census takers increased 146 percent, making it the fastest growing segment of the population. Since 1980 the pace has accelerated considerably, augmented by several large waves of Indochinese refugees. In the years ahead, the "Asian cohort" will continue to grow because of high birth rates and because of the effect of chain migration (i.e., once citizenship is attained by an individual, his relatives move up on the priority list for entrance into the U.S., and many do come).

A hundred years ago the prospect of such a "yellow tide" would have—indeed had—evoked hysterical outcries against imminent inundation, urgent calls for measures to stay the flow, and ruthless attacks on those who were already here. Not today. While some still feel that too many immigrants—including Asian immigrants—are being allowed to enter the United States, concerns about threats to our way of life, when expressed, are far more apt to be directed against those crossing the Rio Grande than those crossing the Pacific.[1]

The images of those who used to be called "Orientals" (they prefer the term "Asian") have changed dramatically. No longer viewed as kowtowing inferiors—the sort of folks Ralph Waldo Emerson once suggested were only good for serving tea[2]—or as inscrutable heathens, Mongolian scabs,

*Originally published as "Asian Americans: From Pariahs to Paragons," in *Clamor at the Gates: The New American Immigration*, ed. Nathan Glazer (San Francisco, 1985), pp. 181–212.

or untrustworthy neighbors loyal only to their motherlands, they are now seen by many as members of "model minorities." In a remarkable inversion, old negative stereotypes have been replaced with positive new ones. "Conniving" has turned into "competitive"; "clannish" into "community-minded." Those who were once seen as inferior have been vested with the most ennobling qualities. The pariahs have become paragons, lauded for their ingenuity and industry and for embodying the truest fulfillment of the "American Dream." Ronald Reagan called them "our exemplars of hope and inspiration."

Such encomiums are reinforced today not only by an increasing appreciation for the carefully made products of the East—electronic gadgetry, photographic equipment, and compact cars—but by the economic success and widely reported accomplishments of Americans with names like Wang, Yamaguchi, Kim, and Tran. Moreover, in recent years there have been a number of glowing feature stories in the national press about the winning ways of recent arrivals, people like Chi Luu, the twenty-five-year-old boat person from Vietnam who graduated valedictorian from City College of New York and won a full scholarship for graduate study at MIT, and Linn Yann, the twelve-year-old Cambodian refugee who placed second in a regional spelling bee in Chattanooga, Tennessee (Linn Yann missed on that well-known English (?) word "enchilada").

Such accounts signal an important phenomenon. Already noteworthy in the fields of science, medicine, and the arts, Asians are increasingly found at the top of honor rolls, high on lists of academic prize-winners and scholarship recipients, and prominent in student rosters of elite universities. They are also beginning to swell the ranks of law schools and to seek careers in politics—areas where, in the past, they were rarely to be found.

Jews of the East?

Often compared to Jews, many Asian Americans do seem to share certain values, modes of acculturation, and patterns of mobility with those once called "Orientals" themselves. The characteristics are familiar: a deep sense of ethnic identification and group loyalty; a high level of filial respect; a heavy emphasis on proper demeanor and on the seriousness of life; a firm belief in the importance of education; a tendency toward extrinsic assimilation (taking on the superficial trappings of dominant groups—speech, dress, musical tastes—while remaining socially separate); and an overriding attitude that one must advance as far as possible not just for oneself, but so that parents can enjoy the Chinese, Japanese, Korean, or Vietnamese equivalent of what in Yiddish is known as *nachas fun die Kinder*, "pleasure from the [accomplishments of] children."

Of course, there are un-Jewish Asian Americans (and un-Jewish Jews) who do not toe the mark, who reject traditional mores, who disobey their parents, who do not want to delay their gratifications. There are those who start work in restaurants, factories, and sweatshops and do not advance up the socioeconomic scale or simply drop out or join gangs. But most do stay the course. Demographic studies show that, along with Jews, Asians are the most upwardly mobile group in the country.[3] As an aggregate, they have caught up to and are even surpassing the Joneses and the Smiths, as well as the Cohens and the Levines.

William Petersen, the demographer most closely associated with the use of the "model minority" term,[4] indicates that their comparative rate of progress is remarkable. He points out that what the Chinese and Japanese had to endure might well have resulted in a pattern of poor education, low income, high crime rates, and unstable families. Instead, notes Petersen, "[they] broke through the barriers of prejudice and, by such key indices as education and income, surpassed the average levels of native-born whites."[5]

In a May 1982 issue of the *New York Times Magazine*, Robert Lindsey profiled a number of Asian American artists, architects, artisans, doctors of medicine, captains of industry, political leaders, and small businessmen. Citing census figures, Lindsey showed that those placed under the rubric "Asian Americans" (members of twenty different "nationality groups") had the highest median family income when compared to all others.[6] Lindsey's account failed to reflect two things: (1) that Asians are disproportionately located in urban areas where wages are higher, and (2) that more members of their families are apt to contribute to the household coffers and are more likely to stay at home for a longer time to do so than those in most other groups. However, such mitigating factors notwithstanding, Asian advancement has a very solid basis. At the time of Lindsey's report, 75 percent of the Asians were high school graduates compared to 69 percent of the whites, 51 percent of the blacks, and 43 percent of the Hispanics. Even controlling for the age distribution of the different populations, those differences are not statistical flukes—they have to do with cultural norms, modes of adaptation, and the manner of seizing available opportunities.

Many others have tried to explain why so many Asians are moving up the socioeconomic ladder with such alacrity. Those who know Asian ethnic groups most intimately—that is, from the inside—often use the same terms to describe them. But they are cautious. While agreeing that many have attained much and that many more will be successful in the future, in certain quarters there is a gnawing disquietude about the image of widespread Asian-American *embourgeoisement*. Close observers have begun to note that both pressures on the young from within the communities and expectations from others outside it are beginning to take their toll. Asian youths, finding themselves on rather narrow career trajectories (requiring a major in math or science, for example) that demand high grades and unstinting effort, and that emphasize the necessity to stay the course or lose face, are feeling the effects of psychological and emotional strain. Reports from college health services indicate that more and more Asian American students are seeking counseling and that their concerns are usually related to the fear of failure.

Public awareness of this phenomenon increased in the spring of 1984 when a series of stories appeared in national news magazines, including the campus edition of *Newsweek*. The lead *Newsweek* article, "Asian-Americans: The Drive to Excel,"[7] provoked several sharp responses from those who felt that the cumulative effect of such reporting was to create a new stereotype, that of neurotic overachiever.

Almost as if anticipating such reactions, the authors of one such piece quoted several social scientists who tried to provide some perspective—or perhaps in a spirit of egalitarianism, to imply that after all Asian Americans are just like everybody else. Russell Endo of the University of Colorado is reported to have said, "In all groups you'll find that some people are sort of in-between. That's true of Asians as well."[8] It is. But such a statement does not address what individuals do with their endowments, especially in those situations where there is a high priority placed upon success and youngsters are socialized to excel by parents and teachers—and expected to do so by everybody else.[9]

A year before the flap over the *Newsweek* piece, Diane Mei Lin Mark and Ginger Chih had already expressed the concerns and ambivalence of many Asian Americans. In their social history, they claimed that one of the primary obstacles to the improvement of conditions for Chinese Americans is the persistence of the "myth of the model minority."[10] They objected not to the praise extended to those who succeed in overcoming great hardships, but to new "exaggerated" characterizations which are seen as being nearly as unrealistic as the old ones. They and others worry about a seeming insensitivity to the inclination of many Asians to mask their real feelings and put on their best face(s) for the outside world. In addition, they point to the persistence of stratification within various communities and continuing problems of health care, housing, employment, and social welfare, especially for new immigrants and refugees, the elderly, and the growing teenage population.

Of late there *has* been a tendency to gloss over the inglorious history of American anti-Asian attitudes and practices, to look at demographic attributes rather than underlying psychodynamic phenomena, and to ignore the continuing division between those now moving into and through the system and those still left behind. The latter is reflected in what some call the "occupational dichotomy" between managers and workers.[11] It is evident in other places, too. Nonetheless, what is most striking is that Mark and Chih and many other Asian Americans writing about the dilemmas of being both a part of and apart from this society return again and again to the model minority motif themselves. They often end their assessments by conceding that, after all, the "myth" is still more real than not.

The sociologist Harry Kitano has said, "the judgment of Japanese Americans as the 'model American minority' is made from a strictly majority point of view. Japanese Americans are good because they conform—they don't make waves—they work hard and are quiet and docile."[12] Kitano suggests, "Ideally, members of the ethnic community should share in any evaluation of the efficacy of their adjustment." In view of this obligation, he concludes:

> In spite of different definitions of what constitutes success and of philosophical discussions that may show Japanese as short of being an "ideal" group, they have achieved a niche in American society. They have been effective in social organization, in socialization, in controlling deviant behavior, and in coming to grips with "success" in American terms. When we look back on the past prejudice and discrimination faced by Japanese we find that even their most optimistic dreams have been surpassed.[13]

Insider Kitano's words echo what outsider Petersen has written: "As extraordinary as have been the positive achievements, the lack of a countervailing negative record is even more astounding."[14] Anyone with a modicum of exposure to American history can understand why this seems so remarkable. No people who came to these shores of their own volition ever suffered as much discrimination or ostracism as did those from China and Japan. None were made to feel less welcome.

Sojourners and Settlers

Things might have been different had this vast land become an oriental outpost rather than an occidental one. The historian George Stewart once whimsically speculated on such a prospect. Suppose, he suggested, instead of the English, Dutch, and other Northern Europeans crossing the Atlantic and settling the eastern seaboard of North America, the approach had been from the West Asians, rather than the Europeans, who would have disembarked and established political control and, for all intents and purposes, cultural hegemony over the new land. In Stewart's imaginary account, a Chinese navigator named Ko Lum Bo stumbles upon the pristine continent, and it is *his* descendants who populate it:

> The Chinese colonists introduced their own well-established ways of life. They continued to speak Chinese and to practice their own religion. Being accustomed to eat rice, they still ate it, as far as possible. Vast areas of the country were terraced and irrigated as rice paddies. The colonists continued to use their comfortable flowing garments, and pagodas dotted the landscape.[15]

Stewart's scenario is a wonderful piece of social science fiction. Had it been real, this country would have been very different indeed.

The Chinese

Of course some of "Ko Lum Bo's" descendants, like many of Christoforo Columbus's, did come here. The Chinese came as early as the 1850s. They labored in gold fields, helped to build the railroads, and sacrificed much to enjoy what others were to take for granted. They were ostracized, demeaned, and rejected; they were also the first group to have their further entry restricted by specific laws. The Chinese Exclusion Act of 1882 was a landmark decision, a crucial watershed in American immigration history and in race relations. It set a precedent for the restrictive legislation of the 1920s that was to prevent many other "undesirables" (mainly from Eastern and Southern Europe) from entering the country.

It is reasonable to assume that, whatever the political motivations for keeping them out, to many unworldly, xenophobic, and competitive Americans, the Chinese "coolies" they saw in the mining areas and seaport towns were a strange lot. They wore pigtails (required at home to indicate their submission to Manchu rule, and since they saw themselves as sojourners, kept to allow their reentry into China). They wore garments that were comical to Western eyes. They ate foods that others abhorred. They spoke an incomprehensible gibberish. But they were also perceived as a threat to other laborers because they were willing to work long hours for low wages. When times were good this was a boon to the railroad magnates and mine owners, many of whom had contracted for them, but it was rarely seen as an advantage for "native" workers, many of whom were, of course, immigrants themselves. (No less a labor leader than the AF of L's Samuel Gompers was a major spokesman against admitting Chinese—or any "Orientals"—to trade unions.)[16] And whenever there was a labor surplus, they were not wanted by anyone.

Convenient scapegoats upon whom to vent all sorts of frustrations, the Chinese became frequent targets for abuse by the rednecks of their day. Anti-Chinese rallies were staged in many western towns—often ending in violent outbursts, the forced "deportation" of the unwanted aliens, and in some instances, such as the Rock Creek Massacre in Wyoming in 1885, brutal killing.

Few raised their voices to protest and the Chinese, numbering approximately 100,000 at the time, deserted the sparsely populated areas. They concentrated—and insulated—themselves more and more in the cities and their own enclaves within them, in what came to be known as "Chinatowns."

Like the Jewish ghettoes of the Middle Ages, the boundaries of San Francisco's Chinatown, and some others, were demarcated by authorities. Those who cooperated by residing within the area, sometimes called a "safe zone," were left to their own devices. In their still predominantly male immigrant societies, life could not center about the nuclear family, but organizations based on kinship and clan membership abounded; so did district associations that were made up of people from the same home area.[17]

The Chinatowns began to develop an infrastructure of their own and a class structure as well: workers at the bottom; small businessmen (restaurateurs, grocers, launderers) in the middle; merchants and professionals at the top. The rank order remains, although the players have shifted. The original workers, many of them the "old bachelors," are now replaced by new immigrants from Hong Kong and mainland China and some Chinese refugees from Southeast Asia. Members of the new bottom rung are sometimes referred to by the "ABCs" (American-born Chinese) as "FOBs" (those "fresh off the boat").

Chinatowns still exist. To outsiders they are exotic enclaves in the city, places to wander early in the evening to peer into odd curio shops and to buy condiments from tiny groceries before "eating Chinese." For the residents, they are enclaves of solace and security, cultural expression, and bustling activity. They can also be places of considerable exploitation. Above and behind the neon dragons and the main rooms of the enamel-red restaurants are tight-packed living quarters and kitchens, factories, and sweatshops where many of those newcomers from Taiwan, Hong Kong, the People's Republic of China, and Indochina often find their first jobs in America.

For some there still exists the problem of what Norbert Wiley once called "the ethnic mobility trap," but it is less pronounced today than in the past. Wiley's idea is that many community members move up through the local stratification systems, sometimes with considerable swiftness, by providing specialized and ethnically specific services.[18] They have far more difficulty moving into mainstream occupations. In recent years more and more young Chinese Americans have begun to spring the trap of confinement mainly by following occupational paths that are viewed with favor both within their community and in the wider society. Even they, however, maintain links to their urban bases. New relationships with non-Chinese college friends, business associates, or professional colleagues often tend to be and to remain, in the lingo of the sociologists, "secondary." Close, comfortable. and intimate relationships are far more likely to be with fellow "ethnics." (This pattern, as shall be seen, is also characteristic of some other Asian Americans, like Koreans, but is far less pronounced among the Japanese.)

In their thoughtful ethnography, *Longtime, Californ'*, Victor and Brett Nee give vivid evidence of the vitality of San Francisco's Chinatown and the people within it. Often quoting at length from those they interviewed, they indicate the character of a community at once riven with political factions and generational rivalries and interdependent, linked by common bonds and organizational structures.[19]

Melford Weiss, author of another ethnography, *Valley City: A Chinese Community in America*, suggested that people in such ethnic neighborhoods may be understood best by putting them into three categories: "traditionalist, modernist, and activist."[20]

The traditionalists are those who adhere to the values and traditions of Chinese society, who try to maintain the "sojourners" lifestyle. It is they, more than any of the others, who embody the old stereotypes of the "mandarin" and the "coolie." The modernists, by contrast, are in many ways mainstreamers who try to adhere to the ways of life of those in the dominant culture. Some might call them "CASPs" (Chinese Anglo-Saxon Protestants) but in many cases their dissident and politically active children, caught up in the ethnic revival, want to be considered Asian and are wont to refer to their parents as "Bananas," yellow on the outside, white in the middle.

Today there are nearly 900,000 Chinese citizens and aliens residing in the United States: 40 percent of them in California, 18 percent in New York, 7 percent in Hawaii, and between 3.5 and 1.4 percent of the rest located in Illinois, Texas, Massachusetts, New Jersey, Washington, Maryland, Florida, Pennsylvania, and Michigan.[21]

Japanese Americans and Korean Americans are also concentrated in many of these same states and, as fellow Asians, are often compared to the Chinese. Examination of their experiences suggests that the tripartite model obtains for them as well, although certain modifications have to be made. For example, neither group is apt to have as high a proportion of "traditionalists" or "activists" in its overall ranks as the Chinese. Most are modernists and many are mainstreamers as well.

The Japanese

Leaving home, even as temporary sojourners was not a common activity for many Asians, at least not until fairly recently. For many it was long forbidden. Nowhere were restrictions tighter than in Japan where, from the sixteenth to the nineteenth centuries, no Japanese were allowed to venture beyond their island home or to have contact with the West.

It wasn't until the period of the Meiji Restoration, which began in 1868, that things began to change. Under the directives of Emperor Meiji's administrators, trade relations began to develop between the Japanese and the *gaijin*, the foreigners the Japanese had long been taught to fear. With the desire to become part of the wider world, to learn as much as possible about the ways of others, especially about their technologies, many contacts were established through official channels and business enterprises. Laborers and students were encouraged to go abroad to work and to study.

In the early years of the opening to the West, a number of Japanese urban dwellers were recruited for plantation work in Hawaii. This did not prove very satisfying either to the workers or their employers. Later, rural Japanese were enticed by the opportunity to improve their financial lots by becoming "guestworkers" of sorts. Like the several million Southern Italians who came to this country during the period (for both groups, the peak decade was 1900–1910), many Japanese saw themselves as "birds of passage"—individuals whose single-minded goal was to make their fortunes and return home. Some did, but many ended up staying in Hawaii, where they eventually became the dominant "minority," or on the American mainland.

The Chinese, who began coming to the United States in the early days of national expansion, found pick and shovel work in the hinterlands and frontier towns of the West. When the economy began to falter, they were driven back into the seaboard cities. The Japanese, most of whom arrived on the West Coast after the Chinese Exclusion Act of 1882, settled in those same cities. Many worked in small businesses and in service occupations. Others began moving out of town to obtain employment as agricultural laborers, tenant farmers, and contract gardeners.

From the early days the Japanese favored self-employment and family assistance. In a relatively short time, the Japanese proved to be "too good" at what they did and were resented not only for their foreignness but also for their skill and industry. Moreover, because they appeared to be more eager and able than the Chinese to become a part of the American system and to assimilate, at least in terms of outward signs of acculturation and economic achievement, they were viewed as threats not only to those in the working class but also to people who themselves were upwardly mobile. The prejudice against the Japanese was pervasive: discrimination was widespread, and restrictions slowed but never quite stifled their own advancement.[22]

The fate of the Japanese Americans is well known. First, the *Issei* (first generation) had to face the enmity of their American hosts when they settled in the United States; second, their community was hardly permitted to grow in the early decades of this century owing to a "gentleman's agreement" between President Theodore Roosevelt and the Japanese government; third, and perhaps most painful of all, they and their children (the *Nisei*) were humiliated and imprisoned in the wake of the attack on Pearl Harbor in 1941 when pervasive anti-Japanese sentiment was turned into legalized harassment. Under FDR's Executive Order 9066, 110,00 Japanese, both American citizens and aliens, were removed from the West Coast and interned in "relocation" centers scattered across the country, some as far away as Arkansas. The majority remained in the internment camps until the Supreme Court, ruling in a case brought against the government by American-born Mitsuye Endo that the federal government had clearly violated the rights of loyal Americans by incarcerating them without proper cause, ordered their release.[23] In the years that followed, numerous other suits were to be brought to correct the injustices and offer reparations for psychic and financial damage.

Those who have studied the episode most closely point to the loyalty to the United States that persisted despite the persecution. While still in the camps, *Nisei* men were offered the option of volunteering for military service. A large number did so. Many of them saw combat in the European theater. Their units suffered some of the highest casualty rates of the entire war and they received an unusually high number of commendations for their valor under fire.

One of those wounded in battle was Senator Daniel Inouye of Hawaii. He, along with Senator Spark Matsunaga, also of Hawaii, and Congressmen Mineta and Matsui and former Senator Hayakawa, all of California, are often cited as examples of the extent to which Japanese Americans were able to survive their ordeal, reenter society, continue their quest for full participation, and gain entry into the highest circles of power.

While there are cases of those who never fully recovered from the camp experiences and of others who are still fighting for recognition as members of a separate and unique ethnic group, there are very few Japanese Americans languishing in poverty in the ghettoes that are home to many other American minorities (including some of the other Asians).

In 1971 William Petersen reported that "of all types of crime delinquency, dependency, or social disorganization about which we have usable statistics, the incidence is lower for Japanese than for any other ethnic group in the American population, including native whites of native parents.[24] That remarkable record remains to this day. Moreover, the evidence of considerable socioeconomic achievement, especially of the *Nisei* and *Sansei* (third generation), are to be found in various studies of the differential mobility of American ethnic groups.[25] Numerous examples of their increasing integration in the wider society are also available.

If, as Milton Gordon has suggested, intermarriage is the last stage in the process of assimilation, then the Japanese Americans are much farther down the road than any other non-whites, including most other Asians.[26] As long as a decade ago, Akemi Kikumura and Harry Kitano found that interracial dating and marriage between Japanese Americans and Anglo-Americans had risen to 50 percent in Fresno, Los Angeles, and San Francisco.[27] How the offspring will define themselves remains to be seen. However, one clue is offered in that some, now entering universities, rather than trying to "pass," seem to be taking pride in their dual heritage and showing particular interest in things Japanese.

Today, in addition to some 800,000 Japanese Americans, there are many Japanese businessmen in the United States, later-day birds of passage who come to feather their nests or those of the companies they represent. The increasing ubiquity of Japanese enterprises has led to a resurgence of animosity in certain sectors such as among the hard-pressed automobile workers in the early 1980s. Frustrations were manifest in calls for protectionist policies and attacks on those thought to be Japanese. An extreme case in point was the vicious murder in Detroit of Vincent Chin—a young man who turned out to be Chinese.

Such rash vengefulness, while quite rare today, is an old story. To a small number of Americans, "A Jap is [still] a Jap"—even if he is really Chinese or Korean. Many remain insensitive to the dual character of individuals who are Asian but also genuinely American. Few *Sansei* and fewer *Yonsei* (fourth generation) know Japanese; most Koreans here are not Buddhists but Christians.

The Koreans

To be sure, there are some historical parallels to be drawn when one looks at the experiences of the major Asian groups that immigrated to the United States. The Koreans, like the Chinese and the Japanese, also began their North American experience in Hawaii and on the mainland as contract laborers.

What is ironic is that in 1882, the very year the Chinese Exclusion Act was passed, the United States became the first Western nation to sign a treaty of friendship and trade with Korea. In the years that followed, some 7,500 Korean workers were contracted by Hawaiian planters to replace the Chinese "coolies" barred from the country by the Exclusion Act. Some of the Koreans returned home; many remained on the islands. And, according to several reports, 2,000 males and twelve females settled in California, for the first Korean community here.[28] Successive waves were to even out and then reverse the gender balance, establishing a pattern of surplus females that was to dominate well into the 1960s.

Between 1907 and 1924 most female Korean immigrants were, like their Japanese counterparts, "picture brides," sent for through marriage brokers by older males. Ultimately this led to the anomalous situation described by Vincent Parrillo as follows: "As a result of the age disparity between the picture brides and the older males, many second-generation Korean Americans spent a good portion of their formative years with non-English speaking, widowed mothers who had had limited formal schooling."[29]

Barred by the Immigration Act of 1924, few Koreans came to the United States between the mid-1920s and mid-1940s. After Japan's defeat in World War II and her forced surrender of occupied lands, including Korea, American armed forces stationed there fraternized with the local population and an increasing number of marriages occurred between GIs and Korean women. The outbreak of war on the Korean peninsula in the early summer of 1950 led to the massive expansion of United States involvement—and to many more liaisons and marriages. With the passage of the Refugee Relief Act of 1953, a steady stream of Koreans began entering the United States. Some were classified as refugees; most were "war brides."

A further surge occurred after the passage of the Immigration Act of

1965, which not only abolished the old country-quota system but liberalized the rules regarding family reunions, accounting for the influx of hundreds of thousands of Asian petitioners. The 1970 Census indicated that there were over 200,000 Koreans in this country. By 1980 there were nearly twice that number.

Perhaps because of the disproportionate number of Korean women married to American servicemen, a higher percentage of Koreans have obtained United States citizenship than immigrants from other Asian countries. And, owing to the strong political and military ties between the United States and South Korea, and the active religious participation of many Koreans in Protestant churches here, there is considerable support for the conservative policies of the current administration within the Korean American community.

Today, as Illsoo Kim and others who have conducted extensive community studies indicate, Korean Americans are employed in a wide variety of occupations; far fewer are laborers than in the old days.[30] Excluding housewives, most of the recent immigrants were white-collar workers in Korea and seek similar employment here. Many try to enter the technical, managerial, or professional ranks upon their arrival in the United States A number have been successful. Others, especially those with language problems or a lack of outside contacts, have gone into small businesses, many into the selling of fresh produce in large cities such as Los Angeles, Chicago, and New York.

It was recently estimated that 900 of the 1,600 greengrocers in New York City were from Korea.[31] In many ways their preponderance in this single industry recapitulates an old immigrant pattern of carving out economic niches, establishing networks, and providing work for family members and other compatriots. (One recent study found that 80 percent of Koreans employed in Los Angeles County worked in Korean-owned firms.) One thinks of Jews in the needle trades; Italian barbers, cobblers, and construction workers; Chinese hand launderers; Greek restaurateurs; Irish barmen and policemen; and Japanese gardeners. Like the others, Korean greengrocers have sometimes been resented by those who see them as chauvinistic and clannish. They have also been seen as threats to established entrepreneurs and as exploiters of other minorities (many of the Koreans' customers are blacks and Hispanics), and, on occasion, the Koreans have run afoul of the law for using business practices inappropriate in this country but perfectly reasonable in their homeland. But by and large they have proven to be hardworking, law-abiding, upwardly mobile, and quite sensitive to maintaining good race relations in the marginal areas where many of their shops are located.

The children of the greengrocers are unlikely to stay in such small enterprises. Rather, they want to join the ranks of those who were able to go more directly into the professions or are now active in the expanding export-import business and in large-scale manufacturing. From all indications, they are on a fast track toward such goals and are using the educational system as a principal stepping stone. Koreans, most of them still foreign born, now represent a substantial percentage of the ever-increasing Asian population in American colleges and universities and graduate schools.

The Other Asians

Aside from the Chinese, Japanese, Korean, and Indochinese (the latter will be discussed further on)—who in large measure share a common racial origin and a common cultural background—there are two other major Asian immigrant groups in the United States. One is made up of the people of the Indian subcontinent (India, Pakistan, and Bangladesh). The other is Filipino, a category of people who share a common nationality but are of diverse racial and cultural background. To many with little knowledge of either group, Indians and Filipinos are sometimes lumped together in the public mind. In fact, they are very different. The popular misconception may stem in part from the disproportionate number of foreign doctors and nurses in America who come from India and the Philippines.

The Filipinos have had a long history of residence in the United States, dating back to 1763 in New Orleans.[32] Most of the Indians, however, are quite recent arrivals. Until 1980, the Census Bureau did not account for the latter group at all.

Many of those who are of Indian origin came (or their parents came) directly from India. Others migrated from East Africa, the West Indies, Guyana, and the United Kingdom, where their families had lived, sometimes for several years, sometimes for several generations.

Some Indians came to the United States early in this century when Punjabi farm laborers settled in California. Many of them left for Canada owing to economic problems and crop failures. A few stayed to form the first Indian settlements on the West Coast. It wasn't until 1946 that Indians were allowed to own land, become citizens, or request permission to bring in relatives. All this changed when the new, liberalizing immigration bill was passed in 1965 and large numbers of Indians applied for and received permission to enter the United States.

While they represent a wide spectrum of ethnic, religious, and linguistic groups, the recently arrived Indians constitute a uniquely high-status group of immigrants. According to several reliable sources, 93 percent were already either "professional/technical workers" or "spouses and children of professional/technical workers" when they arrived.[33] Americans welcomed many to serve in American hospitals, while the exodus of doctors has contributed to the brain-drain from South Asia and, to some extent, from Britain and many former British colonies.

For many years, Indian spokesmen claimed that their official racial designation should be "Caucasian," but the federal judiciary thought other-

wise and repeatedly denied their claims to "whiteness." Maxine Fisher, one
of the few scholars who has studied Indians in the United States, reports
that, even though they were finally permitted to be classified as they had
long wished, some members of the community would now like to change
back to a non-Caucasian designation. She cites "the economic benefits to
be derived from being considered non-white" as a possible reason for
this.[34] Despite the objections of many, there have been efforts to use the
ethnic category "Asian American" to lump such diverse parties as Indians
and Filipinos under the broad rubric "Asian" in order to achieve the benefits of affirmative action programs.

In his book, *Asian Americans and Pacific Islanders: Is There Such An Ethnic
Group?*, Filipino Lemuel Ignacio argues for a common label under which
simultaneously to counteract and emulate the successful movement of
black power brokers. He wants his people to get their fair share of government funding. Because the Filipinos are, like the Indians, a highly diverse,
multilingual, multiethnic community, they need to come together as well
as to ally themselves with others who share their fate if not their history.[35]
Fisher rightly states that "Ignacio is fully cognizant that Asian American
ethnicity—and even Filipino ethnicity to a lesser extent—are artifacts
which he has helped create."[36]

Ignacio sought to present a powerful third bloc of Asians that could
make its own claims for affirmative action in competition with blacks and
Hispanics. In many ways, he was to prove successful. The ostensible rationale for linking these seemingly odd bedfellows was that all had originally come to the United States from the East; all had suffered from some
form of racial discrimination; and, the sentiments of some East Indians
notwithstanding, none were white, nor were they black. They were a separate entity seeking their own "group rights."

That such a move should originate with a spokesman for the Filipino-
American community is not surprising. Of all the large, transpacific groups
that have come here, the Filipinos or "Pinoys," as they often call themselves,[37] are at once among the most marginal and most American of Asian
subgroups. Their marginality *and* their Americanness are a result of their
peculiar history, which has led them to be seen—and in many ways to be—
"the Puerto Ricans of the Pacific."

The Philippine archipelago, situated in a strategic area of the South Pacific, was long a colony of Spain. Spanish *conquistadores*, *padres*, and *patrones*
had left a profound imprint on the culture, religion, and character of the
predominantly Malayan population by the time they were finally expelled
at the end of the nineteenth century. In 1902, after but several years of independence, American forces overthrew the nationalists, took possession
of the inlands, and reorganized the society, its laws and, in many ways, its
mores. After several hundred years of Spanish rule and "nearly fifty years
of Hollywood," the people of the Philippines were subjected to yet another
takeover when the Japanese conquered the country in the early days of

World War II. American forces were eventually to avenge the Fall of Bataan in 1944 and, two years later, the Philippines became one of the many "independent–dependencies" of the victorious allies. It still retains strategic ties to the United States.

To some, the modern Philippines is a case study in cultural amalgamation. To others it is a highly volatile, fragmented, and schizophrenic society that, again like Puerto Rico, isn't quite sure what it is and what it wants to be. No better example of its own confusion is to be found than the practice of many Filipino patriots who, citing the absence of an "F" sound in the their native Tagalog tongue, eschew its use in the spelling of their official names. Often they say they are "Pilipinos," not "Filipinos." Ironically, the same local boosters still render gender distinctions in the traditional Spanish manner ("Pilipino" and "Pilipina") while requiring everyone in the nation to learn English! To confound matters further, once they get to the United States, they are sometimes classified as Hispanics, owing to the preponderance of Spanish surnames.[38]

Since the first "Manilamen" jumped ship in Louisiana in the eighteenth century, Filipinos have been difficult to pigeonhole. They never quite fit into standard schemes and frequently follow their own paths toward integration. They are from the East but are not "Orientals" (save for the many "overseas Chinese" in their midst). They often have Spanish names and some Filipinos of the old, partially European elite can still speak Spanish. Nonetheless, Filipinos are not really Hispanic. They have long been a community unto themselves and yet, since the early days of their immigration to the United States, they have had very high rates of intermarriage with non-Asian Americans.

It used to be said that many Filipinos came because "they lusted after white women."[39] There were other, less disagreeable stereotypes: Filipinos were viewed as diligent workers, ambitious students, and aggressive fighters for their rights.

By 1930 there were over 45,000 Filipinos on the American mainland (and many more in Hawaii), most of them in agricultural work.[40] After the war increasing numbers came to the United States. Many were veterans who had fought in American uniform or served as mess stewards aboard United States ships. Many others were the brides of American servicemen. A decade later they were to be followed by large numbers of countrymen and women who benefited from the changes in immigration legislation (some 250,000 entered the US. between 1966 and 1976). That last group, to which more are being added every year, includes a large percentage of highly educated physicians, lawyers, engineers, and teachers who have come for reasons quite similar to those of their forebears and most other immigrants: to benefit from job opportunities in the new society.

Filipinos still rank lowest among those now labeled "Asian American" in terms of their overall socioeconomic status, but their situation is changing especially for the most recent arrivals. Most Filipino immigrants now come knowing English, already trained in needed skills, and sharing many of the same attitudes about making it in America that other Asians possess. In the years ahead, this enigmatic minority may be more closely identified with Asians (as Lemuel Ignacio would like) than with the other Spanish-surnamed Americans with whom they are often grouped.

The most recent census indicated that, counted according to the country of last permanent residence, some 740,000 Chinese (from China and Hong Kong), 411,000 Japanese, 431,000 Filipinos, 276,000 Koreans, 182,000 Indians, and 134,000 Vietnamese are living in the United States.[41] Not included in these figures are large numbers of American-born children and grandchildren of Asian immigrants, but estimates suggest that there were 895,000 members of the overall Chinese cohort in the country, 800,000 Japanese, 795,000 Filipinos, 377,000 Koreans, 312,000 Asian Indians, and 215,000 from Vietnam in 1980.[42] Since then the numbers of those in the last subset have increased considerably, augmented by the arrival of boat people and other Indochinese refugees, including many who had already experienced life as members of minority groups overseas.

The Newest Asian Americans

A third of all Asian Americans in the United States are Indochinese who have arrived in this country since 1965, a large percentage of those since the fall of Saigon in 1975. To date nearly 700,000 Indochinese have been screened, accepted for admission, and resettled in various parts of the United States. As of May 1, 1984, the heaviest concentrations were in the states of California (estimated to be 254,000), Texas (56,100), Washington (31,800), Illinois (24,600), New York (24,000), Pennsylvania (24,000), Minnesota (21,900), and Virginia (21,300).[43] Other states with anywhere from 16,600 to slightly more than 10,000 Indochinese refugees were Massachusetts, Louisiana, Florida, Colorado, Michigan, and Ohio.[44]

Those from the countries of Indochina—Vietnam, Laos, and Cambodia (Kampuchea)—while often treated as a single entity, are a mixed lot in political, ethnic, religious, and socioeconomic terms. There are former government officials and military personnel, individuals who worked for one of the many agencies of the United States government, "war brides," and Chinese minorities from all areas of Indochina. There are people from the major cities of Vietnam, Laos, and Cambodia; from the rural areas and from the highlands (including the Hmong, Hmien, and Laotung); "old" Khmer who had been part of Lon Nol's forces and "new" Khmer who fled Cambodia during Pol Pot's reign of terror after his downfall, when the country was occupied by Vietnamese forces.

Within groups separated by nationality and divided by ethnicity are French-educated cosmopolites, bourgeois provincials, and dirt-poor peasants; Roman Catholics, Buddhists, Taoists, Shamanists, and Animists.

There are gifted intellectuals, streetwise hustlers, and unworldly fisherfolk and farmers. There are whole families who managed somehow to escape together or to eventually bring in dispersed relatives. And there are single individuals who lost everything but their own lives crossing the "sea of heartbreak."[45]

Though the Indochinese are a varied lot, most of those who have come to the United States since 1975 have shared a common fate and now share a common status. Unlike most other Asians in the West, they are *political refugees* rather than *economic migrants*, a status ascribed to them because they left their homelands after suffering—or fearing—persecution. In other words, they were in a sense driven out rather than pulled away by the enticement of a better life on some distant shore.

Not only are the Indochinese different from other Asians who have set-tled—or resettled—in the country, they are different from other refugees. Unlike most of those who came to America prior to 1965 (Armenians, Jews fleeing Hitler, Czechs, Hungarians, even many of the Cubans who left af-ter Castro's revolution), those from Vietnam, Laos, and Cambodia have been almost completely dependent on direct governmental support or on programs funded primarily if not exclusively by federal departments.[46] This unique situation is related to American response to the defeat in Vietnam.

In April 1975 the United States military airlifted thousands of people out of Vietnam. At transit centers in the Philippines, on Guam, and at four bases in the United States, representatives of voluntary agencies with prior experience working with refugees were called in to facilitate processing and resettlement. Few thought that those who were being assisted would be harbingers of a massive exodus of people escaping from the newly estab-lished Democratic Republic of Vietnam. But they were. The thousands who followed bought or bribed their way on unreliable, overcrowded ves-sels that set out for the nearest landfall. These "boat people" hoped, even-tually, to be permitted to move on to the United States or, perhaps, to France.

Resettling the Refugees

The relatively small number of Vietnamese already in the United States could hardly have been expected to house, feed, and otherwise provide for their countrymen, and certainly not for those coming from Laos or Cambodia, traditionally rival states. Something had to be done—and fast. Moreover, the growing crisis was greatly aggravated by the reluctance of those in the countries of "first asylum" to allow boat people to land, fearing they would not move on but would stay there and drain the local econ-omies, becoming thorns in the sides of the bodies politic and potential fifth-columnists. These fears were expressed in all the countries of the area, but it was Malaysia—worried about inundation by the ethnic Chinese from Vietnam, who could upset the strategic balance between the politically dominant Malays and the economically powerful Chinese—that unintentionally provided the catalyst for a global response.

Americans and others around the world were horrified by satellite-relayed pictures of boats laden with refugees being pushed back to sea by members of the Malaysian armed forces and local militiamen. In a sort of delayed reaction, an international conference was called and an agreement was reached among Western nations and Japan: the refugees would be resettled in "third countries" in the West.

While Canada and Australia took in the largest percentage relative to the size of their populations, the United States accepted the largest number of Indochinese refugees by a factor of ten. Once again, "volags," or private voluntary agencies—the American Council of Nationalities Service, Church World Service, the Hebrew Immigrant Aid Society, the International Rescue Committee, the Lutheran Immigration and Refugee Service, the United States Catholic Conference, World Relief Refugee Service, and several smaller agencies—were called upon to use their expertise to assist the newcomers while the government provided funding and logistical support.

The problems that such an arrangement created were and remain complex and cumbersome, yet a remarkable feat was accomplished and close to three-quarters of a million Indochinese entered the United States to begin their lives anew.[47] Moreover, the relationship of the federal government to the voluntary agencies, a marriage of both convenience and necessity, was institutionalized within guidelines specified in the Refugee Act of 1980, the first comprehensive bill to deal with the plight of refugees as distinct from that of immigrants.

The bill called for the establishment of a coordinator (with the rank of ambassador) to oversee the foreign policy aspects of the refugee program within the Department of State and to work with those in the Immigration and Naturalization Service of the Department of Justice and the newly established Office of Refugee Resettlement (ORR) in the Department of Health and Human Services. ORR was to allocate funds through state welfare agencies and, sometimes, through direct grants to "service providers" who offered ESL (English-as-a-Second-Language) instruction, job training, and employment services. Private voluntary agencies involved in reception and placement were to be reimbursed for "core services" at a rate of $500 per capita. (This has recently been raised to $525 for Indochinese refugees.) Additional money was to be set aside to support a variety of "grass roots" mutual assistance associations. Such funding was to help the refugees to help themselves.

There were some highly successful programs; some that failed rather dramatically; and many that are still struggling to deal with the problems of initial resettlement, first contacts with the wider community, and acculturation. Nonetheless, one thing is quite clear: without the substantial financial assistance of the federal government the Indochinese would have had a much more difficult time once they arrived in America. And without the assurance that aid would be forthcoming, it is doubtful that many American communities would have been as receptive to the influx as they have proven to be—even against the predictions of many that there would be echoes of the cries of a hundred years ago of the "threat from the East."

The American Hosts

A Harris Poll conducted in May of 1975, immediately after the communist victory in Vietnam, indicated that only 36 percent of the American people thought Indochinese should be allowed to enter the United States. More than 50 percent favored keeping them out, and many seemed to agree with Congressman Burt Talcott (R-Ca.), who vehemently opposed their admission because "Damn it, we have too many Orientals." They came anyway. Not just a few, but hundreds of thousands. Yet, unlike most who came before, the newest Asian candidates for American citizenship were greeted with surprisingly little hostility. To be sure, there were instances of difficulties, some of them quite ugly. Nevertheless, considering that the Indochinese refugees constitute the largest non-white, non-Western, non-English-speaking group of people ever to enter the country at one time, and to arrive moreover during a period of economic turmoil, their reception has been quite remarkable. So, too, has their readjustment.

The reception was eased by governmental assurance that the Indochinese would not become financial burdens on American society. But even this cannot explain the unprecedented willingness on the part of thousands to serve as sponsors, guides, and go-betweens for those with whom they had no ethnic ties and did not know. The Indochinese were war victims, and this fact offers a most important clue to American response. As I have hypothesized elsewhere, the willingness to help or, at least, to minimize opposition to the Indochinese is directly connected to the sense of responsibility felt by many in the political establishment and many private citizens.[48]

A number of those who supported America's war effort in Southeast Asia argue that since "we" failed to stop the communists, allowed them to overrun the countries of Indochina, and forced many to flee for their lives, "we owe them something." Many who opposed the war believe that Americans destroyed the countries of Indochina and that it is our duty to provide those who suffered with protection and assistance. The entire situation represents a fascinating example of converging commitments from heretofore rather incompatible bedfellows, both now recognizing that there was a debt that needed to be paid.

It would be naive and wrong to say that all who supported the war and all who opposed it are now as one. Support means (and meant) many things; so does opposition. Many who actually fought in Vietnam are angry, especially draftees who reluctantly went to war and then came home only to be seen as embarrassing reminders of a debacle rather than as heroes of a glorious campaign. They believe that refugees get more favored treatment than they, that increasing benefits are given to those from Indochina while their own are being cut. Most of the bitterness has been contained but occasionally it breaks out in spontaneous acts of violence and, in rare instances, of calculated vigilanteeism. One recent episode occurred in western Massachusetts: a small group of disturbed and disgruntled veterans on a weekend pass from a Veterans' Administration hospital burned a Buddhist temple to indicate their displeasure with the present state of affairs. The nationwide response, especially from Vietnam veterans' groups, was a clear indication that many vehemently disavowed the vandalism. Not only did local branches of major veterans' organizations disclaim any support for such acts, but many offered to contribute money and manpower to help rebuild the religious edifice. (They also used the occasion to remind the nation that the thing that triggers such unfortunate outbursts is the failure to adequately deal with the plight of the veterans themselves—especially those suffering from the malady called "post-traumatic stress syndrome.")

In addition to the troubled veterans, there are two other sources of opposition to the presence of large numbers of Indochinese. Those who might be called "old nativists" and those who are appropriately labeled "neo-nativists." The former are quite familiar to students of North American immigration, those like Burt Talcott and Clare Boothe Luce, who see outsiders, especially those who are quite different from themselves, as unassimilable aliens who could potentially undermine the Anglo-American way of life. Those in the second category are not so well known. They are often members of non-white (and, usually, non-Asian) minority groups who have come to claim that scarce funds for welfare and job training are being squandered on foreigners while Americans like themselves are still being discriminated against and suffering in a depressed economy. They are concerned with what they see as the differential and favored treatment of the refugees and their publicly supported encroachment on their turf.

Voluntary agencies frequently place refugees in the least expensive areas of town. There they represent an alien force to many who least understand who they are and why they came. They are also convenient scapegoats for poor blacks and Hispanics. The fact that many landlords seem to prefer the Indochinese, who, they claim, are less apt to make trouble, exacerbates the potentially explosive situation. Sometimes the seething hostilities burst forth in racial conflict.

Crossing the Threshold

Still, the record overall is quite impressive. Even in the worst of the urban areas, the number of serious confrontations has been relatively few. Perhaps it is because "they don't make waves." Perhaps it is related to the fact that, to the authorities, they are "good" minorities rather than trouble-makers and therefore deserve more protection. Or perhaps it is because of the widespread publicity given to those who seem to be moving into the wider society with such determination and success.[49]

The rapid movement from barely peripheral involvement to extensive participation that has occurred has been quite exceptional, especially when we are reminded that the people under consideration here are those who were rather suddenly uprooted and dispossessed, who came from highly stratified societies with worldviews quite different from those of the West, and who had little preparation for what they were to find.

Not surprisingly, given the socioeconomic heterogeneity of the Indo-chinese who came, some have had an easier time of it than others. The "first wave" Vietnamese, many of whom are two-time refugees, having fled from the North to the South in the mid-1950s and then from the new communist state to the United States in the late 1970s, have had some de-cided advantages. These have included marketable skills, English language capability, a trove of cash, a number of American contacts made during the war, or a combination of these. Likewise, many of the ethnic Chinese have also fared better than many of the others. Some argue that, having always been "marginal men" who often lived in their own separate areas, spoke their own languages or dialects, and maintained their sense of ethnic iden-tity even while serving the economic and professional needs of others, the Chinese from Indochina are more adaptive than those who had been members of the majority groups of the nations of the region.

This is not to say that prior minority status is, *ipso facto*, a boon to adjust-ment in new situations. It depends very much on the placement of the mi-nority in the home society. Thus, while the ethnic Chinese were prospering as "middleman minorities" in Indochina, others were placed far lower in the social order and were often far less worldly. The 60,000 to 70,000 Hmong and members of other hill tribes from the Laotian high-lands now in the U.S. are good cases in point. Along with the Khmer from Cambodia, they have had a far more difficult time adjusting to their new environs.[50]

Between those advantaged because of their place in the status hierar-chies or because of their functional marginality, and those who are most culturally estranged, is the majority, the Vietnamese "boat people." The latter have been here only a few years, but they are already beginning to take on the characteristics of a truly American ethnic community replete with national and local leaders, political organizations, business associa-tions, blocs of solid citizens, and gangs of troubled youth.

Although most Vietnamese left on slow boats and languished for a time in the limbo of the refugee camps, once they boarded the jumbo-jets from transit centers in Bangkok, Kuala Lumpur, Hong Kong, or Manila, they were on a fast-moving treadmill. In twenty-four hours they moved 10,000 miles into the hurly-burly of life in the land of the Big PX. They haven't stopped. Encouraged by sponsors, mesmerized by TV, enticed by the desire to fit in, Vietnamese seem on the whole to be accelerating the pace of acculturation.

In the well-known pattern the first generation, the immigrants, remain in their enclaves living in the past and trying to maintain a semblance of old ways in the alien setting. The second generation, the infants they bring and their American-born children, become the bridges between the world of their fathers and the new society. While often eager to escape the confines of the ghetto and partake of the opportunities seeming to abound beyond it, they are often plagued with uncertainty and anxiety about who they really are. The grandchildren become the new Americans, some abandoning their heritages altogether. However, owing to their appearance if not their aspirations, Asians, including Southeast Asians, are rarely able to be fully assimilated or absorbed. They are now and will remain hyphenates. In this they are unlike many Europeans.

For many Vietnamese families, especially those ensconced in such places as Orange County and San Jose, California; in Versailles outside of New Orleans; or in Alexandria, Virginia, it all seems to be happening at once. The older people still "stay behind." Older children, while far from babes-in-arms, often go through a rapid course in resocialization, learning to assume new responsibilities and to walk the tightrope between the two worlds. Younger children, even some of those born in Indochina or in the camps in the ASEAN countries, take on the dress, manners, and—to the chagrin of their parents—many of the mores of the new society. Yet, even those in the last group (the "third generation") seem to maintain some sense of identity, though it is hardly one their relatives back home would comprehend. They are a new breed, Vietnamese Americans—or Vietnamericans.[51]

It is never easy to make such momentous adjustments or to create what Nathan Glazer once called "a new social form."[52] Ironically, given the strong support provided to the Indochinese, some predicted it would be *harder* for them than it was in the old days when widespread discrimination forced earlier groups from Asia to rely almost entirely upon their kith and kin, when such defensive insulation led to an even greater sense of interdependence and fellow-feeling among members of the same group. Perhaps. But it is also true that that sort of argument sounds strikingly like the one that says that every time Jews find they are about to be fully accepted in the host societies where they have settled, some new wave of anti-Semitism "saves them" from disappearing. Surely the liability of acceptance is far less damaging than the scourge of exclusion. In this, the Indochinese are fortunate to be in a special situation.

While they will continue to face unexpected obstacles, the newcomers have several decided advantages having to do with *who* they are, with *why* they came, and especially with *when* they arrived—a time of philo-Asian-

ism unprecedented in American history. Like other Asians, those from Indochina are coming to be seen by many not merely as "model minorities,"
but as "model Americans": hardworking, achievement-oriented, and, for
the most part, anti-communist.

The Future of Asian Ethnic Groups in America

In the final essay of his *Ethnic Dilemmas: 1964–1982*, Nathan Glazer discusses "The Politics of a Multiethnic Society." He begins by summarizing
what he and Daniel Patrick Moynihan said in the revised edition of *Beyond
the Melting Pot* about what they saw as two alternative paradigms of intergroup relations in the United States circa 1970. One was southern (and
rural), the other, northern (and urban). While in both patterns total assimilation did not occur, the patterns were quite different from each other.
The southern alternative was, essentially, a dichotomous black-white model in which "'separate but equal' [was] an ideology if not a reality."[53] The
northern scheme was closer to the old notion of the multiethnic spectrum
and the idea of *e pluribus unum* (one out of many).

Glazer and Moynihan were quite prescient. While one could quibble
with some of their specific predictions, their major failing was that they did
not see or acknowledge *other* paradigms based on other circumstances.
Their views of the North and South were largely limited to what was going
on—and would go on—from Memphis to Manhattan but not from Seattle
to San Diego.

Perhaps it was because it was an extension of their study of New York's
ethnic minorities that their perspective had such an East Coast bias. Glazer
clearly acknowledges in the new volume in which he offers a third alternative, a western one, which takes into account the experiences and encounters of those large minority groups whose heritage is neither African
nor European.

In contrast to the Mexicans, by far the largest of the newer groups,
others are more alien to us culturally. As Glazer notes:

> [The] newer groups are more distant in culture, language and religion from
> white Americans, whether of the old or new immigration, than these were
> from each other. We now have groups that are in American terms more ex-
> otic than any before. Added to the Chinese and Japanese are now Filipinos,
> Koreans, Asian Indians, Vietnamese, Cambodians, Laotians, Pacific Island-
> ers, many of them speaking languages unconnected to the languages of Eu-
> rope, many practicing religions that have very few representatives in this
> country (though there are many Christians among them), and most [are] of
> racial or ethnic stocks distant from the European.

> A western alternative—or what Lemuel Ignacio might have called a
> "third bloc approach"[55]—could have been advanced a decade ago because the
> trends were already being established then. Today it is even more applicable,
> for the main sources of immigration are not Europe and Canada, but Latin

America and Asia. The third alternative is a complex one, not nearly so par-adigmatically pure as either of the earlier models. While different from both, it contains elements of each.

Importantly, any new "western" model must address the matter of the offering of government protection and benefits to an array of officially des-ignated "minorities" regardless of their actual need. At present, poor Mex-icans and wealthy Chinese can both take advantage of "affirmative action." Any new model must also consider the still viable practice of carving a niche and entering specialized trades, engaging in bloc power, and learn-ing to form coalitions of convenience as well as interest. This leads to the conclusion that there may well be *two* subtypes within the western alterna-tive, or, more accurately put, two divergent paths that will be followed by those minorities living mainly in the western states. One, ostensibly "blackward," will be signposted with phrases like "institutional racism," "second-class citizenship," and by demands that whites be made to rec-ognize the bicultural (meaning in this instance the Latin/Anglo) character of the country to give deprived individuals their just due. Hispanics, who place greater emphasis on power politics, voter registration, and direct ap-peals for governmental assistance, will take this course of action far more often than will the Asians (with the possible exception of the anomalous Filipinos).

Most Asians, despite their own continuing encounters with prejudice, will follow the other path. They will do what they have generally done in the past: that is, they will use communal action less for raising the con-sciences of their own peoples or those in the controlling sectors than for the aggrandizement of kin and clansmen *within* the different and still dis-tinctive ethnic groups. In this they are on a repaved road toward Euro-pean-type assimilation.

Most Asians—newcomers as well as oldtimers—have had ambivalent at-titudes about capitalizing on inherited "disadvantages." To most, merito-cratic principles are the norms by which their lives in the United States have been organized in the past and ought to be in the future. It is this ethos—and the publicity their achievements have received—that causes many to look to them (but rarely to the Hispanics) as archetypes of accul-turation.

And, yet, the paradox remains. While more and more Asian Americans have come to represent the best of what those who promulgate "American-ization" would like to create, they are not and will not be fully assimilated, at least not in the foreseeable future. It will be a long time in Californ' or in any other part of the country before they are simply absorbed (for that is what assimilation is). Rather, like the Jews to whom they are so often com-pared, they will retain their marginal status.

No matter how adaptive in values and aspirations, no matter how sim-ilar to whites in mannerisms and actions, Asian Americans cannot be members of the majority. They can become "Bananas," but they will remain yellow in the eyes of their beholders. Some, like the Japanese of Los Angeles County, will intermarry, thus reducing the issue of racial difference or, more likely, giving it greater subtlety. Most however, will remain relatively endogamous, clearly conspicuous, and fully conscious of their double identities.[56]

The Reagan Years and Beyond

T HE ELECTION of Ronald Reagan in 1980 shifted many national priorities, not least in the realm of civil rights and intergroup relations in
general. It dramatically put the brakes on a course of action that had begun
in the 1940s (with the Fair Employment Practice Act and the desegregation of the military), accelerated in the 1950s (particularly after the
Brown decision of the Supreme Court outlawing school segregation), taken
significant leaps forward in the early 1960s (the civil rights and Black
Power movements being only the most notable generators of changes such
as the Civil Rights Act of 1964), and, for all the concerns about new directives demanding the implementation of "affirmative action" in schools and
workplaces, persisted through the 1970s. That course was, perhaps more
than any other single factor, characterized by ever greater governmental
involvement in the redress of minority grievances.

During the years of the Carter administration, the president from the
Deep South had rekindled the spirit of "welfare-minded" Democrats from
the New Deal days of Franklin Delano Roosevelt through the Kennedy-
Johnson era, lent his weight to a variety of programs to assist the poor,
especially those in racial minorities, and vigorously advocated human
rights at home and abroad. But Carter, an outsider to the Washington establishment, had difficulty in a variety of spheres. Not least was his inability to curb mounting inflation (which reached double-digit heights before
he left office) or to quell the feeling of serious malaise throughout the
country, a sentiment which he sometimes expressed himself. By the time of
the presidential election of 1980, it seemed to many that America was in
deep trouble and needed a change in leadership.

Carter's opponent, Ronald Reagan, campaigned on a "Get America-
Moving-Again" and "Get-the-Government-Out-of-Private Life" ticket and

---

*This is a variation on a lengthier essay originally published as "Values, Beliefs and the
Politics of Ethnicity in America: The Reagan Years and Beyond," in *Commonality and Difference in Australia and the United States*, ed. Glenn Wither (Sydney, 1988), pp. 300–48, 129, then
updated for *They and We*, 4th ed. (New York, 1990), where much of it appeared as Chapter 9.

won handily. Once in control, he moved to keep the promises made during the campaign. Through a variety of economic strategies, not least a massive increase in spending for defense, inflation was reduced, as was the percentage of Americans unemployed. In addition to those firmly on the Right (both political and religious), many "middle Americans"—including numerous white ethnic Democrats—felt that at last there was someone in the White House who understood their plight and was not only willing to articulate it but was acting to stop the drift to "the welfare state."

Under the first Reagan administration, hundreds of programs designed to aid the poor were disbanded, thousands of conservative judges were appointed to federal courts, and millions of dollars were diverted to matters other than human services. The early replacement of Mary Berry with Clarence Pendleton as chair of the United States Civil Rights Commission and the curtailment of its role as both arbiter of interracial conflict and a dynamic force for the advocacy of fairer practices sent a very clear message across the land: activists for group rights beware!

In many ways the representatives of the Reagan administration and their sympathizers were returning to what Michael Lewis has called "the individual-as-central sensibility," in which, it is argued, responsibility for success and failure is highly personal, not collective.[1] (Lewis uses Arthur Miller's *Death of a Salesman* as the fictive representation of this position taken to its logical extreme.) They contended that, in America, one must always be encouraged to strive to be the master of one's own fate, that too much reliance on others, particularly on the institutions of government, threatens the moral fiber and weakens the whole conception of a true meritocracy.

While emphasizing the work ethic and praising individual initiative, the proponents of Reagan policies also stressed the importance of patriotism and the idea that "We are all Americans." Not inconsistently, given the interplay of individualistic and nationalistic themes, many supporters of the administration opposed—openly in some cases, more circumspectly in others—affirmative action policies. These, it was argued, were not only unfair and perhaps unconstitutional because they gave special advantages to certain designated groups (Blacks, Hispanics, Asians and Native Americans), but aggravated the tendency toward polarization along racial and ethnic lines.

All told, those in positions of the greatest power seemed determined to move minority issues low down on their list of priorities. And they did.

Many civil rights advocates were troubled but not surprised. They had seen the writing on the wall. Still, not a few predicted that the anticipated retrenchment would trigger new outbursts of protests from the quarters of those who seemed to be losing the most from new federal action—and inaction! Yet, curiously, the response was not as explosive as many had expected. When it came, very late in the decade, it took rather unexpected forms.

For almost a decade, those still concerned about continued discrimination against racial and ethnic minorities watched in sadness but did little to attempt to stem the erosion of the federal commitment to redress legitimate grievances. There is little doubt that the lack of vigorous response was related, at least in part, to the failure of the civil rights movement's aging leadership to replace itself. There were far fewer spokespersons— and those there were, were hardly the firebrands of the earlier era.

Renewed Debates

Within the ranks of what was left of the old "race relations" community— which still included the remnants of the civil rights movement, a number of mainstream politicians, and several prominent social scientists—an old issue much discussed in the turbulent 1930s, and again in the 1960s, once again became the locus of deliberation. Some called it the "Race v. Class debate."

In its earlier manifestations, it really tended to be an either/or matter. Some argued that racial oppression was a unique phenomenon, relating to particular attitudes toward those viewed and treated as different from themselves ("the White Man's Burden"), and was therefore almost immutable. Others contended that racial oppression was hardly unique, but rather, a clear example of capitalist exploitation, with the contention of "difference" being used as a mask for privilege.

The more recent debate is more complex. The sociologist William Julius Wilson attempted to put it in perspective. In his 1977 book *The Declining Significance of Race*, Wilson argued that, as traditional barriers were removed or lowered as a result of the political, social, and economic activities of the civil rights era, they were replaced with a new set of far more impersonal obstacles, obstacles that "may prove to be even more formidable for certain segments of the black population."[2] He went on to say that, while in earlier periods general barriers were used to control and restrict the entire black population, the new barriers create hardships mainly for the black underclass. Thus,

> . . . whereas the old barriers were based explicitly on racial motivations derived from intergroup contact, the new barriers have racial significance only in their consequences, not in their origins. In short, whereas the old barriers bore the pervasive features of racial oppression, the new barriers indicate an important and emerging form of class subordination.[3]

Those being left behind are what Wilson and others have come to refer to as "the truly disadvantaged."[4] This large and growing cohort has been daunted by the lessening of the need for unskilled workers (the traditional road to stabilization if not instant success), extreme poverty and deprivation of basic amenities of living, the anomic conditions of home environments and decaying neighborhoods, the lack of middle-class role models, diversion from conventional paths by drugs and other means of escape—most of which give but short-term gratification—and increasing dependence on a welfare system that, many feel, undercuts incentive.

Wilson's claim to a growing gap in Black America and, by extension, in other minority communities, was widely acknowledged, but his seeming unwillingness to place all the fault for problems faced by blacks and other non-white members of the underclass in one basket labeled "racial discrimination" rankled many critics. Indeed, the Association of Black Sociologists, a group to which Wilson, who is himself black, had belonged, attacked him for downplaying what, to them, remained the principal issue: institutional racism.[5] They contended that, despite the changes in law and practice, it remained true that, while most poor people in the United States were (and are) white, most black people and most Hispanics in the country were (and continue to remain) poor—and that unemployment rates among such cohorts had hardly changed in the past four decades. Moreover, they posited the resegregation of society (usually citing the increasing number of all or mostly black schools in northern cities—a function, in large part, of "white flight" to the suburbs) as evidence of the shallowness of Wilson's arguments.[6]

Still others linked the "Race v. Class debate" to another issue, the matter of cultural background and social values. Writers such as Thomas Sowell suggested that the real issue is culture not race, pointing to the differential success of those who, while themselves often having to face severe discrimination, including clearly race-based discrimination, were able to rise and even flourish in the system. Citing Jews and various Asian groups, Sowell also singled out fellow blacks, namely West Indians, as exemplars of what others have called, in a related context, "model minorities."[7]

In addition to race, class and culture, other closely related matters were also up for serious reassessment. Among them was a questioning of traditional, and Democratic, approaches to welfare. Increasing numbers of liberals began to rethink the efficacy of programs that seemed to ensure rather than eliminate dependency, programs their more conservative critics had always said "paid people more not to work than to get a job." While such claims were generally off-target, failing to indicate the special needs of many who were not only unemployed but also unemployable, they did raise questions about the overall system. More and more people came to argue for "workfare," a program where the able-bodied poor would be required to do community service in order to earn their allotments.

In actual practice, workfare programs that were instigated varied widely. Most effective seemed to be those which were most sensitive to the conditions under which those in need came to be dependent; which showed an understanding of the problems of poverty and, in many ways, "the culture of poverty"; which were willing to alter outmoded and outrageous stipulations that limited access to certain programs because, for example, a father was present (it was better to be husbandless to obtain AFDC [Aid to Families with Dependent Children] benefits); and which provided two very necessary services: child-care and training.

The "Welfare v. Workfare" debate symbolized in concrete terms the more widespread reassessment of various long-entrenched social policies and practices, many of which focused on services for racial and ethnic minorities. It also led to the realignment of advocates contributing to—and accelerating in a number of dramatic ways—a process that had already begun to take shape in the late 1960s and throughout the 1970s when many old liberals, who in the aggregate were consistently the staunchest supporters of minority causes, became critical of certain trends that deeply disturbed them.

For example, the long-established, mutually reinforcing relationship between the Jewish and black leadership was under increasing strain as a result of continuing disagreements over both the meaning and the usefulness of special programs designed to rectify past discrimination and certain political stances such as those relating to the Middle East, further reducing the effectiveness of united campaigns to consolidate gains already made. The conflicts between certain members of the black and Jewish communities were not the only strains in old alliances.

Labor Movement leadership, often at the forefront of the struggles for human and civil rights in the past, found itself under increasing pressures from rank-and-file members to resist the kind of categorical imperative required by the advocates of affirmative action programs. Those in small businesses also raised questions about the fairness of policies that seemed to be discrimination in reverse.

In 1980, the very beginning of the Reagan Era, the Warren Court upheld a congressional plan that required 10 percent of federal work contracts to be set aside for businesses controlled by minorities. While opposed by many conservatives in the new administration, such set-asides were viewed as a victory for civil rights forces which felt that without special consideration it would remain difficult for blacks and others long excluded from full participation in all aspects of the economy to break the pattern. The opponents saw the set-asides—and other schemes to increase minority participation—as "affirmative discrimination."[8] Many scholars and lawyers debated the morality and legality of programs that were not based on a specific company's acts but rather seen as general ways to redress past grievances.

In a landmark 6–3 decision, early in 1989, the Supreme Court (still known to many as the Reagan court, owing to the several conservative justices appointed by Reagan) ruled that the Richmond, Virginia city council unconstitutionally discriminated against whites in saying (presumably in compliance with the earlier ruling) that a contractor with any city building contract must give at least 30 percent of the value of the project to companies at least one-half minority owned. Speaking for the majority, Associate Justice Sandra Day O"Connor claimed that the city had violated the Constitution because it had relied on past societal discrimination to justify the quota:

> Since none of the evidence presented by the city points to any identified dis-
> crimination in the Richmond construction industry . . . the dream of a nation
> of equal citizens in a society where race is irrelevant to personal opportunity
> and achievement, would be lost in a mosaic of shifting preferences based on
> unmeasurable claims of past wrongs.[9]

Associate Justice Thurgood Marshall, one of the three dissenters, and the only black member of the High Court, bitterly stated that the new rul-ing "sounds a full-scale retreat from the Court's longstanding solicitude to race-conscious remedial efforts" and claimed that "[the] decision masks a deliberate and giant step backward in the court's affirmative action juris-prudence."[10]

Within several weeks the Supreme Court followed its Richmond deci-sion with two other related reversals of prior policy. In the first, the Court set new limits on measures minorities could use to attempt to prove that they had been relegated to less desirable jobs. In the other, *Martina v. Wilks*, a case involving white firefighters in Birmingham, Alabama, who contended that they were being discriminated against because of affirma-tive action policies, the court ruled in their favor.

The new president, George Bush, viewed by many as more sensitive to minority concerns than his predecessor, did not challenge the Court's de-cisions in these critical cases. Many Americans were troubled by this, par-ticularly in view of the very strong stance he took *against* the Court when, but a few weeks later, he expressed outrage at its failure to rule against the burning of the American flag in a civil liberties case. On hearing of the 5–4 decision to uphold the right under protection of the First Amendment guaranteeing freedom of expression, the president immediately called for a constitutional amendment to make the desecration of Old Glory unconsti-tutional.

Campus Trends

The widespread public debate over the flag-burning case and several in-stances of this now-protected form of symbolic protest brought back mem-ories of anti-war and civil rights activities on college campuses in the 1960s. Some commentators predicted that the flag issue might portend new demonstrations on campus in the 1990s. If so, it—and the renewed debates over abortion policy—would be among the first matters to stir stu-dents to widespread political action since the beginning of the 1980s.

Two decades after the tumultuous 1960s, campuses which had reeled under the constant strain of political polarization and confrontation seemed rather oblivious to these real-world debates. In fact, across the country, the onset of the Reagan Era seemed to have signaled a redux of the 1950s—and a final break from the 1960s—as aspiring yuppies (young, urban, preprofessionals) replaced the somewhat sanitized but still committed Yippies (youth for international peace) of the 1970s as the quintessential representatives of the coming generation. For a time, group-based activism gave way to self-centered personalism. The change was noticeable in course enrollments and the choice of majors, especially in the social sciences: sociology, which had flourished in the heyday of civil rights and anti-war protests, lost students; economics gained them; and business administration thrived with a new respectability.

Ironically, it was on some of these same campuses that things began to change yet again in the latter years of the Reagan presidency. According to Shelby Steele, two phenomena led to a heightening of tension and, in many places, repolarization along racial and ethnic lines.[11] The first, he claims, was the result of the *successes* of the group rights campaigns of the 1960s and 1970s which had made even the most elite of universities far more open to the enrollment of individuals from very different backgrounds and thus far more diverse in student composition than ever before. The second was the result of the additional measures taken to further ensure that the trend toward the integration of the schools did not abate even when those minorities best qualified to compete were able to go where they wanted. It was not enough to remove the color bar. Affirmative action policies on college and university campuses, though increasingly under attack, were in fact expanded and more carefully monitored.

But in spite of the significant increase in the presence of nonwhites (now including many Asians) on campuses—or perhaps because of it—in the middle of the decade race again became an issue. In some places it was a positive phenomenon, most dramatically characterized by coalitional campaigns to demand that regents of public institutions and members of boards of trustees of private ones divest themselves of stockholdings in companies doing business in South Africa. But in many places it was not apartheid abroad or segregation at home that brought out the protesters; it was structural pluralism on the campus and challenges to long-lived traditions and "Eurocentric curricula." (A similar charge was made regarding "sexist biases" and parallel demands were made to revamp courses and programs to address the contributions and roles of women.)

Beginning in 1986, on campuses from New England to California there were ugly racial incidents ranging from name-calling and graffiti-writing ("Niggers, spics and chinks: if you don't like it here, go back to where you came from") to cross-burnings to direct physical violence. Minority students, especially blacks (who were most often the main targets) responded with petitions, marches, rallies, sit-ins, and sieges of administrative offices. According to Steele, "much of what they were marching and rallying about seemed less a response to specific racial incidents than a call for broader action on the part of the colleges and universities they were attending."[12]

Many over-forty observers viewed the incidents with a sense of déjà vu, as a seeming replay of an earlier scenario. Black students were again making demands: more African American faculty members, more "black" courses, more attention to the issue of diversity. (In many places across the country, most notably on the West Coast, these demands were matched by those of Asian and Hispanic students.) Yet, for all the similarity, there were differences between the protests of the 1960s and the more recent ones.

> Today's undergraduates were born after the passage of the 1964 Civil Rights Act. They grew up in an age when racial equality was for the first time enforceable by law. This too was a time when blacks suddenly appeared on television, as mayors of big cities, as icons of popular culture, as teachers, and in some cases even as neighbors. Today's black and white college students, veterans of *Sesame Street* and often of integrated grammar and high schools, have had more oppertunities to know each other—whites and blacks—than any previous generation in American history. Not enough opportunities, perhaps, but enough to make the notion of racial tension on campus something of a mystery.[13]

Steele suggested that the mystery may be partly explained by the recognition that the new problem became how to live in an atmosphere of guaranteed equality instead of the old context of accepted, if sometimes challenged, inequality. "On a campus where members of all races are [now] gathered, mixed together in the classroom as well as socially, differences are more exposed than ever."[14]

Henry Louis Gates, in a forceful essay on the debate over the demands to make core curricula less Eurocentric and to include in the basic canon the works of minority writers and women, suggests that much of the conflict has arisen as new voices with significant representation on the campuses have challenged what he calls the "'antibellum aesthetic position' when men were men and men were white, when scholar-critics were white men and when women and people of color were voiceless, faceless servants and laborers, pouring tea and filling brandy snifters in the boardrooms of old boys' clubs."[15] Those leading the campaign to reshape the character of traditional education, challenging the assertions of the new cultural Right, have used the collective strength of newly present groups to assert their critical theories.

Many observers note that, even over issues unrelated to race, individuals seek solace with those who share their label (be it politically or gender- or race-based), leading to what some call the increasing balkanization of the campus. Such politics of diversity is viewed by many as giving further support to those who agree with Harold Isaacs, who worried about too much emphasis on "the idols of the tribe" and too little on integration.

The phrase "idols of the tribe" refers most blatantly to the veneration of kith and kin and erstwhile countrymen; it refers more subtly to the idea of a strain which, if unchecked, could turn the patriotic slogan *e pluribus unum* (one out of many) into *e pluribus plures* (out of many). This is a fear expressed by an increasing number of Americans opposed to giving special treatment to those in certain designated minority categories, as well as by those, to be discussed in more detail below, troubled by the dramatic increase in the numbers of immigrants, legal and illegal, entering the United States from non-European countries.

The Election of 1988

Many observers of American politics believed that the presidential campaign of 1988 would provide an opportunity to hear a thorough airing of many of the debates mentioned above as representatives of the contending parties put forth their positions, especially regarding the character and direction of intergroup relations. Yet, save for the powerful voice of Jesse Jackson, race, class, and gender were among the most significant issues *buried* under Republican rhetoric about good times brought on by peace and prosperity and Democratic rhetoric about helping the little guy access the system. When race was raised, it was by innuendo—such as the Bush campaign's celebrated exploitation of the decision by Massachusetts Governor Michael Dukakis's administration to furlough the black convicted murderer Willie Horton, who committed violent crimes while on leave. The Democrats' counterattack was weakened by candidate Dukakis's reluctance, until the waning days of the campaign, to take strong, identifiably liberal stands.

Both parties used patriotism to rally support, with American flags being more common icons of the 1988 election than bumper stickers or lapel buttons. The Republicans claimed that things had never been better; the Democrats promised (with clear echoes of the campaigns of Adlai Stevenson in the 1950s) greater tomorrows. Although acknowledging that there were still unresolved social problems, neither of the chosen candidates seemed willing or able to specify how he would address the needs of millions of Americans who had not only failed to benefit from the vaunted boom of the Reagan Era but had fallen farther and farther behind. Nor was either specific in speaking to the realities of homelessness, teenage pregnancy, drug trafficking and substance abuse, the ills of the elderly, and continued racial unrest in U.S. cities.

The election itself proved to be a mandate for continuity, as the majority of Americans appeared to be more secure with a team that, to them, had brought stability than with the vague promises of the Democrats. And in the beginning that seemed to be what they got.

However, almost immediately upon his inauguration, George Bush began to send out signals that, in favoring what he called "a kinder, gentler nation," he would be reaching out to those generally ignored, including the members of racial minorities. His words were applauded by many Democrats, including a number who had supported the unsuccessful candidacy of Jesse Jackson in the primaries and who suggested the possibility of some shifting of party allegiances if Bush began to deliver on his newly proclaimed promises. Still, many advocates of minority rights remained skeptical of the new administration's ability to do so, particularly with its continued commitment to avoiding the imposition of new taxes or other means of revenue enhancement, and of its position on those previously mentioned Supreme Court decisions that signaled a continued erosion of hard-won gains relating to improving opportunities for minorities to gain access to the social, political, and economic system.

The new administration inherited a number of old, unresolved foreign policy problems, some of which have indirect if not direct bearings on ethnicity—and ethnic politics—in the United States. Most critical were relations with the Soviet Union and the matter of the opportunities for emigration for Jews, Armenians, Pentecostalists, and ethnic Germans who sought to leave; the forty-year-old Arab-Israeli conflict and the effects of the Palestinian uprising in the occupied territories on the future of the area, its people, and those who supported them in the United States; the much older civil and religious war in Northern Ireland, fought not only in the streets of Belfast and Derry but as the source of some tensions in the homes and community centers of Irish Americans; the powerful impact of the Japanese on the American economy and the growing resentment it has engendered in many parts of the country, especially in the industrial sector; the continuing conflict with Iran, greatly exacerbated in the winter of 1989 by the violent reaction throughout the Muslim world to the publication of Salman Rushdie's controversial novel *The Satanic Verses* and the Iranian leadership's order to kill its author for blaspheming against Islam; the persisting conflicts in Central America and the outflow of people from Nicaragua, Guatemala, and El Salvador seeking asylum as refugees (the same status more easily obtained by those fleeing the countries of Indochina, Cuba, the USSR and—after the violent suppression of the prodemocratic demonstrations in the late spring of 1989 in Beijing—from China); and the general matter of immigration, both legal and illegal, from Latin America and from across the Pacific.

The Issue of Immigration

In addition to the debates about race, class, culture, and cultural values, the realignment of confederates in various civil rights struggles, the matter of the legality and significance of affirmative action and set-asides off the campuses and on them, or the meaning of foreign policy matters for those in various interest groups in the United States, concerns about immigration took on increasing significance with the presence on the scene of large numbers of immigrants, refugees, and "undocumented aliens."

From the early days of nationhood through the post-World War II period, the vast majority of those who entered the United States were white and of European origin. In recent years, in part because of the Immigration Reform Act of 1965—which abolished the old highly discriminatory "quota system," substituting a country ceiling of 20,000 a year—and the Refugee Act of 1980, more than 95 percent of those who enter the United States planning to stay are non-white and non-European. In many ways they are (or seem) more different from those already here than were many who came from southern, eastern, and central Europe in the late nineteenth and early twentieth centuries. Old nativist sentiments have begun to resurface. There is talk, once again, of the influx of "unassimilable aliens." This time, however, other views have been added to those "Old Americans": those of people who might be called neo-nativists. They argue that, until American society takes care of its own, it should not allow others to enter. Some of the neo-nativists are white ethnics; others are members of American minority groups: blacks, Puerto Ricans, Native Americans, and Chicanos. Sometimes their leaders and spokespersons express the view that it is *they* who will have to pay the highest price for assistance to immigrants and for refugee relief. They claim that what scarce government funds there are these days are likely to be diverted to more appealing causes. They also contend that their constituents are at a disadvantage in the job market since "immigrants will do anything" and will often do it well below the minimum wage. Both points sound strikingly similar to what was said by Anglo-Americans in the mid-nineteenth century about the Irish; what the Irish said about the Italians and southern and eastern Europeans; and what those white ethnics have been saying more recently about favoring blacks and other "preferred" minorities.

In addition to debates over entitlements and allowances (such as for the reunion of immediate family members, favoring the recently naturalized, such as Vietnamese Americans, over those who became citizens long ago, such as Irish Americans or Italian Americans), two other critical areas of controversy surrounding immigration are those of Americanization and bilingualism. The former is, of course, an old code word used by many who believed firmly in the idea that forced assimilation into Anglo-American molds was the only way outsiders could ever be accepted.

Critics have long argued that Americanization was responsible for turning ethnic pride into self-hatred and for leaving many immigrants in the unenviable position of being cast adrift on an alien sea. Supporters, by contrast, echoing the ideas of early assimilationists, voice the opinion that only when foreigners cast off their alien skins and forget the customs of the past can they *really* be absorbed. To be sure, they admit, the immigrants have to give up a great deal and make tremendous sacrifices; but, they argue, "Think of what they would be getting."

Bilingualism is a more modern concept. In the nineteenth century, many European immigrants retained their native languages. There were areas where German was the lingua franca; others where Norwegian and Swedish and other languages predominated. However, with the increasing influx of southern and eastern Europeans toward the end of the century, a campaign was mounted to see that everyone spoke English. It became a part of the Americanization process.

Despite ambivalences and insecurities, most newcomers accepted the idea that learning English was recognized as being critical for moving into society. Their children learned it in school "sink-or-swim" style and, highly motivated, many swam. Some of the adults themselves attended night schools where they studied English. Sometimes with those who knew nothing of their culture or native languages, sometimes with those who, in perhaps the first instance of bilingual education, taught them English *as a foreign language.* In order to prevent their offspring from being totally immersed in the new language and culture, some immigrants set up and maintained private after-school language schools. Some of these still exist.

The migration of large numbers of Spanish-speaking Puerto Rican Americans to the New York area in the late 1940s and early 1950s, prompted by the economic boom of the post-World War II period and the availability of cheap and fast air travel, changed the culture and the character of the city, brought about vigorous resistance to assimilation, and more formally introduced the idea of bilingualism. As indicated previously, some sociologists have speculated that clinging to their Hispanic heritage was one way Puerto Ricans could separate themselves from black Americans, with whom they were often grouped. Others say that easy access to Puerto Rico made acculturation less necessary or desirable.

The latter argument also came to be used to explain the reluctance of many Mexican immigrants to Americanize. The closeness of the motherland meant that one could be *in* one world (that of the United States) while in a sense *living* in another (Mexican). Whatever the reason, the result was that many Mexican Americans, like many Puerto Ricans, felt they should be allowed to retain their ways and their language. Some argued that their children should have instruction in Spanish and that their home language should be used as a transitional vehicle for moving along the road to learning to use English in everyday life. (In 1974, in the case of *Lau v. Nicholas,* the Supreme Court ruled that Chinese speaking students of San Francisco were being discriminated against by being taught in a language they did not understand. Schools were required to find bilingual teachers to work with Chinese students.) Others claimed that even such a strategy is too "assimilationistic," that they—and other non-English speakers—ought to be encouraged to maintain their own languages, even to the extent of having them as a recognized alternative to English in all public matters, following the pattern adopted in francophone Quebec.

Because Hispanics make up the largest linguistic minority in the United States, many such debates about bilingualism have revolved around the teaching of Spanish and the provisions for bicultural as well as bilingual programs for them. However, Hispanics are not alone in this controversy.

Other groups have pressed for similar opportunities. (The *Lau* case, cited above, is a clear case in point.)

The reaction against the pressures for bilingualism grew apace in the 1980s, culminating in a campaign to establish the rule of "English Only" not only proclaiming but mandating that Americans have but a single official language: English. The effort has led to the passage of laws in fifteen states and more battles are to be expected in the years ahead. One ironic twist in the controversy is the argument put forth by some of the most fervent supporters of English Only—whose favored rules impose severe hardships on those who must fill out forms not only for medical assistance and welfare but for further schooling and employment—that, once the singularity of "our" language is established in law then we can encourage the teaching of other languages "to enhance the understanding of others."

Americanization and bilingualism are not the only policy debates with respect to new Americans. Others include questions about how assistance is offered and given to newcomers and what hold the service-providers should have on their settlement in this country, especially refugees who are to receive support from federally funded programs. Also how they should be resettled. For example, should Soviet Jews, Khmer Buddhists (from Cambodia), or Cubans be encouraged to cluster, to form and maintain enclaves where they can find security through familiarity, or should they be scattered to encourage their early absorption into the mainstream?

If history is any indication, it would seem most logical to allow people (indeed, to assist them) to form ethnic communities, thereby easing the transition into the American scene from often totally alien cultural milieus. While some immigrants and refugees, especially those with higher education and familiarity with the language and customs of this country, have moved into dominant communities with little difficulty, the evidence suggested that for most, the acculturation process is painful and often prolonged. The support of others who have traveled the difficult road from foreigner to American ethnic has been a proven boon to those who have not made the trip before.

Finally, the most difficult question of all: If not everyone who wants to come to the United States for whatever reason can be allowed to do so, who should be admitted? At a recent conference on The Acculturation of New Americans, sponsored by the Institute on Pluralism and Group Identity, one participant, an economist, asked the assembled corps of policy-makers—representatives of major volunteer agencies that work with immigrants and refugees, members of several ethnic organizations, and some foundation personnel and academicians—how many would favor unlimited immigration to the United States.[16] Not one said he or she would. But the experts could not, or would not, say whom they would admit and whom they would exclude.

Some members of minority groups who were at the meeting commented later that most Americans would probably be willing to welcome as many Indochinese as wanted to come, as well as any number of anti-Communists from Europe, including Soviet Jews and other whites, but would baulk at large-scale requests from Africans or Arabs. They call this racism, pure and simple. Others, also speaking off the record, argued that this was not racial prejudice but cultural bias, a preference for people with an Anglo-Saxon value system or one that is, somehow, its functional equivalent; they wanted to welcome those with high achievement–motivation, who had the skills, or the potential for developing skills, necessary for a modern industrial society.

The issue reached the halls of Congress when, in the last year of the Reagan administration, the Kennedy-Simpson Immigration Bill was introduced. (It passed overwhelmingly in the Senate but failed in the House, and was resubmitted a year later.) The Bill sought to alter certain provisions of the 1965 Immigration Act by including reductions in the family reunion system (there being no such limit under the terms of the 1965 Act) and the addition of an independent category of some 50,000 visas allocated on the basis of a points system that favored those with high educational levels, professionals over unskilled workers, and English language ability. The Bill was denounced by many representatives of Hispanic and Asian communities because of the favoritism shown to English speakers; it was also opposed by the same spokespersons because it would eliminate visas for married brothers and sisters under what is known as the "Fifth Preference," used mostly by Hispanics and Asians to bring in relatives, and by many from all over the world who objected to the proposed elimination of "Sixth Preference" visas, those issued to unskilled workers who are in demand in the U.S. labor market.

Much of the controversy over the proposed legislation reflected deeply felt sentiments in various parts of U.S. society. For some, it is a continuing concern about the changing character of American culture (being directly linked to debates about Americanization and bilingualism), a feeling that "They" are so different from "Us" that things will never be the same, and that a limit has to be imposed on what seems like a threat of inundation. For others, the threat is not that the newcomers are so different but that, whatever they are today, tomorrow they will be too similar: skilled competitors in a society in which ethnic ties remain a primary basis for group cohesion and for social action. The latter sentiment seems especially to underlie the concerns of those who object to the high rate of immigration from Asia.

Addendum (1995)

After a series of bruising primary battles in the Democrats' camp, Bill Clinton was nominated to run against George Bush in 1992. His victory in November of that year was hardly a mandate. The independent candidacy of the millionaire electronics entrepreneur, Ross Perot, syphoned considerable votes of putative Republicans as well as many conservative Democrats. While the Democrats did manage to control both houses of Congress, and though many liberals were elected (more minorities and females than any time in history), many feared the victory would prove Phyrric. In many ways, it did.

Despite a good deal of rhetoric about getting America back on course, solving social problems, controlling spending, and dealing more forcefully with racial issues, only part of the Democratic agenda was realized. Various explanations have been given for the failure. One of the most persuasive is that, for all the talk of commitment to change, for all the involvement of minority representatives, for all the meetings and hype about sweeping reforms of health care and welfare, the Clinton administration did not know how to buck the continuing tide of resentment over what were seen as special treatment for special interests, not least those most vulnerable. Actions relating to those health and welfare reforms were seen by many as litmus tests of the willingness of the new government to temper its "Big Brother" approach and hew more closely to the campaign-based sloganeering about giving the power back to the people. (A theme that ran through the materials put out by all the candidates, including Clinton.)

Toward the end of his second year in office, Clinton, who had never firmly established himself as a leader, became the principal target of the Republicans. In 1994 they swept into office in one of the greatest routs in modern American history.

Led by the new Speaker, Newt Gingrich, and the new majority leader, Dick Armey, the House Republicans tried to implement the very conservative "Contract with America" on which they had campaigned with such obvious success. Not long in office, they threatened—and, in many cases, succeeded in—the dismantling of a raft of social programs that had been hallmarks of Democratic governments and accepted by Republican ones since the days of the New Deal. Among the many that were targeted for extinction or, at the least, drastic curtailment by House committees on Labor, Health and Human Services, and Education were such federally supported activities as job training, assistance to homeless youth, and a variety of educational programs at every level, primary, secondary, and tertiary. Also included in the list of what were construed by many as superfluous bodies or those that were anathema to the ideological stances of the majority party and many of its members was the Corporation for Public Broadcasting. It was all part of what Norman Podhoretz, a neoconservative sympathizer with many of the ideas of the new leadership, called a true "counter-revolution."

The Republican sweep seemed, to many observers, to signal the solidification of a party of reactionary white, males (and many white females too), a cohort that numbered in its ranks not only "WASPs" from every part of the country, including the once solid-Democratic South, but also increasing numbers of Catholic conservatives, Irish, and other white ethnics, many of whom voted for Reagan while retaining local loyalties and were now shifting allegiances across the board. The Democratic Party seemed to be so crippled as to hardly serve as the bastion of succor and support of the non-white minorities it had generally championed. Many surviving members, especially in the House of Representatives and in many state governments, found themselves worried about being seen as too "prominority" and began to echo the sentiments of the Republicans relating to such issues as affirmative action for minorities, the treatment of newcomers, legal as well as illegal, and the sharp recision of entitlements even for those who used to be called "the deserving poor."

While some of the recommended changes were to move specific funding from the federal government to bloc grants for states, where statewide and local authorities who were closer to the scene would determine spending priorities, opponents worried that, with states already burdened with increasing costs of social services, their administrators would divert funds to pet projects. Furthermore, it was argued, when the grants ran out, there would be a natural inclination to close down programs that seemed too expensive. The losers in all such moves would doubtless be the poorest folks, those least able to care for themselves, those already dependent on assistance. This category of often unemployable and even more often only marginally employable people would clearly be disproportionately Native Americans, Puerto Rican and African American citizens, and millions of newcomers, mostly from Asia and Latin America. Here again, the plight of old minorities and new Americans seemed to hang in the balance.

Tempest-Tost

I ASK YOU to use your imagination. Think of the heartrending photograph of the thin, wan refugee mother and her dull-eyed, dying baby, a "mere apostrophe of an infant," as Thomas Keneally has described it.[1]

That image of "The Madonna of the Refugee Camp" is often used by journalists, by publicists for relief and resettlement agencies like UNICEF and CARE and the International Rescue Committee, and by officials of the United Nations High Commission for Refugees to bring to public attention the private suffering of the vast numbers of human beings caught up in the cross-currents of revolution and war. In the 1970s and 1980s the woman and child of the poignant pietà tended to have Asian or African faces. They might as well have been Afghani or Salvadorian. Today they are Hutu and Haitian, Albanian and Bosnian, Burmese Muslims in Pakistan, and Shiite Iraqis in Saudi Arabia.

The specific ethnicity of the emblematic figures may be, and usually is, directly relevant to why they are where they are, but in a transcendental sense, it is less significant than their collective condition. With silent eloquence each singular representation communicates the general pathos of being uprooted and displaced, estranged and afraid.

Here I am concerned with all that that image represents; that special category of migrants—currently estimated to be between 15 and 20 million—who are known as *refugees*. They are victims of racial, religious, or political persecution who seek asylum in safe havens across the borders of their native lands.

While the term *refugee* has only recently entered the legal vernacular, the seeker of sanctuary, driven out by forces beyond his or her ability or control, is as old a figure in the human drama as communal life itself.

Many contemporary refugees are exiles in the original sense of the Latin-rooted term (*exilium*). They are, truly, "outcast," those who, either

*Originally published as "Tempest-Tost: Exile, Ethnicity, and the Politics of Rescue," *Sociological Forum*, 8:1, March 1993, 5–24.

individually like Oedipus—or Solzhenitsyn, or collectively like the ancient Israelites and their descendants in Germany in the 1930s, or the Palestinian dissidents recently deported from the West Bank—have been banished from their homes and homelands for their unacceptable politics or their unacceptable beliefs and practices, the latter often related to membership in a disfavored racial or religious "nationality" group. Many more are "escapees" rather than "expellees." Examples are numerous: the Huguenots, to whom the word "refugee" was first applied; Loyalists who headed for Nova Scotia during the American Revolution; Jews who fled the Czars' pogroms; Armenians; opponents of Franco and Mussolini; victims of Nazi persecution in Germany and in the occupied lands; and most recently, vast numbers of Cambodians who, trying to avoid the wrath of those bent on their destruction, straggled across the border into Thailand.

In addition to such targeted groups, who by virtue of the nature of their selective—and collective—mistreatment are deemed "real" or "convention" refugees (as defined in United Nations' protocols and conventions), there are those, often called "displaced persons," caught in the cross-currents of civil wars and other conflicts that are not of their making, or in many cases, of their direct concern.[2] Some such persons find temporary asylum in nearby lands, but many never cross a border. Their displacement is *internal.* Their plight is especially tragic since they are beyond the reach—or policies—of many international agencies set up to deal with refugees, such as the United Nations High Commission for Refugees, and many other governments reluctant to intervene in the domestic affairs of other states. The Sudan, Somalia, and many other countries on the African continent are the home of millions of such people today.[3]

While it is amply clear that there are factors other than minority status that provide "a well-founded fear of persecution" prompting people to leave their homes and homelands (think, for example, of Haiti today), ethnic conflict has long been recognized as one of the principal root causes of human migration and a particular generator of refugee flows.[4] It still is.

Consider the situation in Sri Lanka, in the east and Southern Africa, in various parts of the Middle East. Think of central and eastern Europe and the human hemorrhaging that is taking place in so many countries in that area today: Yugoslavia, Czechoslovakia, Hungary, Romania, Albania . . . and the various states of the former USSR.

Euphoric reports about the collapse of one communist regime after another throughout the Soviet sphere, watched with such fascination on satellite-relayed television, were most invariable followed by far more worrisome ones. A significant result of the process of dismantling the monolithic controls of state socialism was the fierce assertion of nationalism, and in many places, the blatant display of racial, religious, and ethnic discrimination.[5] Commenting on the situation, Isaiah Berlin made the astute observation that "Nationalism [in Eastern Europe] is not resurgent. It never

[really] died. Neither did racism . . . They are, " he said, "the most powerful movements in the world today."[6] And, I would like to add, they are almost invariably linked.

Chauvinistic zeal, often masked as patriotism, has been accompanied by
the all too familiar ploy of blaming vulnerable others for one's own mis-
eries and by open attacks on minority populations. Such practices, especially in areas where ethnic rivalries had long been held in check by the
slogans and tactics of the state, once unleashed, have provoked actions on
the parts of those claiming sovereignty and reactions by those discriminated against. In some instances minorities are seeking autonomy; in
others they attempt to affiliate with those who share their ethnic identity
(the case of the Serbs in Bosnia is an example). When neither independence nor affiliation seem possible, many try to remove themselves to safer
ground. They, too, become refugees.

Immigrants and Refugees

What all those I have referred to as refugees have in common is that—directly or indirectly—they have been forced out. Immigrants, by contrast,
are people who, it is often said by those constructing typologies (and those
determining legal precedents), are pulled in rather than pushed away. To
be sure, as those who write of labor migrations traditionally point out, opportunities for social mobility often serve as catalysts for consideration for
permanent or temporary residence in other places. But without the attrac-
tion of some Golden Medina, some city of land of promise, few would emigrate or even venture forth as what are today known as "guest workers."
For the dispossessed there is often no such choice.

A stark poster published by the United Nations High Commission for
Refugees shows a brick wall with the words "REFUGEES GO HOME" scrawled
in white paint across it. At the bottom of the poster is a terse response:
"They would if they could."

That is another thing about refugees. Not only must many leave their
homes, but they must leave with the realization that, however much they
might hope their exile will be short-lived, they may never be able to go
home again.

Richard Shelton has expressed this problem with special poignancy in
his poem "The Princes of Exile":

> The Princes of Sacrifice return
>   as rain in a drouth year,
> The Princes of War return
>   as sores on the faces of politicians.
> The Princes of Betrayal return
>   impaled on the swords of their friends
> But the Princes of Exile never return.[7]

Banished, uprooted, or displaced, the princes (and the paupers) of exile are hardly a modern phenomenon. They are found throughout history. We know of them from biblical texts that tell of Exodus from Egypt; in the prayers of those in the Diaspora who, for over two millennia, proclaimed that "next year" they would be in Jerusalem; and in the reechoing lamentations of those once camped by the rivers of Babylon:

> How shall we sing the Lord's song
> In a strange land?

The conditions of "homelessness" is limited to no time or groups of exiles. It is a general condition, as Edward Said, writing on "Zionism from the standpoint of its victims," reminds us.[8]

Stories of the dispossessed are a part of the Western literary heritage. From Tacitus to Tabori, chroniclers have described exile—and the meaning of exile. In age-worn texts and modern commentaries, in historical accounts and personal diaries, and in studies by our sociological colleagues, certain themes appear. They include *memories of persecution; wrenching decisions about leaving family, friends, and familiar surroundings; the ordeal of escape; constant thoughts of who and what was left behind; frustrations of existence in foreign environs; uncertainties of future prospects.* These are related to an all-too-familiar sociopolitical phenomenon: the normative order has broken down, old rules no longer obtain, social groups have been torn asunder, and there is often nowhere to turn. For many refugees *anomie* is the pervasive social reality. (It should be noted that, while it is often assumed that alienation is the result of anomie, here is a situation in which anomie is born of alienation, alienation in its most literal sense.)

The poet A. E. Housman described the dilemma of such estrangement:

> And how am I to face the odds
> Of Man's bedevilment and God's?
>
> I, a stranger and afraid
> In a world I never made.[9]

Whenever people leave kith and kin and strike out on their own there is apprehension. But when they are *forced* to go, there is the added problem of the loss of control over their own destinies, exacerbating the inevitable sense of loneliness.

Loneliness

Of all the words in the extensive "exile literature" I have found none so pointed, so telling, so frequent as "loneliness." It is a word that appears over and over in the stories people tell and in the songs they sing. It is manifest in their dreams and in their nightmares. It is an ever-present companion.

"I'm so sad, so lonely. I cry all the time." The words are those of a new neighbor of mine, a Cambodian refugee who has been in the United States for ten years.[10]

As the Hungarian refugee writer Paul Tabori has stated:

> Exile is the loneliness in the middle of a crowd
> Exile is longing never to be fulfilled,
> It is love unrequited, the loss never replaced
> Exile is a song that only the singer can hear.[11]

Perhaps the reason that loneliness is such a key element in the condition suffered by most resettled refugees, no matter how lucky they might be in having found new homes, it is that they are fated to live on the edges of different worlds.

Like Simmel's "stranger"—and, in a different sense, like Camus'—resettled refugees are persons apart, outsiders who peer into closed rooms. They are the "other."[12] They seek admittance but are ever conscious of their foreignness; they want acceptance but are never sure of their acceptability. They are eager to find niches of their own. Their friends tell them they must not look back, yet in their hearts they cannot help but hear what the Russian exiles often describe as "the evening bells of home." *They are caught in limbo, in an oxymoronic state of permanent instability.*

The refugee is as apt a representation of Robert Park's "marginal man"[13] as one can find. Yet, although all resettled refugees are marginal, not all are equally estranged. Some have easier times than others. It is a sociological irony that those who had been politically, religiously, or socially marginal *prior to their exile* are often better prepared to cope with the new social spaces they must occupy, and with the roles they must play as outsiders within new environs, than are those unused to being seen as belonging to "a people apart." This is especially true of those who were members of what have come to be known as "middlemen minorities" in their homelands.

Historians and sociologists of American society often overlooked the fact that of the millions of traditional migrants to the United States who came seeking opportunities either as permanent settlers or temporary sojourners, relatively few would be classified as minorities in their own countries. *Most migrants become "minorities"—and "ethnics"—after they arrive here.*[14]

Cultural factors are critical, too. Moving to a society much like one's own is far easier than going to an entirely foreign one. Knowing the language of the new society is, of course, one of the most significant boons to acculturation. Also useful is the possession of talents, skills, and training that may benefit the host society. (This is why doctors have easier times in alien environments than lawyers do.)

Lest I seem pollyannish about certain types of "advantaged" refugees, it must be said that, while prior experience with minority status, familiarity with the host society, language skills, and special technical competence may be extremely helpful factors in easing adjustment, even they are not sufficient to ensure it. Many worldly, articulate, highly trained refugees, by virtue of their apparent ability to function in the new society, have misled observers into believing they are well adjusted to their fate. The fact is there is often a considerable gap between public personalities and private thoughts, and as many refugee intellectuals readily attest, cosmopolites can ache for home as much as displaced peasants.

The Armenian writer Antranik Zaroukian made poetry of this simple truth:

> Without a fatherland
> the landless find
> all brown earth an insult,
> all soil rootless.
>
> The exile is a stranger
> even to his grave.[15]

If Zaroukian is correct—and I think he is—that "the exile is a stranger unto the grave," then it means that one who is forced out and remains abroad is never really at home in his new world no matter how welcoming.

But what of the exile's progeny?

Several years ago at a Smith College conference of the "Sociology of Exile," sociologist Lewis Coser, who had lived in the United States for half a century, was asked if he felt at home in America. "Yes and no," he answered. He said he, like many of those he was then writing about in his book *Refugee Scholars in America*,[16] had found a haven, a place to live and to work, but he was still, at the age of 70, "a refugee." "But," he noted, "my children speak without accents. *They are American*."[17]

While many political scientists write of the integration of newcomers (and here I refer to immigrants as well as refugees) in terms of the attainment of *citizenship*, to me the real measure is membership. Belonging is not so much being officially judged acceptable but being made to feel accepted—and *being able to act accordingly*.

For the uprooted, acceptance depends on many factors, not least the kindness, compassion, and assistance of others. Sometimes aid comes from relatives or countrymen already ensconced in the land of exile; often it is extended by unknown benefactors. This, too, has always been the case.

"Refuge" and "refugee," while obviously related concepts, are quite different. Elie Wiesel points this out when he asks,

What has been done to the word *refuge*?
In the beginning the word sounded beautiful. A refuge meant 'home.' It welcomed you, protected you, gave you warmth and hospitality. Then we added one single phoneme, one letter, e, and the positive term *refuge*, became *refugee*, connoting something negative.[18]

While refuge is needed by almost all who flee to foreign soil, the dependency of the dispossessed is a highly complex phenomenon in its own right; so, too, is the idea of an obligation to assist and the source—or sources—of such obligation.

Sacred texts of many cultures indicate how one must deal with the stranger at the gate.

> When a stranger sojourns with you in your land, you shall not do him wrong.
> A stranger who sojourns with you shall be to you as a native among you, and
> you shall love him as yourself; for you were strangers in the land of Egypt.

This sentiment, first stated in Leviticus (19:33) is repeated three times in Deuteronomy (10:17–19; 14:24–25; 22:21). It is a theme that reappears in the New Testament in somewhat different form, often expressed in parables such as the Good Samaritan.

According to many theologians, such teachings have relevance to the plight of refugees today. Here is one example, taken from a sermon by M. Fletcher Davis, an Episcopal priest in Garden Grove, California, a community with a very large Vietnamese population:

> To help the stranger and the sojourner, especially the refugee, victims of social, political, economic, cultural and racial movements which impinge upon people without their consent, is a divine imperative from scripture and from the tradition of the Church . . . the problems of refugees are the basic religious problems: they raise the central question of the meaning of human life.[19]

In a lengthy interview conducted with the late John McCarthy, then head of Migration and Refugee Services of the U.S. Catholic Conference, and president of the International Catholic Migration Committee based in Geneva, I asked him why he does what he does. He looked at me rather incredulously and said, "Because I am a Christian." He said his involvement is based on a basic belief that there is only one reason for a church. It is "bringing to life . . . that's what it's all about . . . and that is what I try to do."[20]

The Judeo-Christian tradition has its counterpart. In Sophocles' *Oedipus at Colonus*, we are told how Theseus, King of Athens, welcomes the beleaguered and blinded Oedipus to his land saying,

> Never could I turn away from any stranger
> such as you are now
> and leave him to his fate.[21]

In modern times as in ancient ones it can be a great help to the estranged when others extend the hand of welcome. It can be devastating to the seekers of asylum when no humble Samaritan or noble king—or "Mother of Exile" (Emma Lazarus's name for what we call "the Statue of

Liberty")—stands by with outreached arm. And yet the historical records show that, too often, wariness had been more prevalent than acceptance, that far more barriers have been erected to prevent entry than bridges laid down to enhance it. Fear of the stranger seems a more common sentiment than compassion.

In his simple and straightforward poetry, Rudyard Kipling, a man well known for his own ethnocentricity, offered a most reasonable sociological explanation for this morally reprehensible tendency.

> The Stranger within my gate
> He may be true or kind
> But he does not talk my talk —
> I cannot feel his mind.
> I see the face and eyes and mouth
> But not the soul behind.
>
> The men of my own stock
> They may do ill or well,
> But they tell the lies I am wonted to,
> They are used to the lies I tell;
> And we do not need interpreters
> When we go to buy and sell.[22]

Kipling was writing of a phenomenon known in Sophocles' time—and in our own—as *xenophobia*, the fear and hatred of the stranger, a far more widely held sentiment than its opposite, *philoxenia*, the love of the foreigner (which, I am told, is often translated from the Greek of the New Testament as "hospitality.")

If xenophobia is—and has always been—so widespread, then sociologists must ask: How is it then that *any* expellees, escaped, or displaced persons ever find refuge in others' lands? Obviously, the explanation lies in broader social structural contexts.

Today, as in the past, most acts of assistance to desperate populations are not offered simply, solely, or even mainly because of biblical injunction of strictly humanitarian concern, but rather for geopolitical reasons—often with diplomatic points being scored or debts being paid or heavy prices extracted for assisting the dispossessed or granting them asylum.[23]

While there is no question that there have always been genuinely charitable people who welcomed the "weary pilgrims," or offered some temporary care and succor, most often assistance and protection and opportunities for resettlement, even temporary resettlement, have been provided on a highly selective basis. Only certain types of people have been permitted to come ashore or cross the frontier, and enter closed communities, city-states, or nations.

In this century, the control of borders has become a major social policy issue in many countries of the world. Restrictions motivated by political concerns have greatly complicated already serious social problems. And problems do not end with the matter of admission.

As the Australian journalist Bruce Grant so clearly shows in his book, *The Boat People*, in many instances

> a refugee is an unwanted person. He or she makes a claim upon the humanity of others without always having much, or even anything sometimes, to give in return. If, after resettlement, a refugee works hard or is lucky and successful, he may be accused of taking the work or the luck or success from someone else. If he fails or becomes resentful or unhappy, he is thought to be ungrateful and a burden to the community. A refugee is especially unwanted by officials: his papers are rarely in order, his health is often suspect; and sometimes, although he claims to be fleeing from persecution, he is simply trying to get from a poor overpopulated country to a rich underpopulated one.[24]

Refugee specialist Bill Frelick explains that, in addition to being a potential financial drain and source of other difficulties, refugees—being the quintessential survivors—have another trait that makes many wary of extending themselves. They end to be self-centered, preoccupied with their own situation and its resolution.

> [The refugees'] concern is not for order, systems of bureaucracies, nor for the general welfare. Their concern, rather, is for survival—their own and that of their families.
>
> Governments, on the other hand, have competing concerns: the sovereignty of borders, relations with neighboring countries, controlling immigration, promoting ruling ideologies, placating public opinion. If offering asylum to a refugee is consonant with those concerns, a government might come to his aid. If, however, the government cannot see a benefit in terms of its own interests, there is little incentive to pay the costs associated with extending protection to the refugee.[25]

This old fact of political life has been brought to public attention again and again in the past 100 years, a period the German writer Heinrich Böll has aptly called "this century of prisoners and refugees." It is an epoch when many governments, including our own, whose public rhetoric stresses "world-wide welcome" to the "homeless, tempest-tost,"[26] have proven reluctant to provide asylum for many who seek it.

Clear evidence of xenophobia is to be noted these days in the rising tide of resistance to strangers in Austria, Belgium, Britain, France, Germany, and Italy, and in the growing strength of those seeking to bar their gates. But it is also evident in certain quarters of our society where, as in Europe, once again, it has become a hotly debated political issue and most likely will become an even more critical one in the years ahead.

The Status of Refugees and Displaced Persons

One doesn't have to look very far to see that here in the United States as in other countries, the criteria for admittance of the dispossessed (to say nothing of acceptance) while presumptively humanitarian are frequently something quite different. Consider the first week of 1992 when a group of middle-class Cubans commandeered a helicopter, and flew it to Miami seeking *and obtaining* political asylum while thousands of Haitian boat people, also claiming to be fleeing oppression, were interdicted, apprehended, incarcerated, and denied it. A month later a number of them were put aboard ships and returned to an uncertain future in Haiti because, it was said, they "were not really refugees" but simply destitute people wanting to have a better life in America. Furthermore, it was argued, they were in little danger of being persecuted when they returned home despite the fact that many had been actively involved in opposing the coup that toppled their legitimately elected president, Jean-Bertrand Aristide, and had "a well-founded fear of persecution."

On December 23, 1991, Edward B. Marks, chairman of the U.S. Committee for Refugees, boldly—and, I believe, accurately—states, "Our Government's position on Haitian boat people is clearly discriminatory." In this indictment Marks was expressing a sentiment held not only by advocates for particular groups of asylum seekers but by many close observers of U.S. Refugee policy. Moreover, increasing evidence of abuse, including death threats, to those forcibly repatriated in early February 1992, indicated that the peril was political and not "merely economic" as the officials of the Bush administration were then arguing.

It is not exaggeration to say that, under American refugee policy, the quality of mercy has long been strained by overriding economic, social, and political considerations. Our reception and treatment of would-be asylees is—and has long been—a textbook of situational morality.

Of course, Machiavellian cynics would say, as much as purists might want to separate politics and morals—the former being tied to strategies of governing and norms of expedience; the latter to ethical standards about what is right, or good, or just—what is theoretically separable hardly matters in the everyday affairs of states. Politics is a multifaceted game, and policies carried out by governments and their agents involve congeries of factors that invariably blur such distinctions.

The moral justifications of social behavior are one of the oldest of societal scams. It has long been evident in the use of ethnocentric expressions like *Gott mit uns;* in sanctimonious rhetoric about "the white man's burden"; in jingoistic sloganeering about saving ourselves from everything from "the Yellow Peril" to Japanese carmakers (which, for some, is but a modern variation on the same old theme); and in cold war biases that led to a policy of defining refugees in American law—from the years 1952 to

1980—not as people fleeing persecution "on account of race, religion, nationality, [or]membership in a particular social group or political opinion"
(as the law reads today) but as "people fleeing communism." In those not-
so-distant days, to have found acceptance as a bona fide refugee in this
country it was important to have fled from the right (read "left") place.

Breaking Waves

Such "calculated kindness," as political scientists Gil Loescher and John
Scanlan[27] have labeled it, and its rationale, is an old story in this country;
so, too, is the tendency to distort history itself to serve various social and
political needs.

For example, along with Columbus's great "discovery" 500 years ago,
the Landing of the Pilgrims (almost always written in caps) is one of our
many "creation myths." Its central theme is the quest for a refuge from
persecution and the success in finding it in this New Jerusalem.

In a stirring paean to those early settlers titled "The Landing of the Pilgrim Fathers in New England," the nineteenth-century poet Felicia D.
Hemans asked,

> The breaking waves dashed high
> On a stern and rockbound coast
> When a band of exiles
> Moored their bark
> On the wild, New England shore.

> What sought they thus afar?
> Bright jewels of the mine?
> The wealth of seas, the spoils of war?

> [No!]
> They sought a faith's pure shrine. . . .

> Freedom to worship God.[28]

Those Hemans called that "band of exiles" came to be viewed in the
hoary hagiography of the Founding as the first Americans. For generations, every year, a special day is set aside to celebrate the event. Families
from coast to coast gather together, and sing the English words to the old
German hymn asking the Lord's blessing and reminding themselves of
those brave and buckle-shoed refugees and their befeathered guests, with
whom they broke bread and ate wild turkey and pumpkin pie—and whom
they tried to civilize.

In the early days of nationhood, those early settlers and the many others
whose families had come to the Massachusetts Bay Colony and to any one
of the twelve others, came to call themselves "native Americans."

I note, for those interested in the sociology of sociology, that those of us trained in survey techniques in the 1940s and 1950s had a common label for what were later to be known as "WASPs." Our label was "NAM"— native American!

Returning to the eighteenth century, those earlier NAMs—ignoring both their indigenous neighbors and the Africans who had been here almost as long as they and already constituted 20 percent of the population—worried about how others, meaning Europeans, might fit it. Not surprisingly, they favored those who were similar to themselves in looks and outlooks. A naturalization law, passed in 1790, specified that only free white immigrants were to be eligible to become American citizens.

Early ideas about who was acceptable to be viewed as a "real" American, and the rules about who could become one, persisted as part of the social convention and the legal structure, well into the nineteenth century, even when Ralph Waldo Emerson described the country as a "smelting pot."

When Emerson was middle-aged, the biggest perceived threat to native American hegemony was the flood of Irish Catholics driven off their land by the devastating effects of the Great Famine. Their presence evoked concerns about conflicting loyalties; their manners and mores were viewed as offensive. Many considered them to be "unassimilable aliens" and sought to protect America from the likes of them. "No Irish Need Apply."

Most of the Irish were eventually to escape the wrath of the nativists— and not a few were to adapt quickly to the racial mores of the day. They, too, joined in the persistent debates over whom to welcome and whom to exclude. Many of the rivals of Irish immigrants, and the rivals of other new Americans who worked on the railroads and in the mines were less fortunate than they. The first restrictive legislation against any specific group enacted by the U.S. Congress was the Chinese Exclusion Act of 1882, the year of Emerson's death. It was a portent.

During the Great Migration that began in the early 1880s, millions of Slavs, Italians, Greeks, and Poles seeking economic opportunities, and Jewish refugees seeking freedom to be themselves, crossed the Atlantic, entering New York through Castle Garden, and beginning just 100 years ago, through the portals of Ellis Island's reception center.

> "Listen! Can't you hear the roaring and the bubbling. There gapes her mouth—the harbor where a thousand mammoth feeders come from the ends of the world to pour in their human freight. Ah, what a stirring and a seething. . . ."[29]

The colorful words, precursive of what would someday become multicultural celebrations, were those of the English writer, Israel Zangwill, in his famous play about the New World and the place he called *The Melting Pot.*

In point of fact, many of the immigrants who came between 1880 and 1920 found their new country no Golden Medina but a harsh and often hostile environment. In Yiddish, Italian, Polish, and brogue-heavy English, they cursed Columbus. They said they wished he had never discovered the place! But they made the best of their precarious situation and continued to struggle to make new lives and find acceptance.

Many of those whose society they sought to join feared the influx of what Madison Grant was to claim represented "the weak, broken and mentally crippled of all races drawn from the lowest stratum of the Mediterranean basin and the Balkans, together with hordes of wretched, submerged populations of the Polish ghettos."[30]

Kenneth Roberts, the historical novelist from Kennebunk, Maine, spoke for many. "If," he wrote, "a few million members of the Alpine, Mediterranean, and Semitic races are poured among us, the result must inevitably be a hybrid race of people as worthless and futile as the good-for-nothing mongrels of Central America and southeastern Europe."[31]

In 1911 the presidentially appointed Dillingham Commission came up with a number of suggestions, all of which reflected the view that too many foreigners were being allowed into the country, especially those from southern, central, and eastern Europe. Its findings were supported by testimonials of a number of prominent eugenicists and sociologists.

Writing in *A Connecticut Yankee Speaks His Mind,* John Rowland voiced the sentiments of many anti-immigrant, anti-foreign, and clearly racist Americans.

> The Nordic stock in America seems doomed to extinction in competition with the ancient, generalized stocks from southeastern Europe and Asia minor. . . . What shall we do about it? If our race is worth saving, it is worth saving at all costs. . . . We must break with some of our idealistic tenets. We can no longer subscribe to the doctrine that this land shall lie open to all comers without regard to race or color. The one thing we can do right now is to lock and bar the gate. For every Slav, Armenian, Turk or Jew that you welcome to this country, you may be sure that you are killing an American as yet perhaps unborn.[32]

Rowland's essay was published in 1924, the same year that the most restrictive immigration law in American history was passed, a law that closed the "golden door" to millions of Europeans. For most intents and purposes, it was not to be opened again for forty years.

It is important to note that, at the time of the so-called Quota Law, there was no separate status accorded refugees. This meant that the restrictive legislation not only kept out those who today would be called "economic migrants," but also denied entry to many who had been forced to flee because of racial, religious, or political persecution.

Refugee specialist Julia Taft and her colleagues put it tersely when they wrote:

> If they met the admission criteria of the time they would be admitted; if not, they were excluded. Thus, Jewish refugees from the pogroms of Czarist Rus-

sia fit into a class of admissible aliens during the first decade of this century and were accepted. Many Jewish refugees from Hitler's Germany, thirty years later, did not so qualify, and were not admitted.[33]

The relative few who were able to obtain visas, many of them scholars and scientists, were given little assistance by any official agencies of government—save, in some instances, the War Department. Instead they were assisted by private agencies and services such as the Hebrew Immigrant Aid Society, the International Rescue Committee, and the National Refugee Service.

Changing Course

After the war things began to change. A series of acts passed during the days of the Truman presidency allowed a specified number of displaced persons and war orphans to be admitted outside the quota restrictions. In the 1950s and 1960s, the authority of the office of the Attorney General was used to "parole" a large number of Hungarians and Czechs. That most who were admitted were from communist countries was very much in keeping with both cold war attitudes and immigration statutes, including the 1952 Walters–McCarran Act, which defined "refugee-escapees" as persons who, "because of persecution or fear of persecution on account of race, religion, or political opinion . . . have fled from any *Communist or Communist-dominated country or area* [emphasis mine] or from any country within the general area of the Middle East and are unable or unwilling to return to such country or area on account of race, religion, or political opinion."

The national quota system was finally done away with by the Immigration Act of 1965, but the 1952 definition of refugees remained. Thus, while one significant bias in America's admission policy was dealt with, another was still to be altered. This was not to be addressed until the late 1970s during debates over an act prompted by the fall of Saigon and the aftermath of the war in Indochina.

Under the terms of the Refugee Act of 1980, refugees (i.e., political refugees) were finally defined according to criteria nearly identical to that of the United Nations—that is, as those who have suffered discrimination because of their physical attributes, religious beliefs, or political affiliations and activities, or being out of their countries, have a well-grounded fear of persecution should they return or be sent back. This new definition—new, that is, to Americans—was a major step forward in bringing government policy into line with schoolroom oratory about America as a haven for those "yearning to breathe free."

Yet, as Alejandro Portes and Rubén Rumbaut indicate, formal rules may change but old principles remain.[34]

For years the undercurrent of East-West politics remained the most prominent factor enhancing the opportunities of some and inhibiting the access of others. It was not the only one.

Special interest groups have long been a part of the American political scene. "Bloc power" is an old factor that still must be reckoned with. Generally it is thought of in terms of domestic affairs (such as pressures to advance the cause of civil rights, to legalize abortion, to get prayers back in schools, to provide bilingual education), but pressures have long been exercised by powerful and specific constituencies that affect American immigration and refugee policies. They still are. A very recent example is reflected in the unified stance of a group of black leaders who charged that the Bush administration's policy toward Haitian escapees was in violation of both the letter of America's immigration laws and the spirit of our tradition of safe haven for the oppressed. "If the President will not act, " said the spokesperson for the coalition of organizations including the NAACP, the SCLC, the National Council of Negro Women, TransAfrica, the National Coalition of Black Trade Unionists, and such individuals as Jesse Jackson, Mary Berry, Coretta Scott King, and several U.S. representatives, "Congress must enact legislation to prevent the repatriation of Haitians, at least temporarily."[35]

There is little question but that some of those who sought admission to the United States benefited not only by getting out of the right place at the right time, or because they are more attractive than others or assumed better able to fit in, but also because they have such very strong and effective lobbyists championing their causes.

Indeed, lobbying is often necessary. But is rarely sufficient to ensure special—or even equal—treatment. Being able to "fit in" is also deemed important by many who make and enforce the rules of acceptability. Official denials to the contrary, there is little question that rules about refugee admittance are rather elastic. They may be—and are—stretched to assist certain individuals or groups, contracted in order to exclude others. The racial designation and social class background of petitioners and asylum seekers are among the most widely discussed variables. As in the case of would-be immigrants, there are still favored and disfavored refugees. And the least favored are the immortalized "tired and poor," the "huddled masses."

Eleanor Myer Rogg has commented that "[The migrant] arrives not only with the values and attitudes distinctive of his country of origin but . . . also . . . with values and attitudes distinctive of his social class."[36] Her view is supported by Alejandro Portes who notes that those who first came to Cuba after the Castro Revolution created an economically favorable context of reception for later arrivals. "The bulk of the early Cuban migration, composed of displaced members of the bourgeoisie rather than laborers, brought the capital and entrepreneurial skills with which to start new businesses; later arrivals followed a similar course, leading eventually to the consolidation of an ethnic enclave economy in south Florida."[37]

In recent years even such successes have been called into question as the isolationist phrase "America First" has begun to reecho in the arenas of political debate. The expression conjures a specter that harkens back to earlier campaigns—nativist in name, racist in character—in which many tried to specify who should be permitted to enter the society and participate in the system, and often succeeded in curtailing the influx of "undesirables," like those Patrick Buchanan has charged with making America "so vulgar and coarse, so uncivil and angry."[38]

What is noteworthy is that, as in the past, concerns about newcomers have been raised not only by traditional advocates of restricted entry—some aptly referred to as "paleoconservatives"—but by Americans of varying backgrounds and political persuasions, some of them not too far removed from Ellis Island themselves. Such persons have been joined in recent years by members of various minority communities from Overton in Miami to Monterey Park in Los Angeles who feel that outsiders (like Cubans and Mexicans, for example) "are taking over *our* country."

The few words are laden with proprietary feelings ("our country") and a sense of usurpation—and often by betrayal. ("They said our problems were the highest on the agenda but the damn immigrants get all the jobs.") Such sentiments remind us of Lipset and Raab's discussion in 1970 of the anger of the "once hads" who feel *they* are being displaced, and of the "never hads" who say, "If it weren't for the [Mexicans, Koreans, etc.], we would be much better off."

What is significant in the context of my narrower theme is that—worried about the fact that Americans are no longer in control of the borders, and worried about competition from the outside—those who wish to draw up the gangplanks and close the gates make little distinction based on the motivation of the migrants—that is, whether they are being drawn in the classic manner of economic migrants or expelled and forced into exile by direct persecution or by the collapse of the political order and random violence.

The Politics of Rescue and the Sociology of Exile

The politics of rescue and the resettlement of refugees in this country and others are clearly a multidimensional problem raising issues of theoretical and practical significance for sociologists and for policymakers. Unfortunately, too few of the former have focused on the experience of exile. But this is beginning to change as the importance and urgency of the problem are at last being recognized, and as more and more sociologists begin to address the complex relationships between foreign affairs and national politics—often centered on ethnic rivalries; the dependency of the dispossessed and the proclivities of others to offer or to deny care and succor; and the very nature of community itself, seen in terms of a reexamination of the meaning of ingroups, outgroups, acceptance, and exclusion.

The matters I have discussed here, while focused—especially in the last section of my remarks—on the United States, may be about borders, but they are hardly circumscribed by them. The issue is a global one, and the rise in social conflict, particularly, ethnic conflict means that great as the refugee flows are today, they may be expected to increase dramatically in the future. . . .

How, we must ask, will they—and we—face the odds, of *Man's* bedevilment, not *God's*?

"Of Every Hue and Caste"

N OT LONG AGO, after years of refurbishing, the immigration facility at Ellis Island was rededicated. In one celebration after another, Americans of different backgrounds—European, African, Asian, and Latino—paid homage to all those things that that portal to America was said to represent: shelter, opportunity, liberty, justice. One person after another extolled the wonders of "the world's oldest democracy"; "this haven in a stormy sea"; "our nation of nations"; "the house that we call Freedom."

Yet some who attended the festivities and many more who heard the speeches on radio or television found it all a bit disingenuous. While acknowledging the fact that there had been remarkable advances in intergroup relations in the century that had just passed, especially the integration of the children and grandchildren of the "tired and poor and tempest-tost" who came through Ellis Island in the years between 1892 and 1954, and great successes in the realm of civil rights for all citizens, especially during the last three decades, they knew that just across the harbor—and throughout the land—there were struggles that belied the lofty rhetoric of acceptance, inclusion, and unity. There still are. Wretched slums not all that different from those that existed when the reception center was first dedicated still pock the cityscape. These days, however, instead of the babble of German, Italian, Polish, Yiddish, and brogue-heavy English, so confusing and offensive to the ears of many old Americans who felt they were being overrun with "queer and repulsive"[1] alien elements, the urban centers resound in Spanish, Chinese, Korean, Vietnamese, and Black English. These days the voices of the ghetto poor are more often than not those of people whose skins are considerably darker than those of the "swarthy" Italians, Poles, Slavs, and Jews who came in great numbers in the late nineteenth and early twentieth century. But what many face—

*Originally published as "'Of Every Hue and Caste': Race, Immigration, and Perceptions of Pluralism," in *Interminority Affairs in the U.S. Today: The Challenge of Pluralism*, ed. Peter I. Rose, *The Annals of the American Academy of Political and Social Science*, 530, November 1993, pp. 187–202.

poverty, alienation, rivalry with others in similar straits, and envy for those who have managed to escape—has a depressing familiarity, particularly to those close at hand.

City councilors, police authorities, social workers, schoolteachers, factory managers, storekeepers, journalists, bail bondsmen, welfare mothers, gang members, local residents, and nearby neighbors are the real experts in urban sociology. They know that the melting pots are seething caldrons of competition and intergroup tension, and, to paraphrase Bob Dylan, they do not need outside pundits to tell them that they are boiling over. Consider the headlines: "FROM KILLING FIELDS TO MEAN STREETS"; "BLACKS VS. BROWNS"; "LATIN MASS"; "BONFIRE IN CROWN HEIGHTS"; "DANGEROUS LIAISONS"; "THE NEW POLITICS OF RACE." The last phrase suggests that something is different in the ways various groups interact with one another.

Dramatic changes have occurred, especially in the relativity of poverty, the deterioration of communal structures, the intensity of the violence, and the technology of intergroup combat in the inner-city areas, but, in certain ways, it may be said *plus ça change, plus c'est la même chose* —the more things change, the more they stay the same. At bottom, what is called the new politics of race is more a variation on an old theme, one that has been heard since the earliest days of nationhood.

The Old Politics of Race

Alexis de Tocqueville, a great admirer of American democracy, predicted that, even with the emancipation of the slaves, the racial situation in the United States would be a continuing source of domestic unrest. Writing in the 1830s, Tocqueville expressed the fear that the majority of whites would never overcome their views of the innateness of their own superiority and that the majority of blacks would never lose their enmity for the humiliation and suffering they had experienced.[2] Tocqueville claimed that what we now call "racism" would "perpetually haunt the imagination of Americans, like a painful dream."[3]

Nearly a century and a half after Tocqueville's famous visit to America, another Frenchman, the sociologist Raymond Aron, offered another assessment.

> As far as I am concerned, the greatest achievement of American society is to have drawn millions of people from the lower classes of Europe and made them into good American citizens. That is an extraordinary performance, an unprecedented marvel of acculturation. But you didn't do it without paying a heavy price. . . . You have a permanently un-integrated fringe, consisting chiefly of blacks and Puerto-Ricans. . . . You did very well in assimilating national minorities, but not nearly as well with racial minorities."[4]

Aron, highlighting the dramatic demographic changes that had occurred between the 1830s and the then-present day, made specific reference to the fact that America had long ago ceased to be a society whose principal groups were an Anglo-American majority and a black minority. It had become "a nation of immigrants."[5]

Despite the poetic ring to the expression, historians of the period point to the fact that not all or even most of the newcomers, including those millions of "lower-class" Europeans, were welcomed with equanimity. Once in the United States, they often found themselves ranked and treated according to a congeries of criteria that determined their collective as well as individual place in a hierarchy of acceptability and acceptance. Time of arrival, region of origin, cultural attributes, religious preferences, and physical appearance were among the factors that determined how they were greeted and how they were treated. It was already an old story.[6]

When this country was established, the new nation, like the original colonies, was overwhelmingly white and Protestant, and most citizens hoped it would stay that way. There was great resistance by the Anglo-Americans—who came to call themselves "native Americans"—when émigrés from poverty-ridden Ireland sought refuge in this country. Their presence triggered the first major attempt to restrict immigration, but no formal, specifically targeted restriction against the Irish or any single "nationality" was imposed. That dubious distinction came in 1882, when the Chinese Exclusion Act was enacted. Not long afterward, renewed fear of foreign agitators combined with deeply rooted sentiments against certain groups led to the formation of the Immigration Restriction League. Founded in 1894, it lobbied against those regarded by many as members of "unassimilable races."

The campaign to stop or, at the least, significantly curtail the flow of immigrants continued unabated as more and more newcomers appeared on our shores. Finally, the trend was reversed by the outbreak of war and the subsequent passage of highly restrictive immigration laws, the first passed in 1921, the second in 1924.

The second law succeeded in effectively closing the already heavily guarded gates, keeping millions of immigrants and would-be refugees from entering the United States. By 1929, when the Reed-Johnson National Origins Act of 1924 was fully operative, a grand total of only 165,000 persons were allowed to enter in any given year; 82 percent of those eligible were to come from countries of Northern and Western Europe, 16 percent from Southern and Eastern Europe, and only 2 percent from the rest of the world.

Those who had managed to enter before the heavily biased Quota Law was implemented had hardly been unfamiliar with deprivation or exploitation prior to their emigration. Indeed it was the promise of a better life that drew so many poor people to America. Yet, with the exception of the East European Jews and those in several other much smaller groups, most who came—either as temporary sojourners or to settle here permanently—had had little experience with categorical discrimination because of their own cultural distinctiveness, their religious affiliations, beliefs, or practices, or their politics, nor had they had much experience interacting with persons unlike themselves. They quickly learned that in the New World they were different from those in the dominant group and different from other so-called minorities.

The consequences of this were several. Not surprisingly, coping with both phenomena contributed to the strengthening of in-group allegiances as newcomers found themselves increasingly dependent on countrymen who shared their ascribed identities. This led to the development of networks for employment and welfare and for taking collective action against rival groups. It also led to the adoption of community-based political tactics to press for rights, services, and recognition. These developments, in time, would enhance the acceleration of their entry into the wider society as they evolved—psychologically and politically—from being immigrants to becoming American-style ethnics.[7]

While group rights were not to be officially recognized for more than half a century, many had developed skills for engaging in bloc power to ensure the ability of those like themselves to overcome barriers of prejudice and discrimination. Yet it is also true that, despite the fact that they had often faced considerable racist sentiment and blatant discrimination themselves, it was rare for the new ethnics to identify with the African Americans, to see their situations in any sense as analogous. On the contrary, whatever else was going on, part of their general acculturation involved taking on many of the prejudices of those in the dominant society.

In time, overcoming the considerable hostility to their presence, most of those known as "national minorities" did succeed in becoming "ordinary" Americans,[8] and saw themselves as such. So did many others.

> Wherever our parents came from, whatever language we spoke at home, we reached for a common overriding identity. Those born abroad, or to immigrants, understood that in part it was an identity given to us by the country. We took it with pleasure, when we sang ". . . land where our fathers died" we knew it was not our fathers we were singing of but it was sure our country. Our teachers knew that. Everybody knew that.[9]

The descendants of the involuntary migrants from Africa who, in many ways, had long been quite ordinary Americans in manners and mores and religious practices were not so lucky. They remained marginalized. This paradoxical reality has not only continued to affect relationships between black and white people including those now called "white ethnics"—but also those relationships many African Americans have had with other newcomers, including those who, while frequently categorized as racial minorities themselves, were and remain nationality groups, too.

The Idea of Pluralism

The immigrant-to-ethnic metamorphosis of the newcomers and their politicization, while strengthening communal ties and enhancing leverage, served to many outside their communities as evidence of persisting clannishness, feeding fears of disloyalty or, at the least, conflicting allegiances. Those in positions of power and authority worried aloud about subversion, about the fragmentation of the polity, about the possibility that the "hyphenates" might be responsible for "the disuniting of America." "Americanism is a matter of the spirit and of the soul. Our allegiance must be purely to the United States. The one absolutely certain way of bringing this nation to ruin . . . would be to permit it to become a tangle of squabbling nationalities."[10]

Theodore Roosevelt and others who agreed with his remarks and his view that "there is no room in this country for hyphenated Americanism"[11] advocated the acceleration of procedures that would discourage any thoughts of separatism while holding out the carrot of full partnership. Integration was to depend on eshewing distinctiveness and fully accepting the ways of the dominant group.

The promoters of such a policy sometimes invoked the image of the melting pot, but savvy listeners would realize that they were less interested in what the new Americans would bring to any new social alloy than in controlling the damage the immigrants might inflict on the body politic. Regardless of the colorful rhetoric, it was forced assimilation rather than fusion that was most favored.

Some of the immigrants and some of their supporters, seeing through the rhetorical legerdemain of what came to be known as Americanization, offered alternatives. Perhaps the most thoughtful and surely the most effective came from a group of liberal and radical intellectuals, a mixed group of old Americans and new ones. The concept of cultural pluralism was to become the watchword of an ideology first formally presented in 1915 by the philosopher Horace Kallen, himself an immigrant from Eastern Europe.[12]

The basic premise was that there is strength in diversity, that being proud of one's past and appreciating where one came from complements rather than compromises membership in an ever more heterogeneous society. To Kallen and such allies as Jane Addams, Lillian Wald, Randolph Bourne, and John Dewey, the United States was not a fondue of amalgamation but a symphony of accommodation.[13] Pushing his own metaphor, Kallen saw the orchestra—that is, the society—as consisting of groups of instruments (nationalities) playing their separate parts while together making beautiful music resonant with harmony and good feeling.

Kallen's pluralism was especially appealing to the immigrants from Eastern and Southern Europe. At the time, others, including those in the small Asian communities and the growing Latino ones, seem to have paid it little mind. The same was true of the far larger black community. For good reason. It was heavily biased, "encapsulated," as John Higham aptly put it, "in white ethnocentrism."[14]

While generally sympathetic and frequently in league with supporters of better treatment to those still called Negroes,[15] few of the pluralists had had much to say about the contribution of those from Africa, or, for that matter, from Asia or Latin America, to the society they liked to characterize as "the new America." As Bob Suzuki and Nicholas Appleton point out, when first proposed, "pluralism in the United States was concerned with liberty and equality [of European immigrants] and not with promoting the historic identities of non-English subcultures."[16] The latter was not to come until the last decades of the twentieth century, when, as shall be noted, "multiculturalism" became an alternate shibboleth, a slogan most enthusiastically endorsed by nonwhite Americans and looked upon with considerable suspicion by many others.

The acculturation and acceptance of the "national minorities" to which Raymond Aron referred did occur, but not overnight. It was a slow and uneven process, taking place mainly in the four decades between the mid-1920s and the mid-1960s, a time when immigration from outside was almost at a standstill and debates shifted from the rights of foreigners to the rights of Americans; a time when the society underwent a series of dramatic political and economic reversals as well: boom, bust, war, peace, prosperity, and the wrenching conflicts in Vietnam and on the streets of America. Affecting the speed of the integration were a number of cultural, social, and situational factors, many related to these ups and downs.

Despite periodic resurgences of old prejudices and the implementation of new ways of blocking entry to neighborhoods, jobs, and social institutions, and a number of serious interethnic conflicts,[17] white ethnics did begin to move from the margins into the mainstream. Especially after World War II, often abetted by such entitlements as the G.I. Bill for armed service veterans, the arrivistes faced a world of expanding opportunities and took advantage of them. While some were left behind, increasing numbers moved to new homes in new neighborhoods where they were to enjoy life as proud, patriotic Americans, often defining themselves in class terms rather than strictly ethnic ones.

One result of their "making it" was the loosening of many bonds to old communities. But they were rarely severed completely. Even in what some saw as a "twilight of [white] ethnicity,"[18] there was almost always a glow of nostalgia and the retention of symbolic ties.[19] Yet, ironically, for many who were also well on the way to what Milton Gordon once called "structural assimilation,"[20] the dying members were to be fanned afresh in a reaction to three trends that occurred in the 1960s: the Black Power or Black Consciousness movement, the renewal of immigration, and the contentious debates over the meaning of multiculturalism.

Black Migrants

Toward the end of the period of the Great Migration, the sons and daughters of former slaves and their grandchildren began moving north seeking to find acceptance in what, like the immigrants, they, too, saw as a "promised land."[21] It was in the north where those who were in so many ways the least foreign but still the most alienated of all—save, perhaps, for the native peoples—often came face to face with a new problem: ethnic diversity. It was in the cities of the North where the seeds of considerable interminority tension so often highlighted in the press today—blacks versus members of the old white ethnic groups, such as the Irish in Boston, Italians in Brooklyn; blacks versus Jews, as in Crown Heights; blacks versus Latinos, as in Miami; blacks versus Asians, as in Los Angeles—were sown alongside, and, in some instances, in lieu of, more traditional black-white conflict.

In the segregated south, those called Negroes had been well aware that they were a people apart. But their separateness was largely a harshly enforced relegation to a fixed subordinate status, an ascribed and maintained marginality based not so much on cultural differences as on far more base assumptions of absolute inferiority. Jim Crow laws that emerged in the wake of the brief post-Civil War period of Reconstruction returned them for many intents and purposes to their preslavery status as America's *Untermenschen*. One result was to institutionalize an apartheid system in which the South would formally remain—at least until the mid-1950s—along with much of the rest of the country, what Pierre van den Berghe once aptly labeled a *"Herrenvolk* democracy."[22]

When the African Americans started to move north, it was a given, a fact of life, that white people, like those they had known back home, no matter how poor, were privileged members of the society, privileged enemies. Thus even the optimism with which they undertook the city-bound movements to New York, Philadelphia, Cleveland, Detroit, and Chicago was always tempered by the realization that northern whites might not be all that different from those in the south. They were more or less an already known entity to be guarded against. The immigrants were something else altogether.[23]

Owing to the precariousness of their economic situation, the African American migrants sought housing in the cheapest parts of town. By the time of their movement, many of the areas were already heavy with the presence of Jews, Italians, Slavs, and the others who looked stranger, sounded stranger, and acted stranger than the sort of white folks they knew and knew about. In a number of cities, it would not be long before some of those who settled in these mixed communities would have their confusion compounded by the fact that the ghettos that seemed to be serving as way stations for the others were, for them, more characteristic of their original, medieval form, that is, places of confinement.[24]

Recognition of the relativity of their freedom was further aggravated by the belief—which sometimes had a sound basis in truth—that it was the "foreigners" who were most directly in control of their lives. They were frequently the people who employed them, sold to them, rented to them, loaned them money, and in general leapfrogged their way to positions of even greater power and influence in the economic nexus, politically, and in public institutions—as policemen, welfare workers, and schoolteachers—and, frequently, right out of the neighborhoods.[25]

For many, immersed in their own struggles, the fact that the immigrants around them had had hard lives before, that many of them had also been persecuted and continued to be discriminated against, meant very little, if they were aware of such situations at all. Seen either as agents of The Man or as interlopers, and sometimes as both, the Jews and other white ethnics[26]—and, in time, others, such as Cubans in Miami[27] and Koreans in New York and Los Angeles[28]—were close-at-hand targets for their bitter rage at the "oppressive system," a rage often expressed in what, heard from the mouths of others, would be called "nativist sentiment."

In the 1950s, Ralph Ellison spoke of the black migrants in the northern slums, who "like some tragic people out of mythology . . . aspired to escape from its own unhappy homeland to the apparent peace of a distant mountain; but which, in migrating, made some fatal error of judgment and fell into a great chasm of mazelike passages that promise ever to lead to the mountain but end ever against the wall."[29] He knew who they were but, he argued, others did not see them; they were "invisible."

In the early 1960s, Michael Harrington identified them as part of "the other America."[30]

By the mid-1960s, those in that "other" America, in particular those who were black, were not only known by all but heard by all. The cries for justice, sounded mainly in the southern campaigns led by traditional civil rights leaders, mingled with other cries—for assertiveness, for retribution—as the civil rights movement for inclusion turned into a Black Power revolt and as a spirit of ethnicization spread through the African American communities.

Many white Americans, including numerous children of European immigrants and many others now living at some distance from what Kenneth Clark called "the dark ghettos,"[31] were, by then, firmly imbued with the spirit of Kallenesque pluralism. Yet they were quite unprepared for what blacks—and those in some of the other racial minorities who often used Black Power advocates as their models and frequently adapted the tactics and rhetoric of Black Consciousness to their own conditions—began to demand, and to do, often in the name of cultural recognition. Organized struggles for community control of neighborhoods, requests for assurances of representation in jobs and on campuses, demands for special programs in universities and equal time in the curriculum are examples of the sorts of activities that seemed particularly threatening.[32]

Jules Feiffer captured the essence of the changing mood in a cartoon in which one of his white liberal characters says, "Civil rights used to be much more tolerable until the Negroes got into it."[33]

Of course, not all blacks in the 1960s were militants, and not all militants were poor, ghetto-dwelling members of what has become known by the controversial term "urban underclass." Nor are they today. There are many, probably the majority, who want to have what so many others simply take for granted; who wish to be judged, in the words of Martin Luther King, Jr., not "by the color of their skin but by the content of their character."[34] Yet it remains a fact of life that the bus drivers, nurses, auto workers, schoolteachers, and social workers, even the lawyers and doctors and professors among them, are, to this day, far from free of color-based prejudice, far from free from distorting assumptions about how they got to where they are—and what they are doing there anyway.[35]

In the eyes of others, and often in their own eyes, even at the dawn of an era when the president's cabinet, for the first time in history, "looks like America," most black Americans still remain a people apart. "Black students at Yale University, black members of the Omaha police force, even black passengers on an airline flight," Andrew Hacker reports, "never cease to be aware of their white surroundings."[36] Rich, poor, well-educated or illiterate, having police records or Ph.D.s, they are reminded of this fact of American life by both blatant and subtle indicators at every turn. It is something Hacker rightly claims that most white Americans, even those intellectually well aware of how black people have suffered due to the inequities imposed on them, simply cannot fathom.[37]

The Renewal of Immigration

The second unanticipated phenomenon that marked another turning point in race and ethnic relations was the passage of the Immigration Reform Bill of 1965.

When it was being debated, those working most diligently for the removal of quota restrictions imposed in the 1920s assumed that the beneficiaries of the lowered barriers would be, in the main, Europeans, as had most immigrants before. Yet one of the unexpected consequences of the act [as discussed at length in the essay "From Pariahs to Paragons"] was the entry of millions of newcomers from Asia and Latin America.

Many who worried about what such changes might portend would agree with Ellis Cose's observation that "Congress had ended up with a most expansive result—one ensuring that an already steady stream of strange people knocking on America's door would swell into a torrent, heightening not only the potential for ethnic enrichment but also for ethnic turmoil."[38]

The last five words highlight an old and familiar problem that, in recent years, has taken on renewed urgency, that is, finding a way to reconcile diversity—the most recent flow of immigrants contains the largest influx of nonwhites of any time since the peak years of the slave trade—with the potential for a renewal of group-based competition so characteristic of the years of the Great Migration and their immediate aftermath.

The recent tensions between new immigrants and old minorities, especially African Americans, in cities across the land are pointed indicators of the sorts of conflicts Cose fears. But there is something more, something suggested by Nathan Glazer. The latest "newcomers" may be, as he put it, "more distant in culture, language and religion from white Americans, whether of the old or new immigration, than [they] were from each other,"[39] but, as I have argued in an earlier essay, many of the Asians and some of the Latinos—especially Cubans who, of course, are in the Southeast, not the West—have tended to take a path that seems quite northern in character, reenacting in a variety of instances the strategies and proclivities of the European immigrants.[40] This has included methods of dealing with racism directed against themselves; patterns of intergroup competition in city neighborhoods; differential mobility based on class, contacts, and cultural values; assertions—and reassertions of historical identities (this time as Chinese, Japanese, Korean, Filipino, Vietnamese Americans); and, in many cases, in attitudes toward and in relationships with blacks.[41] Moreover, many Asians and, again, some Latinos appear to be recapitulating the white ethnics' movements from the peripheries of communities into ever more direct involvement at the centers. But their acculturation as new, clearly hyphenated Americans has not been without difficulty, and it is far from complete. There is resentment on many sides—as there had been for their white ethnic counterparts. The most successful of the new foreigners are particularly threatening to the status quo of both whites and blacks, but especially the blacks, as they—like their earlier counterparts from Europe—move in, up, and over.

Racial animosity is very sharply felt. Not surprisingly, those caught in its complex web are seeking ways to protect themselves and whatever hard-won gains they have achieved. Intergroup rivalries are nothing new. Once again they are proving to be "both an enduring American phenomenon and an invaluable political tool . . . [one that] has more resembled a virus that at times lies dormant but can suddenly erupt with vengeance—particularly during periods of stress."[42]

Half a year after the worst urban American riots of the century, Los Angeles seems to be a city coming apart rather than coming together. Though there are some signs of progress and hope, there are others that the violence and destruction served only to intensify competition and mistrust in this most diverse of major American cities.

Black, Hispanic, Asian, and white communities have withdrawn into themselves, more aware than ever of their differences, competing for scarce resources, aid, jobs, and political power.[43]

Going to Extremes

A decade ago, Milton M. Gordon, the sociologist who had written so insightfully about cultural and structural assimilation, seemed to reconceptualize the old idea of pluralism, suggesting that there were, in fact, two kinds, one "liberal"—which sounds, to this writer at least, rather conservative—and the other "corporate."

"Those who favor the liberal form," Gordon argued,

> . . . emphasize in their arguments the ethical and philosophical value of the idea of individual meritocracy and the notion that current generations should not be expected to pay for the sins of their fathers or, at least, those who lived here before them, whether genetically related or not. They also point to functional considerations such as the possibility that measures such as forced busing and affirmative action to ensure group quotas will create white backlash and serve as continuing major irritants in the relationships between racial and ethnic groups. Those who favor policies which fall, logically, under the rubric of corporate pluralism emphasize . . . the moral and philosophical position which posits group rights as well as individual rights, and the need for major compensatory measures to make up for massive dimensions of racial discrimination in the past.[44]

Gordon predicted that deciding which approach to pluralism to adopt, or which path to follow, would become an issue not only for scholars of American culture but for the society as a whole. Resolving this "new American dilemma," as he referred to the problem, "will have much to do with determining the nature, shape, and destiny of racial and ethnic relations in America in the twenty-first century."[45] More recently, Arthur M. Schlesinger, Jr. suggested that the time had already come to make the choice. He posited the dilemma as a challenge to the inclusive trend of American democracy by those fostering an ideology of balkanization, one that clearly plays on the sorts of tensions that have been reappearing on the streets and on the campuses in recent years.

> Instead of a transformative nation with an identity all its own, America increasingly sees itself as preservative of old identities. Instead of a nation composed of individuals making their own free choices, America increasingly sees itself as composed of groups more or less indelible in their ethnic character. The national idea had once been *e pluribus unum*. Are we now to belittle the *unum* and glorify *pluribus*? Will the center hold? Or will the melting pot yield to the Tower of Babel?[46]

While seeming to alter the basic premises of the old pluralists, especially the core idea that the hyphen connects instead of separates, the polarization that both Gordon and Schlesinger posit is the topic of intense debate. Their distinctions are not only philosophical but strategic, depending, in large part, on the class, status, power, and, especially, the race of the antagonists.

It ought not to be at all surprising that those who have become successful, particularly but not exclusively the old white ethnics, favor what Gordon calls the liberal approach and see the other one less in terms of enhancing the richness of the society—as many of their own parents and mentors might have argued—than as the vehicle for its disintegration. On the other hand, it is equally understandable that those who are still on the outside and who have suffered discrimination generally greater than that ever conferred upon the others—want to use collective action to satisfy a desire for acceptance on their own terms. It is something that another pluralist of "The Hyphen-Connects School," W. E. B. Du Bois, said in 1903, before pluralism was an ideology—and before John Dewey's felicitous expression had ever been uttered!

Du Bois's famous statement that "one ever feels his twoness,—an American, a Negro" ends with a desire: "He simply wishes to make it possible for a man to be both a Negro and an American, without being cursed and spit upon."[47]

Horace Kallen once said that "men may change their clothes, their politics, their wives, their religions, their philosophies to a greater or less extent: they cannot change their grandfathers. Jews or Poles or Anglo-Saxons, in order to cease being Jews or Poles or Anglo-Saxons would have to cease to be."[48] The same sentiment is now again being expressed not only by newcomers but also by many spokespersons for those old, very old, Americans—from Africa.

Few engaged in the new movements for group recognition want to tear down the foundations of society, but they do favor altering the structures to truly be more inclusive. But their opponents, often using the most extreme examples, claim that the would-be multiculturalists are, in fact, "polarizing particularists" or "subversive separatists." They further argue that the corporate tactics are alienating members of their own groups from still-needed allies while accelerating the disintegration of the United States into a fractured mosaic. If it continues, it is argued, only cohort membership will be the sine qua non of identity and power.[49]

While concerned about the "centricities" of all who are making demands,[50] there seems to be an underlying motif in the expressions of many who worry about "the cult of ethnicity."[51] Their most strident language is often used in objection to the rise of black chauvinism and, as Schlesinger puts it, "the guilt trips laid on by champions of cultures based on despotism, superstition, tribalism, and fanaticism, especially, the Afrocentrists.[52]

It should be noted that, even for opponents of multiculturalism, somehow the demands of Native Americans to recapture their old ways, the assertions of those from Japan and China and India to have their presence acknowledged and to be granted special recognition, even certain cultural proclivities of Mexican Americans once viewed, as were those of Italian

Americans and French-Canadians, as being too peasant-like seem more tolerable to many white Americans—including the old-fashioned liberals—than the claims of blacks. The old argument that "the Negro has no culture of his own"[53] is now transmuted into one that states that he has no culture worth resurrecting or reasserting: not the African heritage; not that of the diaspora, which, of course, would have to include so much of the music, literature, and icons of the popular culture now regarded here and throughout the world as quintessentially American. The persistence of what George Frederickson has called the peculiarly American "arrogance of race"[54] continues to diminish the significance of Afro-American culture and the significance of those who want to celebrate their own contributions to a society that claims to be one that appreciates those "of every hue and caste."

There are many parallels to what was going on in the waning days of the last century and what is happening today. But whereas the main fault line in the society, north and south, had long been between whites and non-whites, the ground now is shifting. In the future, the sharpest divisions may well be between blacks and non-blacks.

Blaming the Jews

I

"O F ALL PEOPLE, why the Jews?"
This question, often prefaced with the phrase, "Given all they have done and their close alliance with civil rights causes," is now being raised in many public symposia and private discussions on Black-Jewish relations in the United States and in response to a number of anti-Semitic attacks recently made by certain African Americans in university lecture halls and over public airwaves in many parts of the country.

One straightforward and only half-facetious answer is "Why not?" After all, even in America, where they have achieved unprecedented success, Jews remain a vulnerable minority and ready scapegoat. For all their achievements in business, the professions, the arts—or, more likely, because of them, Jews are still viewed with considerable ambivalence, especially by those Seymour Martin Lipset and Earl Raab once called "the never-hads."[1]

Many such never-hads, particularly those who are more formally described today as "disadvantaged, non-white minorities," see Jews as models to emulate. ("If they can do it, we can do it.") But others within the same cohort, have taken a different stance; a position shocking to many Jews who long saw themselves as the primary advocates of integration.

In an "Op-Ed" piece in *The New York Times* in March 1990, Lipset noted that "In America, blacks are the only major ethnic community in which some spokesmen voice anti-Semitic stereotypes."[2] Since then an increasing number of those who have listened to such voices seem to have been caught up in the fervor of accusation, turning bitterness at the barriers that thwart black advancement and resentment at others' attainments

*Originally published in *Society: Social Science and Modern Society*, vol. 31, no. 6, September/October 1994, pp. 35–40, this expanded and updated version appears in "Black Anti-Semitism and the Rhetoric of Resentment," in *Performances in American Literature and Culture: Essays in Honor of Professor Orm Øverland on His 60th Birthday,*" ed. Vidar Pedersen and Zeljka Svrljuga (Bergen, Norway, 1995).

into a causative relationship. ("The only reason for the Jews' success is that it was achieved at somebody else's expense; namely, ours.") Going even farther some have been waging vitriolic campaigns against these "Jewish profiteers." The most virulent rantings of antipathy sound strikingly like the sort of things white anti-Semites have said for years. Once again, Jews are grotesquely characterized as everything that is underhanded and loathsome. Added to the all-too-familiar caricatures of "hook-nosed, lox-eating, money-grubbing vultures," particularly prominent in homegrown as well as foreign-sponsored anti-Jewish campaigns of the 1930s, they are sometimes portrayed today as even being so diabolical in their deviousness as to have been responsible for the Holocaust. Here, for example, is Khalid Abdul Muhammed, an assistant to Louis Farrakhan, speaking at Kean College in Union, New Jersey in November of 1993: "everybody always talks about Hitler exterminating six million Jews. But don't nobody ever ask what they did to Hitler. . . . They went in there, in Germany, the way they do everywhere they go, and they supplanted, they usurped. . . . They had undermined the very fabric of society."[3]

Some of the charges are more specific to the history and current conditions of the African American spokespersons and those they claim to represent. Included in the many sweeping generalizations are these: in times long past, Jews were the leaders among slave traders and the principal slave owners; for years they were the main exploiters of blacks in the ghettoes who "drained their patrons of their lifeblood before turning over the task to Arabs, Koreans, and others"; today they control everything in the private sector, from the banks to the communications industry, as well as most government agencies. Jews are also said to be the leading opponents of government policies which favor blacks and other designated minorities through affirmative action practices, while being the principal supporters of the suppression of Palestinians and other Third World peoples.

While the expressions of the extremists are hardly the views of the majority, recent surveys indicate that many African Americans have perceptions of Jews that are hardly complementary. They contain some variation on one or another of the aforementioned themes. Often such ideas are even found, in one form or other, among those who would be assumed to think differently. This is especially disturbing to those Jewish and African American intellectuals and religious and political leaders worried about the breakdown of trust and the growing tendency to revert to identity politics. There is reason for such concern.

The long-documented generalization of an inverse relationship between levels of education and levels of anti-Semitism[4] is being challenged by evidence of high negativity even among well-educated blacks, especially teenagers and young adults. Recent surveys show that nearly one in four black respondents under thirty, including those who are highly educated, are unfavorably disposed toward Jews.[5] (In older age groups, the "education correlation" still appears to be holding.) Much of this may be attributable to the success of the campus crusades mounted by Louis Farrakhan and other charismatic advocates of communal pride, spiritual uplift, political mobilization—all seemingly dependent on the need to define an enemy. Using the very same words Adolf Hitler penned in *Mein Kampf*, they, too, are saying "the Jews are our misfortune."

While it is doubtful that Farrakhan or Khalid Abdul Muhammed or Leonard Jeffries of the City University of New York or others who have been widely quoted for their diatribes against "Jewish interests" and, not infrequently, Jews themselves, ever read the writings of the German sociologist Georg Simmel, like so many others who need scapegoats to advance their own causes, they clearly understand the concept of "the third element."[6] Third elements not only greatly complicate social relationships and provide "opportunities for transition, conciliation, and the abandonment of absolute contrast," as Simmel put it[7] they also offer a vehicle for considerable manipulation of the other parties, even by the weakest member. What the black demagogues are seeking to do—and to gain—is what many others have tried before.

In a comment in *Time* magazine, published along with those of others on February 28, 1994, Midge Decter put it differently, but the implication of her remarks was clearly similar. The sharply focused attention on Jews as enemies, she says, offers a kind of political methadone for African Americans in an environment in which other forces are difficult to control.

Jew-baiting by blacks (at least certain black leaders) may be more a placebo than a panacea but it is bitter medicine, leaving a terrible aftertaste, and not only for those who swallow it. It contributes to a significant backlash, the latter most noticeable in the increasing reluctance of Jewish Americans to take traditional liberal stances in explaining (some would now say "explaining away") many of the extreme actions of those most long saw as victims of an oppressive and unfair system.

Other commentators, including among them Leon Wieseltier, Cornel West, and Michael Lerner, who were also quoted in the same *Time* forum on "The Rift Between Blacks and Jews," offered different interpretations from Decter's, though, it should be noted, almost all, regardless of their racial or ethnic identity, made distinctions between attitudes about and relations between blacks and "whites" and those about and between blacks and Jews. Such distinctions are a central theme in Paul Berman's widely discussed article, "The Other and the Almost the Same," published in *The New Yorker* on the same day in February 1994. (They reappear time and again in "Jews, Blacks and Others," a special symposium prompted by Berman's essay, that appeared in the social science journal *Society* in November of 1994.)

II

Without using the word triadic, Berman notes that the relationship between blacks and Jews (and other whites) in the United States, at least in the twentieth century, has been precisely that. In his essay, he removes Jewish Americans from the rubric "white"—but he does not put the nonwhite Jews and the blacks together in a single category. While members of both groups are literally as well as sociologically speaking minorities, they have very different backgrounds and cultures and have had very different experiences in trying to make it in America.

Berman goes even farther and suggests that "American Jews and the African Americans have never looked or sounded alike and the difference in economic conditions has become more pronounced since the days of bedbug-Jewish-tenement poverty."[8] Although there are numerous exceptions, seen most clearly in similarity of outlooks, manners, mores, and politics of substantial segments of today's black and Jewish middle-classes, Berman's contention is quite valid. There is little doubt that the significant gap related to the rates of mobility within the two groups has long been and remains an underlying source of tension. It is not the only one. There is also the matter of "relative suffering."

While it has been argued that the two groups do have a common bond owing to their confrontation with bigotry and discrimination, even here, as Berman says, "The shared history of having someone's boot press on their vulnerable necks . . . has taken such different forms for blacks and for Jews as to be barely comparable."[9] This is evident even in the most cursory review of their respective experiences in America.

The first blacks arrived in the American colonies in 1619; the first Jews in 1654. The former were indentured servants, the latter, merchants and professionals. The relative status of those early representatives was, in a sense, prophetic, for regardless of how far some blacks were to move up the ladder of social mobility in the centuries ahead, Jews generally would be on a higher rung. Even the Jewish immigrants who arrived between 1880 and 1925, impoverished refugees from Czarist pogroms and general economic blight, were still better off than the black Americans who had been in the country for more than two centuries. While the new Americans had come from traditional societies where the serfs had only recently been emancipated, they had never been in peonage. Their marginal status, whatever its negative consequences—and there were many—meant that they had learned to care for themselves while having to cope with the others around them. They had survived in part by playing the classic role of "middleman minority." That was to carry over into the United States.

Many of the East European Jews (who were to constitute well over 90 percent of American Jewry) began their new lives as peddlers and tradesmen or garment workers, struggling to survive and to give their families a new lease on life in what was often a quite hostile environment. Despite a variety of obstacles, not least anti-Jewish prejudices and restrictive practices, they worked hard to prove themselves and to improve themselves. By the 1940s, the dramatic mobility of the Jewish segment was beginning to be noticed. Within another decade Jews were to be rated as the most successful of all ethnic groups in the United States on the basis of achievement, and professional status.[10] Their continued success was marked by increasing prominence in government circles, first as advisors, and then as elected members of Congress, and, most recently, in the administrations of many of our most prestigious colleges and universities. (Currently, the presidents of Barnard, Dartmouth, Harvard, Princeton, Trinity, Williams, Yale, the University of Chicago and Pennsylvania are all Jewish.)

Americans from Africa have had a very different history. They did not choose to come, and their entire existence was shaped by the reason that they did. The mark of their oppression left a bitter legacy. Slavery was replaced by segregation and blacks remained beyond the pale of social acceptance, far down in the stratification hierarchy and outside the mainstream of American political life. Yet, owing to the nature of their particular acculturation experiences, they were to internalize many basic Protestant American values regarding achievement and mobility. What most blacks came to want was not very different from what Jews sought, namely, a legitimate place in American society; still, despite the famous Supreme Court decisions of the 1950s and the Civil Rights Acts of the 1960s, categorical discrimination persisted, institutionalized in a variety of contexts in what George Fredrickson has aptly called "a culture of racism."[11] This meant that the majority of African Americans continued to be handicapped in trying to realize their hopes for full acceptance and inclusion. Even today, when the president of the United States has a cabinet that, as he says "looks like America," the legacies of slavery and segregation are still all too present.

Andrew Hacker's recent book shows just how pervasive racism is today, affecting and infecting almost every sphere of social life—economic, political, social, familial, even religious. Its institutionalized nature is shown to consistently favor those born white over those born black leading to significant differences in life chances. Hacker borrows Benjamin Disraeli's famous phrase about the sharply divided and mutually ignorant classes of Victorian England to refer to the United States as two nations, one white, one black, separate, hostile, and decidely unequal.[12]

In such a context, blacks would surely see Jews as a well-entrenched part of the "white nation." Many whites would too. While in many ways they are white, if asked, many Jews would point to the fact that they are also quite different from many others who check that box on questionnaires and census forms. Moreover, if you pressed them some would claim that those on the two sides of America's great racial divide are quite similar to one another, more similar than they are to Jews. The main reason for this is that, despite the circumstances that forced them to come to America as involuntary migrants and the caste lines that formally kept them apart, most contemporary African Americans share a common rural, Protestant tradition and culture quite different from that even of those few Jews who grew up in the South.

Although quite ignorant of Jewish suffering in medieval and modern Europe, in segregated parishes, those who used to be called Negros did share a sense of biblical affinity for they long identified themselves with the time "When Israel was in Egypt's Land" and with the call to "Let My People Go." The imagery linked the beleaguered blacks to Pharaoh's Jewish slaves. Yet, on the occasions when they did meet or interact with real-live Jews, they did not encounter Moses—or Joshua or David, the Giant Killer, but dealers and doctors, none of whom seemed to have little connection to their spiritual icons.[13] And while it may well be true that, as many blacks claim, they could not tell who was Jewish merely by looking ("white folks are white folks"), many still allow as to how, though they didn't know many Jews personally, they knew about them, and knew that they were different from those in the dominant sector, the white Christians.

Those differences, couched in varied ways—some religious, some political, but mostly economic—are well fixed in the folklore of the Old South where, as Harry Golden once said, "the Jewish store is as commonplace as the Confederate monument that stands in the town square." Black storytellers frequently acknowledged the Jewish presence, limited though it was, in their very regional *Weltanschauung*. A common opener was: "One day a Negro, a white man, and a Jew. . . ."

In the North, where more than 98 percent of Jewish immigrants had settled in the years between 1880 and 1925, the greenhorns from the cities and shtetls of Eastern Europe constantly compared themselves and measured their own progress against that of the "real Americans" (meaning, of course, old, native-born white people, not Indians) and other newcomers, too. Rarely were African Americans, then in the early stages of their own Great Migration, such referents.

For their part, when the black migrants started to move north, it was a given, a fact of life, that white people, like those they had known back home, no matter how poor, were privileged members of the society, privileged enemies. The optimism with which they moved to the cities of New York, Philadelphia, Cleveland, Detroit, and Chicago was always tempered by the realization that northern whites might not be all that different from those in the South. And black Southerners often proved to be quite prescient. While not legal, segregation was a de facto aspect of life within every nook and cranny of their new Promised Land. Owing to their precarious economic situation, the African American migrants generally moved into the cheapest parts of town, into areas often already heavy with the presence of people who looked stranger, sounded stranger, and acted more strangely than the sort of white folks they knew so well.

If those who were white were an already known entity to be guarded against, the immigrants, among them large numbers of recently arrived East European Jews, were something else altogether. In a number of cities, it would not be long before the very blacks who settled in mixed communities or in nearby enclaves would have their confusion compounded by the fact that the ghettoes that seemed to serve as way stations for the foreigners, were, for themselves, more characteristic of their original, medieval form, that is, places of restriction and confinement.

The recognition of the relativity of their freedom vis-à-vis the immigrants' was further aggravated by the belief, which often had a sound basis in truth, that it was those newcomers, sometimes of Jewish origin, who were most directly in control of their lives. While they did not run the cities or own the banks, by the 1930s, Jews were becoming increasingly prominent among the people who employed blacks, sold to them, rented to them, loaned them money, all the while preparing for their own or, more often, their children's move outward and upward.

In a frequently cited essay about his Harlem childhood, James Baldwin noted, "The grocer was a Jew, and being in debt to him was very much like being in debt to the company store. . . . We bought our clothes from a Jew and, sometimes, our second hand shoes."[14] Baldwin's image was that of thousands of others who grew up in similar circumstances. It is not hard to see how easily it could be asserted that what Jews accomplished could only be done by contrivance and connivance at the expense of those in the weakest power positions, like the blacks. This assumption received added credence by the fact that, more quickly than the offspring of other newcomers, second generation Jews soon began to achieve power and influence in the political and economic arena, in politics and in public institutions where they became welfare workers, schoolteachers, and local government officials. Moreover, many of the stereotypes already held about their intentions and involvements, their talents and their proclivities to push themselves and their children appeared to be reified wherever blacks looked. Jews seemed to have a knack for taking hold of their own lives and those of others.

During the same time period, Jews were developing their own perspectives on their "colored" neighbors. Some shared the views of the majority, others adhered to their own. Some of their notions were quite positive; others quite negative. Almost all were about people who were different than they themselves.

Blacks were seen as long-suffering, religious, physically strong, athletically and musically talented, and "cool." Not a few immigrant kids looked favorably at such traits, especially the latter ones. But the Negroes were also thought to be irresponsible (a variation on "shiftless"), untrustworthy, prone to violence, and sexually aggressive.[15] American Jewish humor often reflected these mixed perceptions. It was evident in the jokes exchanged on the mean streets of the old ghettoes and the whispered jibes made about "the shvartzes." It was standard fare on the "Borscht Circuit" in the resorts of the Catskills region near New York and in the clubs of eastern cities but also in Los Angeles. It is still evident in the vulgar slurs as challenges to "political correctness" in Jackie Mason's latest Broadway show.

Jews, so sensitive to slights and stereotypes themselves, were not—and are not—exempt from criticism for their own prejudices.

III

It seems quite remarkable that, given the fact that blacks and Jews were really such strangers to one another, and one another's culture, they ever managed to have any sort of significant relationships or that they ever got together for common causes. But as is well known, both these did occur.

As Paul Berman, among many others, rightly suggests, this point should not be dismissed as just so much rhetoric. However great the differences of history and culture and temperament, real as well as symbolic bonds helped to establish and then maintain one of America's most important and long-lived progressive confederations. The now-so-mightily strained (many call it the "broken") alliance was once so powerful as to have been a model for coalition building. It had started quite modestly.

In northern cities, in league with early advocates of organized defenses against racial and religious injustice, increasing numbers of educated and politically active children of Jewish immigrants, few of whom knew much about Africa or the African Diaspora, came to relate the enslavement, segregation, and ghettoization of America's blacks to their own past history. From the earliest decade of the twentieth century, Jews and blacks were tied together in the battle for civil rights and against the common foes of bigotry and discrimination. Many Jewish philanthropists and many more less well-endowed Jews joined forces with black leaders in the earliest days of the struggle. Jews were prominent among the founders and funders of the National Association for the Advancement of Colored People, the NAACP's Legal Defense and Education Fund, and numerous related organizations.

From the mid-1930s to the mid-1950s, the very period when the close-at-hand economic symbiosis was most acute, prominent representatives of both groups were key figures (and rank and file members) of both leftist and liberal organizations fighting for human and civil rights. Throughout the Civil Rights Era, many Jews marched and some of them died alongside blacks in the dramatic campaigns to overcome segregation. In a kind of paean to the whole connection, Martin Luther King, Jr., once said, "It would be impossible to record the contribution Jewish people have made toward the Negro's struggle for freedom; it has been so great."[16]

For many African Americans today, especially those too young to have experienced the turbulent conflicts and bittersweet victories of the 1950s and 1960s, words of praise and thanksgiving like those voiced by King have a hollow ring. Even before King's assassination, other, more flamboyant spokesmen had began to say they were growing tired of hearing how much Jews had done for them and many began saying things that were much worse. These revisionists further began to proclaim that, even in the very specific social settings and political contexts where blacks and Jews had marched together, they had not really been partners. They (the African American critics) claimed that, instead of that, they were merely pawns; causes to be taken up; people to be pitied or manipulated for others' psychological needs ("guilt trip" became a common expression), or for more nefarious purposes.

Needless to say, most Jews vehemently disagreed with such characterizations, feeling and sometimes stating quite openly that they were hurt and puzzled and terribly disappointed by the failure of those who criticized them to recognize all that they had done in fostering the cause of *integration*.

Perhaps a significant part of the problem lies in that key word "integration." For many years, to many Jews *and many blacks*, when it came to the plight of African Americans' integration, it was generally considered something more akin to the old one-way process of assimilation than to acceptance and mutual respect. Integration was more than desegregation (breaking down the legal barriers); it was an ideological commitment to lift those who were stigmatized and labeled "culturally deprived" out of the misery of their estate, enabling them to benefit from full access to the advantages of mainstream (read white) society. Going to white institutions, joining formerly all-white clubs, finding employment in once-segregated organizations, and similar goals were all seen as ways of enhancing fulfillment. Integration meant leaving the past behind and becoming a part of the future. However reasonable its intent, it is likely that such an orientation unintentionally denigrated much that was—and, even more, was to become—meaningful to these Americans, especially after the sea change that took place in the middle of the 1960s. With the onset of the consciousness-raising movements of the 1960s, many came to resent the noblesse oblige assumptions of the so-called integrationists much as Jews and other newcomers had resented the schemes for their "Americanization" early in this century.

For years, the majority of American blacks who led or joined the fight for civil rights, like their allies, saw progress in movement from the margins of society to the center. Because their marginality was related to the basest caste-like distinctions prescribed by the color bar rather than cultural and religious ones, "overcoming" seemed far more important than asserting uniqueness of culture or character. Save for the early nationalists and Garveyites and the intellectuals of the Harlem Renaissance, a phenomenon Langston Hughes said "ordinary Negroes hadn't heard of . . . or, if they had, it hadn't raised their wages any,"[17]few blacks spoke of "cultural pluralism" and fewer still of "separatism" until midway through the 1960s. (Talk of "multiculturalism" or "Afrocentricity"—a heavily politicized variation of the earlier them of "Negritude"—was to come much later.) But a series of events, catalyzed by the shooting of James Meredith, during his ill-fated march across Mississippi, and electrified by the strident call for "black power" which reverberated around the country, signaled the birth of a new era that would cause whatever rifts there had always been to begin to yawn wider and wider with each passing decade. Beginning with what Kenneth Clark once called their own "Declaration of Independence," many in the movement broke rank with their most steadfast supporters in the struggle.

IV

Julius Lester, an African American convert to Judaism and astute observer of both communities, once put the changing climate into bold relief: "While Jews consider themselves liberal, blacks consider them paternalistic."[18]

Within a year or two many of those "liberal" stalwarts, including a disproportionately large percentage of Jews, were eased or pushed from positions of civil rights leadership. Soon other events contributed to the growing estrangement: urban riots in predominantly black neighborhoods, some of which were still inhabited by Jewish old-timers—or whose shops were owned and run by them; mounting demands for community control of New York schools, where many teachers and principals were Jewish; pressures for "open enrollment" in public city universities; and growing disagreement over the efficacy and implementation of affirmative action policies mandated to ensure greater representation of those who, along with Asians, Hispanics, and Native Americans, had come to be officially designated as "minorities."

The specific of institutionalized targets and goals, however "benign" these quota-like objectives were said to be, was (and remains) particularly upsetting to those all too familiar with Nuremburg racial laws and *numerus clausus* first imposed by Harvard President Lowell and copied by many other university administrators and corporate leaders ostensibly "to keep a balance." (In an ironic twist, this old device to keep Jews out is now having a replay in some parts of the country where highly qualified Asian Americans are finding that they are not being accepted at the colleges of their choice because including them would contribute to furthering their "overrepresentation." This, among many other things, has led to the widely publicized increase in tension between Asians who, while themselves members of a recognized affirmative action category, are enduring reverse discrimination, and others, who are not only wanted but wooed in order to meet certain "diversity" targets.)

Withal, there is little doubt that what many blacks are thinking about Jews today is, in large measure, a narrowly focused reflection of a deeply rooted triple sense of *powerlessness, dependency,* and *envy.* It implies being left behind, the persistence of discrimination, an increasing sense of isolation, and a growing feeling of desperation. Jews have made it and they, whom Jim Sleeper (1991) has called, "the closest of strangers," have not.

Many African American leaders know all this and are seeking to confront it in constructive ways, not least by trying to engage in dialogues with still sympathetic (if not always empathetic) outsiders, especially Jews. Their goal is to re-form alliances based on mutual respect and common commitments. But many others seem too willing to accede to demagoguery and demonology to blame the Jews for all their problems, or, if not that, to remain still when they hear of or personally witness expressions of either. They and the members of what is in fact a highly stratified and quite diverse community, and the now-wary Jews, are not the only players, of course.

In keeping with the triadic formulation that is far more than a heuristic distinction, the third party (actually the first—for it is truly the most powerful), gives new meaning to the sobriquet "silent majority." Few voices have been raised to counter the campaign of vilification. The lack of strong opposition to Jew-baiting in much of the white community is most unfortunate but hardly surprising. But to see such a lack of public reaction as agreement with the extreme expressions of hate is to grossly misread the situation. If there is any Machiavellian plan underlying the statements of Farrakhan and his minions holding Jews responsible for every conceivable wrong within society and, most specifically, the current condition of black America in order to win white support, the effort will prove futile, even counterproductive. Those few white Christians most apt to resonate to rhetoric of the African American anti-Semites about Jewish control are likely to be most vehemently anti-black as well.

Thus, aside from instilling pride by increasing group chauvinism—and group narcissism at the expense of further alienation of those who have been most helpful in the past, it is highly doubtful that the net effect of the tactics being used on the streets and on the campuses will serve either the purpose of *divide et impera* (one of the ploys outlined by Simmel) or help to overcome the real problems of African Americans, especially those in the seething caldrons of the urban ghettoes. More likely, they will deepen the divisions between blacks and others—"white" as well as Jewish.

INTERVIEWS

Caretakers, Gatekeepers, Guides, and Go-Betweens

HAD A reincarnated George Orwell gone to Southeast Asia to observe the refugee relief and resettlement operation in 1980, he might have thought that "newspeak" was already the order of the day. The paths to the clinics, food distribution points, registration desks, transit camps—indeed, to the United States or any other "third country"—were signposted with acronyms most confusing to the uninitiated. To trace the resettlement process from the time a boat is spotted or a muddy border crossed to Anytown, U.S.A., as I did in the fall of 1980, first required the decoding of these neologisms and then learning where each of the organizations represented by the shorthand expressions fit in the complex system.

After a few intensive weeks in the field I found I could speak like a pro and even knew, more or less, what I was talking about. Here is one conversation I had with an American government official in Thailand (I was checking to see if I understood how the "processing" of refugees worked): "So," I said, "after the UNHCR gives permission, you have your people from the JVA (who, I understand, are mostly ex-pats working under contract to the IRC) do the prescreening to prepare the biodata for ACVA in the States and for the INS officers out here. If they are accepted, ICEM will handle the medical checks and prepare to move them. Cats I and II being given top priority, right?" He smiled, then said, "Well, you forgot that they have to have visa falcons before they are INSed. And, if they're rejected, we have to internationalize them. But otherwise you've got it down pat."

What I had said, in the argot of the "in-group," was that, after the representatives of the United Nations High Commission for Refugees—the nonoperational overseer, funding source, and legally responsible body, give permission, caseworkers from the Joint Voluntary Agency, an American refugee organization contracted by the Department of State (in this case, the International Rescue Committee) which employs many Americans already overseas (rather than recruiting them from the U.S.), begin

*Originally published as "Links in a Chain: Observations of the American Refugee Program in Southeast Asia," in *Migration Today*, vol. IX, no. 3, 1981, pp. 7–23.

processing the potentially resettleable refugees. They prepare background information for the American Council of Voluntary Agencies, a consortium that coordinates sponsorship and facilitates resettlement as well as for the Immigration and Naturalization Service, the organization ultimately responsible for passing on eligibility for entry into the United States. When people are ready to move to the United States—or to another country in the case of those wanting or, more often, having to go elsewhere the Intergovernmental Committee for European Migration (now called the Intergovernmental Committee for Migration) gives medical examinations and makes arrangements for transportation from the camp to the point of resettlement. Priority is given to those who are spouses, parents, and children (Category I) or former employees of the United States government (Category II). There are two other categories; III is for those of high risk such as former South Vietnamese soldiers and employees of the deposed government; and IV is a sort of residual rubric under which such persons as spouses or married siblings are placed.

I was told that I had gotten things pretty straight but should not have forgotten that a security check (the visa falcon) is always required before the Immigration and Naturalization Service officer can even consider the case. And, should he or she find a person ineligible (a rare occurrence), the application would be rejected and the case turned back to the UN High Commissioner's staff for consideration for placement elsewhere. "Internationalization" is the euphemism that describes such a search for a welcoming host society.

I was learning. I was to learn and see much more and to conclude that this operation was not a prelude to an Orwellian nightmare but a superhuman response to the trauma of those caught up in the aftermath of an incredibly protracted war. The use of the acronyms was but a superficial sign of involvement in a motley corps of refugee workers, international civil servants, U.S. government officials, local employees, and representatives of the various international organizations (the IOs) and voluntary agencies (the volags) that were all links in the rescue-relief-resettlement chain.

The purpose of the trip was to get a first hand look and feel for the way Indochinese refugees are received, cared for, and, when eligible, readied for resettlement. It was part of a large study of the sociology of exile, the politics of rescue, and the psychology of altruism on which I had been working for some time.

Unlike many who had already visited the anchorages and border camps, the holding centers and transit camps, my focus on this trip was not on the refugees per se but on the agents and agencies that were involved with them. Much had already been written about the victims of the Vietnam War and of Pol Pot's genocidal policies in Kampuchea but surprisingly little about those who provided care and processed the mountains of papers to help them on their way to becoming new Americans—or provided temporary assistance to the thousands of displaced Khmer who were housed on the border of Thailand and Kampuchea. As an official of one of the vo-lags put it during an interview early in the trip, "For every ten minutes of time we spend with a refugee family, it takes hours of work to assist them." This readily became apparent as I interviewed, observed, and accompanied a cross section of American refugee workers and saw members of international teams, including those from the UNHCR.

My odyssey began in Hong Kong and took me to offices, ministries, and refugee camps in that Crown Colony and in Macao, Singapore, Malaysia, and Thailand. All of these countries, as well as Australia, Indonesia, and the Philippines have programs in which refugees are granted first asylum status and processed for onward movement to third countries. Thailand also has huge border camps for displaced persons.

Resettlement procedures generally follow the course I described previously, but in each of the countries there are vast differences in the actual operations. As the people living in the countries of first asylum differ in appearances and in attitudes, so do the ways they address themselves to the refugee problem and to those who have come to assist. Today [meaning early in 1981], care, maintenance, processing, and movement are handled in somewhat different ways by host governments in cooperation with the designated or accepted IOs and volags.

Hong Kong

Immediately after arriving from the States I had several brief meetings with people in the Office of the Refugee Coordinator, representatives of several agencies, the staff of the High Commissioner, and various officials in the Hong Kong government. My introduction to the refugees themselves came, appropriately, at a place called Dockyards, an old row of *go-downs* or warehouses taken over by the Hong Kong Prison Authority to hold the boat people picked up by the harbor police and others. It was a warm, sunny day and the "camp," which had held as many as 10,000 at one time in three long, dark, and cavernous buildings, had fewer than 2,000 on the day of my arrival. Most of the people were then living in one building with rows of oversized bunkbeds each deck of which was a temporary home for a family of tired and bewildered newcomers. Most had been at sea for a number of days. Some had arrived on one of the celebrated ships that had run aground; many had come on small junks. Still others had come by small boat but only from the nearby People's Republic of China. It was they, more than the others, who troubled Hong Kong authorities already worried about the continuing flow of illegal immigrants from mainland China. While acknowledging that many of the boat people may well have fled Vietnam originally, since they had sought refuge in China, that was their country of first asylum (the Hong Kong government representatives gave all indications that the colony was not about to become a "third country" for them).

All those who are brought to Dockyards are initially screened by UNHCR representatives as well as Hong Kong Immigration. Health checks are also conducted there. A decision on the status of each individual or family is made almost immediately. However, the inmates are not told their fate until they are about to be moved—a period of up to several weeks. Movement from the compound depends on several things, not the least of which is the available space in the refugee holding centers. When the time comes, some of those who came "through" China are to be taken to detention camps for eventual "repatriation." Most, however, would go to one of five centers set up under UNHCR auspices and run under contract by various organizations, including several American-based volags. One such camp is Jubilee, operated by the International Rescue Committee.

Jubilee is located in the Shim Shui Po area of Hong Kong (another camp called Shim Shui Po run by a Hong Kong religious organization is right beside it). The camp is an old four-story forlorn-looking block of army quarters, grey and shabby and filled to the rooftrees with the human flotsam that await sponsorship and resettlement.

Moving past the gate into the camp area itself I was immediately struck by the contradictions encountered. For example, at first glance it seemed to be a place of listless older people and whimpering babies who stared out into the hardly empty space of their overcrowded digs. Suddenly the air was alive with laughter and the milling of children. They looked happy and healthy and quite well dressed. Some were on their way to or from classes. We followed one group past a playground outfitted by a Dutch organization, into a school set up in a prefabricated building donated by a German church group. Inside there were classrooms where teaching was conducted with a sense of familiarity that caused me to momentarily forget where I was—and who the pupils were.

Moving back to the central area I was surprised to note that there seemed to be almost no male adults around. It flashed through my head that they didn't exist, having been annihilated during the war. But I knew that such was not the case.

I learned that in Hong Kong refugees were allowed to work and all who could did. They were employed in garment and electronic factories along with the Hong Kong Chinese. This unique and unprecedented situation was possible because of the constant need for cheap labor in the colony. For the refugees it was a godsend. It meant that the men had a chance to maintain their dignity by contributing to the family coffers. The money was used mainly to buy the food (that is cooked in large kitchen areas where each family has its own gas stove) and clothing. Jubilee's camp manager, Augustine Leung, was a thirty-five-year-old Chinese, a former group worker who had studied sociology at an American college in Hong Kong. While employed by the International Rescue Committee, he was given a certain amount of autonomy which he seems to have used well. A staff of professionals, mainly social workers and teachers, was supplemented by volunteers from many countries (including a number of young American women who work mainly in child-care programs) and a council of refugees. The latter serve as both section leaders and liaisons. They enforced the rules of the camp and, within prescribed limits, set up some of their own, especially regarding punishment for petty crimes.

The other camps in Hong Kong, while physically different, had somewhat similar organizational structures. Still, the physical environment, the attitudes of the representatives of the agency in charge, and the personalities of the administrators and workers leave their marks. Innovative ideas also stand out. For example, Jubilee was the first camp to have a cooperative store run by and for refugees on a profit-sharing basis. Soon after it was established, others followed suit.

At the time of my visit to Hong Kong the Refugee Coordinator, Anne Henshaw, was a USAID lawyer with a wealth of experience in Southeast Asia during the war and with refugees from that area ever since. She had been at Fort Chafee when the 1975 wave came through; so, too, had Dick Shinn, the head of JVA/Hong Kong office, a minister and representative of the Lutheran Immigration and Refugee Service (and, so it turned out, had the Hong Kong IRC Director, George Goss). The circles form a significant network of individuals (many of them old Southeast Asia hands—some military, some missionary, some former Peace Corps volunteers) whose paths have crossed many times. They represent a significant part of the first substantial corps of refugee administrators since the post-World War II European programs.

On meeting such people I was struck by their keen sense of fellow-feeling. They were members of a rather closed fraternity who had undergone lengthy initiation rites. It was not that they were reluctant to share their views but, rather, possessed an apparent suspicion that, not having "been there," it was hard for outsiders to understand. Yet, whatever the official and unofficial lines, I left Hong Kong thinking that I had seen the inner workings of a smooth running machine, an operation that, it turned out, was beginning to wind down as the numbers of boat people had begun to decline.

Macao

Macao was a different scene altogether. Not only was the program on a much smaller scale than Hong Kong's, but it is dominated—as apparently are most of the social welfare efforts in that Portuguese outpost—by one man, a gregarious priest appropriately named Father Lancelot.

The people who land in or are dropped off in Macao are little different from those who enter Hong Kong at the Dockyards, at least when they arrive. However, visits to two camps, "Casa" and "Green Island," made it readily apparent that they do not fare as well. If there is a single reason it is probably related to the fact that refugees do not work outside the camp. The Portuguese authorities do not allow it and, presumably, the economy could not sustain it. So, crowded in camps, though no more crowded than those in Hong Kong, they sit—sometimes for two years.

The Catholic Relief Service (CRS), an arm of the U.S. Catholic Conference, the agency that—through its Migration and Refugee Service (MRS) handles over 40 percent of all Indochinese refugee resettlement in the United States, operates three camps in Macao (again, under UNHCR authorization and with their financial support). There, as in Hong Kong, I was impressed by the commitment and dedication of the various participants in the rescue, relief, and resettlement efforts. These included an Irish social worker, who had come out of retirement to go back into the field and was in headquarters, and an ascetic middle-aged priest, who ran "Casa," a holding center which was once a church school building and was condemned to be demolished when appeals were made to allow it to be used to house refugees. The priest, Father Yuen, kept apologizing for being able to do so little to assist his charges who lived in the chapel, in the classrooms, in the wine cellars, and in the corridors of the old school, tightly packed in bunk beds.

Richard To, a former merchant seaman with an engineering degree, had come ashore to help "Father" and became assistant manager of Green Island. He showed me around the holding center on the edge of the city. It was a compound of five buildings, three for ethnic Chinese from Vietnam one for ethnic Vietnamese, and one for administration. They were separated at Green Island because, it was said, there had been tensions and a near-riot several months before and it was felt it would be better to maintain some social distance. (Actually, the buildings were very close together and people could move freely about. However, they seemed to stay in their own area.) Here, unlike Casa, people seemed somewhat busier. While they could not work in the regular labor force, they could do some piecework in the camp. Casa's "workers" were making beautiful paper flowers of which they were very proud.

Singapore

Lee Kuan Yew's tiny island Republic was the next stop. It did not take long to find out that if Hong Kong and Macao authorities were concerned about refugees, those in Singapore were—or had been—almost paranoid. Refugees are not welcome in Singapore and those rescued at sea are the only ones permitted to enter the Republic, and then for only 90 days. I learned that shortly after my arrival in separate meetings with a CRS staff person working in the JVA office (CRS is the contracted volag for processing in Singapore; the American Council of Nationality Societies, ACNS, handles Indonesia out of a Singapore office), the U.S. Refugee Coordinator for Singapore and Indonesia, and representatives of the UNHCR and

ICEM, who were all in one convenient location, a fifty-story building directly above the wharf where refugees are brought ashore. I also sat in on a morning review session attended by persons from each of the links in the chain.

Owing to the special circumstances imposed both by Singapore's strategic location and the reluctance of the government to offer anything more than temporary sanctuary while processing for resettlement takes place, a greater degree of coordination between the UNHCR and the American JVAR was evident there than elsewhere. For example, when a ship is reported to have picked up refugees, someone from the UNHCR office and someone from the JVA office rush to the wharf to board the vessel as soon as it has dropped anchor in the harbor. They are there often as quickly as the Singapore authorities.

The rule is that no one may enter the Republic unless already guaranteed third country resettlement. Since refugees are picked up by ships carrying flags of many nations, it is expected that the countries will provide the guarantees. There are two notable exceptions. First are those who have relatives in the United States or worked for the U.S. government, i.e., "Cats I and II." They are automatically accepted for the U.S. program regardless of the flag their rescue ship is flying. Second are those aboard ships under flags of convenience such as those of Liberian or Panamanian registry. These people are "internationalized" by the UNHCR. (Many of the boat people sail down from Vietnam and into the main shipping lanes knowing that international law requires that they be picked up. Normally they hope to be rescued by an American ship or, at least, one from a Western nation. It is ironic when the ploy backfires completely and fugitives from Communist Vietnam are taken aboard an East European or Russian ship. They are aware of the problem—the grapevine is incredibly effective. "They know everything, every rule and rule change," said one refugee official. But there is little they can do for one regulation is that once accepted for resettlement one cannot apply elsewhere.)

Once registered by UNHCR and the JVA/Singapore, the boat people are moved to Hawkins Road Camp on the other side of the island. Another old army encampment, Hawkins Road looks quite different from Jubilee in Hong Kong. It is far more isolated and spread out. (While there, I kept thinking of the descriptions of the Japanese occupation after the fall of Singapore where British soldiers became inmates in their own compounds.) In Singapore, the JVA's biggest task is to get those considered acceptable for resettlement in the United States through the processing as quickly as possible and then get them out of the country so more can enter without exceeding the stringent limits under which they are allowed to operate. Knowing this, I expected very tight restrictions on the refugees. Yet, such did not seem to be the case. Hawkins Road is pretty much an open camp. People may leave during the day and go into the city. But they do not work. No matter, they are not there long enough to fall into the deep depressions etched in the faces of many in Macao and some in Hong Kong. They know they are assured a place of asylum in the Western world.

The camp itself was bustling with activity; its stores overflowing with all sorts of foodstuffs. The crowded barracks were cooler than the even more crowded tent areas near the offices, clinic, and library. But many seemed to prefer to be where the action was. That sentiment was corroborated by the refugee selected camp leader, a Vietnamese refugee with an M.A. from a southern university in the States. (He was about to depart for resettlement in California.) His job was to coordinate activities and to supervise section heads, also refugees, who kept tabs on their units and handled many administrative tasks, including the allocation of money provided by the UNHCR for food to be purchased either at the exceedingly well-stocked camp store or on the local market.

At Hawkins Road I also met several other central characters and bit players in the resettlement drama. I sat with a JVA caseworker, an INS officer, and an interpreter as they went through the required formalities to determine acceptability, the man from the INS asking all the questions and the refugees responding. As the interviews progress, the INS officer is guided in large measure by what is written in the file as prepared by the caseworker.

In addition to observing the INSing in Hawkins Road, I also managed once again, to talk to a number of workers—in this case, Americans with varied backgrounds, including prior experience in the area as Peace Corps Volunteers. The most impressive thing noted was the ease with which they interacted with the refugees, their lack of aloofness or status consciousness, and their obvious efforts to try to communicate in halting Vietnamese while trying to teach bits of English to those about to leave for the United States directly or to one of the Resettlement Processing Centers (RPCs) situated in Indonesia and the Philippines. (Not only an increasing percentage of people who land in Singapore find themselves moving toward their final destination in stages, so, too, do those who land in other countries of first asylum. Usually they are flown out but some, such as a large group from Malaysia, have been sent by sea.)

Malaysia

In Malaysia things were again different. While not much publicity had been given to Singaporean recalcitrance to admit boat people, the whole world knew about Malaysian resistance and the stern measures taken to keep refugees out, at least in the beginning.

Malaysia is a Muslim country with a precarious balance between the politically dominant Malays and the economically powerful Chinese. The numerical balance tips slightly in favor of the Malays but only slightly, wherein lies much of the resistance to the Vietnamese, many of whom are ethnic Chinese.

While it was true that boats were pushed away and, in several infamous cases, large numbers drowned in sight of shore, the policy was changed with the assurance of onward movement. New camps were set up and old ones expanded throughout the peninsula and in Sabah and Sarawak and on off-shore islands, the largest being Pilau Bidong, to which boat people were still taken.

There is also a camp called Cherating near Kuantan on the east coast which had recently been changed from a holding center for Vietnamese boat people into a resettlement camp (the first of its kind in the area) for a select group of Khmer Muslims allowed to enter from camps in Thailand.

In Malaysia the central government sets policy regarding refugees but the state governments carry them out. While the UNHCR funds the operations, it keeps a low profile; so does everyone else, save the Malaysia Red Crescent Society (nee the Malaysia Red Cross), the agency designated to care for those in the camps, and a Muslim social welfare body that works with MRCS in Cherating. The IRC works under MRCS as do medical teams from the League of Red Cross Societies, an organization that is often confused with the International Committee of the Red Cross. (The League is a consortium of national Red Cross societies of which MRCS is a member. Normally, it goes into the field or arranges for country teams to do so in the realm of natural disaster relief. The ICRC is a separate Swiss-based body that gives medical care in war zones, deals with political refugees, and provides tracing and other services under the terms of the Geneva Convention.)

While in Malaysia I spent a considerable amount of time with IRC head, Mark Ice, a young American with prior experience working with two other agencies and with MRCS people. I was especially impressed with the dynamism of Datin Ruby Lee, the Secretary General, a Chinese woman who kept things moving, working closely with her dedicated staff which included a soft spoken but tough Indian physician, Dr. T. Visranathan, who is the Medical Director.

Limited time prevented me from visiting more than the two camps mentioned above. Sungei Besi Transit Camp, divided into two sections, one for those going to the States, one for those going elsewhere, was more akin to what I had grown used to than to the special Khmer camp at Cherating. In Malaysia I spoke to many refugee officials and volunteers about the broad cultural differences between those from Vietnam and from Kampuchea about which I had read so much beforehand—and had been observing. The clothes were different. The food was different. The signs were different. I was to see much more of such ethnic differences in Thailand.

Thailand

Thailand is unique in many ways. It is the country in the area into which members of all groups fleeing communist dominated Indochina are to be

found in significant numbers. Bordering Cambodia and Laos and across
the Gulf of Siam from Vietnam, thousands upon thousands have sought
sanctuary in Thailand. They have rarely been welcomed with equanimity.
Like neighboring Malaysia to the south, Thailand has often taken a hard
line. However, it is much more vulnerable to outside and, specially, American pressure.

Unlike Malaysia, Thailand was deeply (some would say intimately) involved in the Vietnam War. Large numbers of American servicemen and
support forces were stationed in the country; many others went there for
"R and R." While sometimes strained, relations with the United States remain based on mutual interests of security, especially against Vietnam's ex-
pansionist policies. Most important for refugee affairs is the American
ambassador, Morton Abramowitz. While on record as favoring improving
conditions within Cambodia, Abramowitz is an outspoken advocate of protecting the right of asylum, a facilitator of resettlement to those eligible,
and a prime mover in the manpower program to feed the hungry who
crowd the border camps. His persistence and that of his staff, led by an imaginative and experienced Refugee Coordinator, Lionel Rosenblatt, has
persuaded the Thais into taking a more humanitarian stance than might
have been their wont. And, skillfully, he has seen they are credited for doing so.

The magnitude of the operation in Thailand—for Vietnamese, Lao,
Hmong, and "old" Khmer refugees and now for "new" Khmer just inside
the border—is difficult to imagine. Figures released in March 1981 reveal
that over 150,000 had entered the country from Laos and Kampuchea
since 1975, many to be eventually resettled in other countries. At least
137,000 new Khmer, the overwhelming majority of whom had come in
1979, were being housed and fed in holding centers on the Thai-Cambo-
dian border. (It was recently estimated that approximately 160,000 persons
are on the Kampuchean side of the border.)

One need only walk into the modern apartment complex on Wireless
Road in Bangkok to get a sense of the American involvement in these operations. In one building, marked with a permanent-looking sign "Joint
Voluntary Agency," was the operation center for the JVA/Thailand with
six sections, one each for Vietnamese, Lao, Highlander (Hmong), Khmer,
Transit and unaccompanied children from all groups, plus Statistical, Financial, Research, and Computer units, the last of which is rather extraordinary as is its section head, a bilingual (Thai and English) American
computer whiz who had revolutionized data processing for the entire
American refugee effort in Thailand. All told, in October 1980 there was a
staff of approximately sixty-five "ex-pats," many of these case workers who
move back and forth from various camps to the headquarters in Bangkok,
and 100 locals, most of them involved in clerical work. Next door to the
JVA offices is a duplicate building which houses the Refugee Section with
the U.S. Government management team led by the Refugee Coordinator,

plus the JVA staff and KEG, the special Khmer Emergency Group which monitors relief for those in holding centers and along the Thai-Kampuchean border and is a part of the Refugee Section.

William Sage is the present director of the JVA office in Bangkok and coordinates the largest resettlement program in the world. Prior to being named head of the JVA/Thailand, he worked for the U.S. Catholic Conference in San Francisco, California, as a resettlement caseworker. His agency, the International Rescue Committee, the contracted volag in Thailand, also had a separate office in Bangkok from which a young lawyer coordinated and directed medical programs and some educational and tracing services in various camps scattered throughout the country.

IRC is one of many volags in Thailand. Most of these are American. Almost fifty agencies are united in their common effort through the offices of the Committee for Coordination of Services to Displaced Persons in Thailand (CCSDPT); a number of others have "Visitor" status in the organization. CCSDPT has taken responsibility for coordinating many activities in an attempt to avoid conflicts and duplications that, not surprisingly, occurred in the early days of the crisis.

That fairly smooth running machine did not come about overnight. It only seemed that way in retrospect. It was the result of negotiating a host of jurisdictional disputes between American officials and those in such international bodies as the UNHCR and the ICRC which, respectively, controlled camp management throughout the country and relief operations, including food distribution, on the border. One main source of disagreement with the ICRC and other IOs, including UNICEF, which maintain their presence only with the concurrence of the host governments, was their constant worry about upsetting delicate arrangements for getting food directly from Phnom Penh. The Americans were not averse to direct shipments of food into the capital but wanted to assure that those on the border were also supplied. For this they were often accused of attempting to destabilize the Vietnam-controlled Cambodian regimes. One of their most effective programs was distribution of rice and rice seed on the border itself. While undoubtedly some "undesirables" received the seed, given out to whomever lined up to receive it, there is little question that it helped to improve the harvest in 1980 and had some effect on stemming the outflow of Khmer from Kampuchea.

Today, representatives of international organizations and volags are found in almost all of the camps. Let me describe four different types. The first is a holding center, most similar to those visited in other countries. Called Phanat Nikom, it is located in eastern Thailand near the town of Chon Buri. The camp is closed but the people inside have ample access to all sorts of foods, soft goods, and even some hardware sold to them by Thai traders whose little shops line one fence of the encampment. I was struck by the incredible sight of refugees sitting on stools, arms on the counter of noodle stands whose owners pass the food through the wire that separates them. I was also impressed with the intensity of life in Phanat Nikom. More than any place I had been, everyone seemed busy. People were active whether in one of the ubiquitous U-shaped compounds of three prefabricated buildings facing an inner common ground or in the schools, play areas, clinics, or offices.

In addition to the ex-pat relief staff, many Vietnamese and Khmer refugees assisted in the wide variety of programs, including sports, crafts, traditional dance, and English language training. As in all such camps there were also a number of young Americans and some Thais working on reprocessing under the direction of the JVAs.

In Phanat Nikom, once again, I sat in on a series of interviews with JVA field-team workers who, in this case, were doing prescreening for preparation of files for presentation to the INS. With interpreters they gently but firmly asked the necessary questions, often prodding people to answer honestly. False statements are grounds for being barred from acceptance.

There are more serious issues that come up in the interviews such as evidence of having been in the service of the communist forces and being a bigamist, both grounds for exclusion from the U.S. program. Such cases are generally turned over for internationalization, that is, to search out those willing to accept them.

The refugees in Phanat Nikom, like those in other holding centers, were awaiting word that they had sponsors and could be moved. When the word finally would arrive they would be readied for departure by ICEM representatives, then taken either directly to the airport or to Lumpini Transit Center in Bangkok.

Lumpini is a grim place in the middle of the city. It is near a magnificent park not far from "Embassy Row," but the people inside do not get out. Thai authorities are very strict. No pictures may be taken here. This proved to be understandable (from the perspective of Thai officialdom), since it would be easy to do an exposé on the crowded and unkempt conditions.

In Lumpini people tend to separate themselves by ethnic group in barrack-like buildings marked "Khmer," "Hmong," "Lao," "Vietnamese." Instructions are printed in five languages. For many, this is the first time they have lived in such close proximity with Indochinese refugees from different backgrounds (most camps, with some exceptions like Phanat Nikom, are ethnically specific).

However, once called for their flights, the refugees are grouped according to where they are going rather than where they have been or are from. The new life really begins at that point.

Lumpini has a small UNHCR staff, a few nurses who run a clinic, members of an American women's club which provides some warm clothing in preparation for the first few days, and several volag representatives who answer questions (mostly about why individuals are not moving).

Representatives from the JVA check in constantly to look for people who are there for two or more weeks.

The then-current chief of the Transit Section of the JVA office was typical of many Americans who work as liaisons between camp residents and the officials. A social worker from a U.S. Catholic Conference office in California, Bunny Hedrick had gone out to Bangkok for six months and was just ending her tour when I met her. She, and others, stressed the importance of carrying back not only impressions of the camps but the message that resettlement only begins there and that far more needs to be done in the States to aid in the acculturation process.

Khao I Dang is a world of its own. Not a refugee camp but a gigantic holding center for displaced persons from Kampuchea, it, too, is run under the UNHCR with many contracted agencies and organizations working within its large perimeter. I visited the camp with a Khmer-American who served as guide and interpreter.

Before entering we had lunch at a noodle stand across from the camp's main gates and spoke to members of medical teams from at least five different countries, most prominent among them being Germans from the *Malteser-Hilfsdienst Auslandsdienst EV* (known as MHD). I was somewhat troubled to observe that there was little mixing of the national groups. Wary of snap judgments, I said nothing to my guide but, seeing the same phenomenon again and again, I did ask various people with experience in places like Khao I Dang about what I had observed.

I was told that, for a variety of reasons, not least the variation in medical practice and procedure, it was felt that different wards and units were best managed by country teams. Since people also worked with their compatriots, most of the free time, like working hours, was spent with them. There were many exceptions but, by and large, fraternizing among the medical staffs was not widespread.

Not only did I observe the doctors and nurses at their leisure (and at work) but also saw a good deal of the camp, an instant city of street after street of thatch and bamboo houses occasionally broken by stores, schools, clinics, religious compounds (Buddhist and Christian), and illegal stands selling all sorts of contraband. Near the Buddhist temple, a makeshift tent-like structure, I spoke to an old man sitting in a house with a number of children and Buddhist nuns. Through the interpreter I carried on a conversation. Part of it included the following exchange:

"Why are you here?"
"Because we were afraid of the communists. Because we were starving. Because of the conditions in Kampuchea."

"How did you get to Khao I Dang?"
"We came on buses from Nong Chan [on the border]."

"When?"

"About a half year ago."

"How is it here?"
"All right for us, the older people. But not for the children."

"Why not? They look pretty healthy and pretty happy."
"Because they will lose their way. They will forget about their traditions."

"What will happen to them?"
"If they stay here they will be people without a country—not Khmer, not Thai."

"Do you think that is likely, do you think the Thais will let you and your children stay here?"
"Never."

"Never?"
"Well, they may let us stay until the regime changes. I hope so."

"Then what?
"Then we go home."

"Do you want to go anywhere else?"
"Well, some people wish to go to America. Some, who speak French like I do, wish to go to France. Not me. I want to go home. I am Khmer."

After a while I changed the subject and asked:

"Who runs Khao I Dang?"
"The UN, but the Thai authorities control it."

"Who takes care of you?"
"Everyone. The whole world, America, France, Germany. . . ."

Was this an accurate indication of feelings? I asked others similar questions and then checked with colleagues. All echoed many of the same sentiments. While some want to go to the United States and elsewhere, many—perhaps the majority—were truly displaced persons or exiles longing for a chance to go back home. A new life is not to be found in America, they said, but in a new and truly democratic Kampuchea—not the "Democratic Kampuchea" of Pol Pot. (Whether anyone could really go home again seemed very questionable at the time. Still the Khmer of Khao I Dang seemed to want to try.)

Near Khao I Dang is Nong Chan. Nong Chan is the fourth type of camp found in Thailand. It is part displaced persons camp and part (mainly) an encampment for transients, Khmer who wander back and forth across the border seeking protection and food, mainly rice.

Like Khao I Dang, Nong Chan is under the control of the Thai Supreme Command and is guarded from outside by checkpoints and heavily armed Thai soldiers. The approach to the place is like going through the looking glass for nothing seems as it should be. There are the soldiers, true, but in between their checkpoints are tranquil farms and rice paddies with Thai peasants netting fish or washing water buffalo in them. And there are young boys zooming up and down the road on brand new Honda and Kawasaki motor bikes. Affluence abounds within sight of what has been described as the Valley of Death. The motor bikes and other signs of new wealth are explained as one moves farther down the bumpy road. Thai traders are lined up as far as the eye can see. These are people from the district who bring foodstuffs, cloth, transistor radios, and all manner of goods to exchange for the gold and jewelry some of the Khmer still manage to bring out. The authorities seem ambivalent about them and, I was told, vacillate between toleration and suppression tempered a bit by periodic shakedowns.

After crossing a tank-trap and a muddy, often washed out and much repaired corduroy road, another jarring sight comes into view: thousands of half-bamboo, half-plastic shelters scattered about a barren plain next to a large bamboo hospital. This is Nong Chan.

The interpreter and I walked the length of the camp, stopping occasionally to chat with the people, especially with transients who had just crossed into Thailand reporting that things were difficult for the trails were very muddy and the oxen could not get through. The Americans working for CARE were worried, too. They had the rice to distribute but the oxcarts weren't coming (a week before there had been 15,000 people and they were overwhelmed).

Those Americans, including three Yale graduate students studying management the hard way, were models for others interested in doing refugee work. They had a dual mission: to assist and to learn. One, a woman of about twenty-five, was in charge of a feeding program for unaccompanied children; the others, two young men, distributed rice. They had been at their jobs for CARE for six months and planned to stay at least three more.

There were many other Americans in Nong Chan, mostly working for relief agencies, and many foreigners, too, mostly on medical teams.

The JVA does not work in Khao I Dang or in Nong Chan or other border camps. However, representatives of the Khmer Emergency Group (KEG) do spend considerable time interviewing people on the border, monitoring the U.S.'s international relief effort. They often learn of people whose relatives are in the United States or who worked for Americans. In such cases they are advised to contact UNHCR or to write to the U.S. Refugee Section giving more specific details. If a person or family is then found qualified (usually for purposes of family reunification), they are transferred to a transit center like Phanat Nikon.

Outprocessing for those old Khmer, Vietnamese, Lao, and Hmong people who are eligible (in contrast to the vast majority of those in camps like Khao I Dang and Nong Chan) is the joint effort of the JVA office and that of ICEM. Here is how it was done in Thailand. The ICEM representative upon learning that a case was acceptable would have all members of the family photographed separately and as a group (each holding a slate on which their case number is chalked). They also fingerprinted them for identification purposes.

After INSing is completed, all pertinent data on each case is telexed or pouched via courier to the American Council of Voluntary Agencies (ACVA) in New York. At biweekly meetings representatives of the eleven resettlement agencies there would review what has come in. A scan search is made to pick up "interest cards," that is, notifications that a particular agency already knew about a person (often because it had already resettled other family members). In such a case the interested volag would get the case. Otherwise the cases were distributed and the volag's own staff and volunteers work on arranging sponsorship in the States.

In point of fact, the volags vary in the sorts of services they provide and in the way in which sponsorship is arranged. The U.S. Catholic Conference, for example, resettles the most Indochinese—approximately 40 percent—and offers the widest variety of services and sponsor-programs, including parishes, civic groups, families, and private organizations. The Lutheran Immigration and Refugee Services (LIRS), Church World Services (CWS), and World Relief Refugee Service, a branch of the national Association of Evangelists, work primarily through church groups.

The International Rescue Committee (IRC) acts as its own sponsor. The American Council for Nationality Service (ACNS) does some of its own sponsoring but also uses private individuals and local groups. The Hebrew Immigrant Aid Society (HIAS), which has resettled some four to five percent of the Indochinese refugees, works directly with local Jewish Family Service agencies or Jewish Community Centers, congregations, community groups, and families providing sponsorship for HIAS. In addition, the American Fund for Czechoslovak Refugees (AFCR) and the Tolstoy Foundation, while doing only a minimal amount of work with those from Southeast Asia, do arrange sponsorship for some, mainly through group and family sponsors.

When notified sponsorship is obtained, the JVA office in the field is notified by ACVA and the person is ready to move.

The actual outprocessing begins when ICEM gets the word, in fact a list of cases which need transportation. The UNHCR as the ultimate party responsible to the host government also receives a copy. Depending on the local arrangements, when people are finally called for movement they are brought from holding centers to transit camps (in the case of Singapore where there is only one camp, they are separated from the others). In the meantime, the Operations Section of ICEM has been working out all the travel arrangements from the port of embarkation (and, in some cases, to that port from the camp) to the point of resettlement. To see their operation is most impressive. They are readying people for movement, portal to portal. In the fall of 1980 a number of Category IIIs and IVs and some Is were being moved to the United States in stages, sent first to Resettlement Processing Centers (RPCs) in Bataan in the Philippines or Galang, an island in Indonesia not far from Singapore. There they have several months of orientation and English language training. Others, still the majority, fly directly to the United States.

Sixty percent of the flights arranged by ICEM are American charters. The rest, regularly scheduled flights of American airline companies on which blocks of seats are bought for refugees who all sign promissory notes for eventual reimbursement. (I was told that the record of repayment to date is better than that of Americans who owe on college loans.) The ICEM-chartered planes all land at Oakland, California. Others are planes bound for Seattle, San Francisco, Los Angeles, and New York (usually via Europe). ICEM also arranges onward flights or other means of transport almost to the sponsor's door.

Reflections

The entire procedure of refugee processing is a fascinating study. It involves asking all sorts of questions about who seeks asylum and why, about how escape is enhanced or inhibited by official bodies and unofficial networks (and the effectiveness of worldwide publicity focusing attention on one problem instead of another), and about who gets involved in assisting others and what motivates them to do it. These subjects are of special concern to me. In fact, they served as guides to my interviews and observations. But, of course, one cannot get involved in such a project and expect to maintain the cold aloofness of the detached scientist. I didn't expect to nor did I want to. However, there is a critical difference in being what many social scientists call a "non-participant observer" and a "non-observing participant."

We caution our students not to become so involved that they can no longer maintain any sense of distance. On my recent trips to Southeast Asia, as well as in other visits to refugee areas, I found I had to constantly remind myself of that old shibboleth. It is especially crucial in gathering information and insights into a process so filled with poignancy and pathos.

Like anyone trying to get backstage in the drama of refugee rescue, relief, and resettlement, I was bombarded with many messages and had many different reactions. Sometimes it was anger at the stupidity of human beings who created the conditions that led to the situation. Sometimes it was awe at the sheer magnitude of the problem. Sometimes it was astonishment at the patience of the people who languished in the centers and in the camp. Perhaps because of my special interests, it was often pride, pride in the effort that many were making to alleviate the suffering of others. Too frequently the efforts of those I have elsewhere called "the Descendants of Theseus"[1] go unheralded. They should not. Without the assistance of the corps of refugee workers life would be far worse than it is for thousands of suffering human beings.

And they do suffer. It is hard to say which of the myriad images deeply etched in my brain is the most heartrending: the starving people at the border; the vacant stares of young women who had been repeatedly raped by pirates and bandits; the giggling children who seemed so incredibly resilient once their bellies are full; the disoriented Buddhist priest; the anxious teenagers who had known nothing but the struggle to survive and were still hustling; the former professor now huddled with his family of six in the second tier of the triple decker in a space of three square meters in a corner of a small room with 25 others; 300 anxious faces lined up for a 4 A.M. flight with their few possessions and their plastic ICEM bags containing documents and tickets to places they could hardly pronounce much less fathom, places to which they were to fly on jumbo jets even bigger than the B-52s that may have brought their first messages from America; or the apprehensive looks of refugees and sponsors as they furtively scan each new face in a crowded air terminal each wondering which stranger will become a part of their lives and how they will be received.

And yet, owing to the efforts of so many of those I saw in action and to the thousands more in Southeast Asia and in the United States, wonders never cease. The Indochinese do make it to America and, by and large, make it in America.

The movement to the United States and the initial stages of acculturation is the subject of the following essay, "Long Night's Journey." Suffice it to say here that the repeated success of the Indochinese refugee may be hypothesized to be related to two factors: first, something the refugees bring with them; second, something that Americans provide. What many, though surely not all, Indochinese take along are cultural values, norms of behavior and aspirations that are highly adaptive to American society. Most have a strong family sense and are eager to see that their children have a better life than they. They will spare no time nor energy assisting their offspring to achieve. Together the various groups are an assemblage of proud people, eager to prove themselves, eager for a chance to start life anew.

Long Night's Journey

T HEY SIT and stare. A forlorn looking group, 550 strong—or weak, weakened by painful decisions, by dangerous passages across ill-charted seas, by the thoughts of those left behind, by the grieving for family members who died alongside them, by the long months—even years—of waiting, by the shunting back and forth from camp to camp, by the uncertainty of the future. These estranged people are Indochinese refugees. They are at the International Airport in Bangkok, Thailand, waiting, once again. This time they are waiting to take the biggest step of all. They are frightened and anxious, and very, very quiet. Long accustomed to waiting, they are almost zombie-like as they hunker by their few possessions all tagged and bagged ready to go.

The tags have their names and other critical information including final destination. The bags, square plastic ones about 20" x 20" and marked "ICM," contain their documents, visas, tickets, and papers relating to their new status as legal refugees about to enter the United States. Interviews with American caseworkers from the JVA (Joint Voluntary Agency); communiqués back and forth from the JVA representative to ACVA (the American Council of Voluntary Agencies) for Foreign Service in New York (the coordinating body of the eleven principal resettlement agencies); State Department clearances on their security; screening by field representatives of the INS (Immigration and Naturalization Service), and health checks by the ICM (Intergovernmental Committee for Migration) doctors are all behind them. Sponsorship has been arranged and temporary homes in places as disparate as Sacramento and St. Louis, Boise and Baltimore, have been found. They are finally about to be moved.

How the Indochinese refugees got to this stage and one observer's views of those who facilitate the rescue, relief, and processing of refugees and some of their reactions was the subject of an earlier report. This essay deals with the second phase of resettlement—movement from Southeast Asia to

*Originally published as "Southeast Asia to America: Links in a Chain, Part II" in *Catholic Mind*, April 1982.

the United States and the first confrontation with Americans on American soil. Once again, the focus is as much on the refugee workers—government officials and representatives of Egos (non-governmental organizations), especially the "volags" (voluntary agencies), as it is on the refugees themselves. However, unlike the earlier report ("First Asylum"), this is not a country-by-country assessment but, rather, a look at the situation of those leaving any Asian country of first asylum and the journey either directly or indirectly to the United States. (At the point of disembarkation there are few of the differences discussed previously for, by and large, movement is handled by the Intergovernmental Committee for Migration under UN authority.)

In the fall of 1980 I spent a considerable amount of time visiting refugee camps and holding centers in five Southeast Asian countries: Hong Kong, Macao, Singapore, Malaysia, and Thailand. A second journey in May and June 1981 took me back to some of these same countries, to the Philippines, and to the Bay Area of California—once more to look and to listen, to analyze and to report. The second trip was focused on movement itself with special attention to one- versus two-stage resettlement.

Familiar with asylum-processing, that is, the registration and interviewing of "boat-people" coming from Vietnam or across the Mekong from Laos and "land-people" coming directly from Kampuchea (or directly from Vietnam via Kampuchea), I wanted to see how those eligible for resettlement in the United States were readied for transport and prepared for their new lives. Since the largest operation was in Thailand, I focused on this operation.

Waiting and Wondering

Once refugees have been deemed eligible for consideration for admittance to the United States, qualifying under one of four categories of eligibility—Category I, immediate relatives; II, former U.S. government employees; III, "high risk"; IV, other relative (such as sister-in-law)—security checks, called "visa falcons" are run on them. They also have "pre-INS" interviews used to gather biodata prior to interviews to be carried out by the Immigration and Naturalization officers in the field. This is often done in the first-asylum camps to which these refugees come—such as Nong Khai in Thailand or Pilau Bidong in Malaysia or Palawan in the Philippines. Sometimes the interviews are conducted in holding centers or in transit camps like Phanat Nikom in Chon Buri, Thailand, or Sugi Besai outside of Kuala Lumpur in Malaysia. Once a case is cleared, all essential information is sent to ACVA in New York for sponsorship. If there are relatives in the country, they are frequently the sponsors of preference. (Even when they cannot assume the financial responsibility they usually become involved in the process, aided by the agency that settled them.) Refugees may also indicate acquaintances they know in the States. If there are no relatives, and no other contacts, the choice of sponsoring agency is more or less arbitrary. Indeed, there is a hard and fast rule that agencies—and their personnel—cannot preselect individuals for special resettlement. This policy is the result of the desire of many field workers to help certain individuals or families they have befriended. The refugees may, however, ask to be settled by or near them—as that is doubtless taken into account.

When the match is made and medical examinations have been given, refugees are ready to move. Outprocessing begins.

In some countries, those eligible to go are moved to transit centers. The largest of these is in Phanat Nikom, several hours south of Bangkok. Phanat Nikom looks different from most other camps, having a sense of permanence and order. It is surrounded by a wire fence and, like other camps, under the control of government officials, in this case, representatives of the Thai Ministry of the Interior. Some observers say it reminds them of the Interior. Some observers say it reminds them of internment or prisoner of war camps in the 1940–1945 period, but to those who have seen the camps from which the people there have come, it looks like a bustling, if overcrowded, new town complete with schools, recreation facilities, stores, and hospitals—and ethnic neighborhoods: Vietnamese, Lao, Khmer, Hmong, and ethnic Chinese. Phanat Nikom is also like an army base where "hurry up and wait" is SOP. (Mostly, the word is "wait.") The people who come into the camp, knowing they are eligible for movement, are eager and anxious. There are some especially among the Vietnamese, who express their impatience in repeated queries to resettlement and relief workers: "When am I going?" Many others, while perhaps harboring similar feelings, keep them to themselves, and they wait.

Return to Bataan

Approximately 60 percent of the refugees are sent directly to the United States from Bangkok or from the capitals of other countries of first asylum. Their means of transport is usually a special charter—a World Airways or Flying Tiger, lines made famous and very rich by the Vietnam War when they or others were contracted for troop transportation. Charters taking off from Bangkok, Kuala Lumpur, Singapore, or Hong Kong land in Oakland, California, from which most refugee passengers are then moved to Hamilton Field for a day or two before going on. (Those with relatives in the Bay Area are usually picked up at the Oakland Airport.) Others may be placed on regular commercial flights bound for the West Coast cities on which blocks of seats are purchased in the names of refugees. They are known as "proflights."

For many refugees, there is another way-station en route to America. In fact there are two: one, a camp at Galand in Indonesia, the other in Bataan, the Philippines. These are called RCPs or Refugee Processing Centers, and are used both to "stem the flow" and to orient the refugees to the manners and mores and, especially, the peculiar language of Americans. Proflights from the various first-asylum countries transport people to Singapore and Manila for transfer to the RPCs.

Almost every day planes fly into Manila airport partially loaded with refugees. Those who fly with the refugees report on the excitement, bewilderment, awe, and, for some, sheer terror on the faces of old and young. The flights are short (the longest is from Bangkok). Upon arrival in Manila they are hurried through the crowded old airport and herded into blue buses which briskly move down busy Roxas Boulevard to park, sometimes for hours, across the street from the United States Embassy, until the drivers are told to move out ("Hurry up and wait"). Finally they leave for the RPC five long hours away from Manila over a twisting road through the very same mountain made famous in the early days of World War II. (The refugees pass by the Great Cross, a memorial to those who lost their lives in the Japanese rout and infamous Death March. But the symbolism is lost on them. They are dazed and dozing, exhausted from their travel.)

Upon arrival at the camp in Bataan, a series of in-take interviews are conducted. JVA/Manila's caseworkers are there to review and update the files and to assign them to English classes. All refugees between the ages of sixteen and fifty-five are required to attend eight weeks of ESL (English as a Second Language) classes and four weeks of CO (cultural orientation), before they can be moved from their new homes. At the time of the in-take interview, the JVA workers write down the day of departure. Eventually the names will be turned over to the ICM representatives for final medical checks and movement.

The Bataan RPC, like other refugee camps in the area, is under the joint authority of the UNHCR (United Nations High Commission for Refugees) and the national government. In the center of the camp, two flags fly; that of the United Nations and the Philippines'. (The U.S. government has no official role here.) The Filipino contingent consists of both military personnel and representatives of the Community Development Administration, a body charged with creating new settlements (which, it is said, the Bataan camp will become once its current functions have been served).

The incoming refugees are assigned billets in one of two large areas—Phase I and Phase II, each of which can house up to 10,000 in prefabricated low-rise barracks with small living spaces and sleeping lofts for approximately six persons. The barracks are grouped in neighborhoods each containing classroom buildings and latrines. There are also administration buildings, food distribution centers, and dormitories and mess facilities for staff. Refugees cook their own food in impoverished kitchen areas behind their rooms. (This is a common practice in most refugee camps.) There is also a market where some food may be purchased by staff members or refugees.

While the U.S. government has no official role in administering the camp, it is the principal funding source and American workers are found in almost every section. These include individual JVA caseworkers, hired by ICMC, the International Catholic Migration Committee's American branch, USCC (the U.S. Catholic Conference). ICMC is the "contract volag" in the Philippines. ICMC also holds the contract for the ESL-CO program for the sixteen to fifty-five-year-olds. When I was there, the 160 teachers hired by the ICMC were almost all Filipinas, teachers of English or another foreign language, whose coordinator, a fellow Filipino, was a professor seconded from La Salle College in Manila. Under them was one supervisor for every eight to ten teachers. At the time of my visit there were fourteen expatriates, all former Peace Corps volunteers, on the teaching staff. The cultural orientation program had a more diverse staff with some Filipinas and many American teachers, most of whom were also former Peace Corps volunteers or UNVs, volunteers from the Peace Corps—recruited workers who were under the UN authority. The administrators of the CO program were also Americans hired by the Joint Voluntary Agency authority back in Manila.

There were many other refugee workers in the camp, including language teachers from CARITAS, preparing some 1,000 refugees for movement to Germany. (So far as could be determined, they were the only large group not bound for the U.S. from Bataan.) And there was also an ICM staff—medical personnel and transportation facilitators—who, like most JVA caseworkers, were going back and forth from Bataan to Manila, usually staying in the camp for four or five days at a time.

It takes a while for the refugees to settle into the camp routine. First they must fix up their modest rooms which are often denuded of some of the original fixtures, invariably said to have been taken away by previous tenants. Then they must get into camp routine which involves more than attending mandatory classes. Sometimes they have to wait several weeks before starting their schooling. There are four schools running simultaneously, one class every two weeks for 800 to 850 residents in ESL classes of twenty and CO classes of forty. In any month there are then approximately 3,000 students enrolled in the JVA's ESL program.

The neighborhoods in which they live, and they did seem like neighborhoods, are for the most part ethnically specific, places that in another place might be called "Little Vietnam," "Chinatown," "Lao Village," and so forth. People are recognized by language and dress and, say the refugee workers, "by demeanor."

The cultural (and class and education) difference clearly shows up in the ESL classes where most are divided by ethnic groups and by level. Some prescreening determined where to place people. "A1" is non-literate, a situation most frequently found among the Hmong but sometimes among other groups. "A2" means literate but not in English. "B" indicated some English; "C" more; "D," fair competence in the language. "E's," are "those," one teacher explained, "who are so good, they shouldn't be here!" But when I was there, some were—and they were used to help teach and to serve as interpreters for both caseworkers and cultural orientation instructors.

When the refugees have completed their training they should be able to communicate in basic English and know something about the United States. In cultural orientation classes they learn bits of geography and history, but mostly they learn about housing, work, legal and local services, and the lifeways of Americans. Talking to them at the end of the course, and talking to those who knew them best, I got the impression that the program is neither an overwhelming success nor a wasted effort. Rather the orientation program seemed to be a faltering first step in dealing with the very difficult acculturation process. (Seeing people at the other end, I felt that those from Bataan at least had a somewhat more realistic understanding of what they could expect and, since few had any English before going to the Philippines, some sense of the language and an ability to communicate if, generally, at a most rudimentary level.)

With ESL classes and CO behind them and everything else in order, they are ready to go. JVA representatives interview then again and ask if they know where they are going. Most are very confused although they smile politely. The interview lasts about five to ten minutes. At the end of the session, each refugee signs off on a sheet, is given a map of the United States with a red mark indicating where he or she and the family is going and is handed a printed paper that says they are refugees who have been cleared by American authorities. The paper must be invested with magical qualities in the eyes of some of the refugees, for one caseworker I observed told one person after another, "If you have any problems, show them this paper." (I thought to myself, "Would that it could be so easy.")

In that last interview the refugees are also told when they will be going to Manila—and to America.

"You will be leaving tomorrow, so get your things together," the caseworker tells them. Many respond with a shy smile, as if to say, "At last." Many others nod rather dully. They will believe it when they see the blue buses. But the buses do come, usually on schedule, and they are off for Manila and a new life in a new world.

To the Promised Land

Whether coming from an RPC or directly to the United States from the country of first asylum, the airport scene and the flight are quite similar. Arranged through ICM, the refugees are herded aboard 747s for the long transpacific flight. On board the overcrowded charters include over 500 refugees, flight attendants, and two ICM nurses. No one else is allowed to go with them and so I can only report what I have been told. Consider one typical flight. This one is ICM Flight #50 out of Bangkok on June 15, 1981. It is boarded by 501 refugees, most of whom had been in Phanat Ni-kom for at least four months, some longer. A motley assemblage. There are representatives of all the ethnic groups in the area. There are large families and small ones; single adults and unaccompanied children. Some are headed for the States and family reunions. Others hope to join friends. Some have individual American sponsors; some have none, for the VO-LAG which has assumed responsibility for them. But all are ready and eager if very apprehensive—apprehensive not only because they are about to take the big step but also because, for many, they will be taking off on their first flight.

According to the ICM nurses, if one word describes the passengers on Flight #50 (or others on which they have served) it is "quiet." There is little talking as the people board the jumbo; little talking as they make their way to their small seats, which, as one pilot told me, "are in a one-class 'refugee configuration.'" There is little leg clearance, in a ten across, 3–4–3 set up throughout most of the plane.

There is little talking as the plane taxies and lumbers into the air. The stoic passengers clutch the armrests, close their eyes, or stare blankly.

The trip itself is usually twenty to twenty-four hours long, with layovers for refueling in Tokyo or Taipei and Anchorage. Few passengers get much sleep. But many are airsick and some have serious problems. There would be an effort to see that they were the first to be processed after touchdown in Oakland.

On the morning of June 15, 1981, I drove out to the Oakland Airport to meet Flight #50 which was scheduled to land at 11:05 A.M. I was late; the plane had come in at 8:30. "They didn't stop at Narita [Japan]," explained a tall blond American, Bob Carroll, an ICM worker with several years of experience in Southeast Asia and in the airport. Carroll and Nguyen T. Nguyen, a Vietnamese-American who works for the International Refugee Committee, had paved the way for me to be there, to observe, to question, to record reactions.

When I arrived I learned I had missed very little. The refugees had been taken off the World Airways charter and led into a large holding area where they were seated. Those who were ill had been cared for but the others sat in stony silence. "This is how they were all the way," said one of the ICM nurses. It was 9:30 and they were waiting for the immigration of-ficials and quarantine officers from the U.S. Public Health Service. Repre-sentatives of the ICM office in San Francisco, caseworkers from several of the volags, and a few interns from a special Georgetown University Refu-gee Program were already on hand. Once the rest of the principals in the entry-into-America drama were in their place the processing could begin. The sequence proceeds as follows.

First refugees are called by family groups to a desk where an ICM worker checked their credentials against the flight manifest and other information and assigned several numbers to each party. These were crayoned on the precious ICM bags which were still clutched at the side. In addition to the writing, color-coded stickers were affixed to the bags. Those called up first were with particular medical problems and those with relatives in the Bay Area who had requested an airport pick-up.

After it is found that the papers were in order, the refugees go to the quarantine officer to have their medical records checked. Those with flagged records, indicating active TB, for example, are held up—from a few minutes to several hours—while telexes are sent to the facility nearest to their final destination to alert authorities to the imminent arrival of these special patients. Once released by quarantine officers, the refugees then proceed through "Immigration." An INS officer reviews each individual's or family's documents and stamps the I-94 form, the slip of a paper that serves in lieu of a visa and, for a time, will be the main source of official identification.

Customs is next. The check there is not perfunctory for some inspection of luggage and packages is made; but it is not a very long or thorough search. The refugees then pass through the doors. They are now bona fide registered aliens and they have legally entered the United States.

Beyond those portals to America is not Nirvana but, for many, something akin to it. There, eagerly scanning the faces as the refugees pushed through the heavy double doors, were relatives of some of those on Flight #50. The reunions were moving to observe; a pat on the back from an older brother; a stare of disbelief from a teary daughter on seeing her parents for the first time in several years, then an awkward embrace; a solemn handshake from an old grandfather.

But most who come to Oakland on these flights are not met by relatives or friends. They are either to be settled in various parts of California or elsewhere. For all of them there is more waiting.

Those who left from Flight #50 (at least 90 percent of the passengers) were moved to various sections of a large room outside of the restricted area from where they had just come. In groups of approximately forty they waited for buses to take them and their belongings to Fort Hamilton in Marin County. It is an old military post now used as an ICM transit facility. Waiting for the bus for Hamilton, the refugees were all quiet and relaxed (or, more likely, numb). Many children fell asleep in the arms of equally exhausted parents or curled up on the floor. Finally their bus arrived and they were told to board. They walked out of the stuffy airport into the brilliant California summer sunshine and onto the bus. At this point, the refugees, having gotten through the ordeal of entry-processing now seemed particularly eager to be certain that all their possessions got on board too. Several stepped off the bus to check.

The trip to Hamilton, up route 80, across the San Raphael bridge, past

San Quentin, and into Marin, one of the wealthiest counties in the country is, for most, a blur. They are dazzled and confused and wondering where they are now being taken. Once they arrive at Hamilton they are greeted by the ICM workers and representatives of various agencies who, using interpreters, explain where they are, what is going to happen, and when they will move again, most likely back to Oakland or to San Francisco for onward movement. (Few will stay more than one night.) They are given bedding and toilet articles and shown to their rooms in one of the barracks. And there they collapse.

In the evening they are given an Asian meal served by a contracted caterer. Then they go back to their rooms to try to sleep. They have a hard time for, despite their fatigue, their biological clocks still say it is daytime, tomorrow actually, in far away Southeast Asia.

The tomorrow that will be their first in America comes early. Their odyssey is about to take a new turn. This is the day the Hamilton hostelers will become part of their new society.

T-152902

To get a clearer appreciation for those initial hours and days in America, I decided to follow a single family that was to be resettled in San Francisco by one of the volags, the International Rescue Committee. A representative of the IRC went over the list of "their people" on Flight #50 and found "my" family: Manychanh Kenh, T-152902, a thirty-nine-year-old from Laos, his wife, Yinh, 33, and four children; Ing, 9, Khamlianh, 8, Chianh, 7, and Khamla, 5. According to the personal information available, the Manychanhs were ethnic Chinese and Buddhists. Kenh had had six years of education and had been a merchant of some sort before leaving Laos in June 1980. His wife had also finished elementary school and had worked as a seamstress. (I later learned that Kenh was a peddler who had sold software—towels, mats, pillows, and cloth.) While one must always be wary of single-case analysis, my days with the Manychanh family proved most helpful in understanding "Phase Two," the second stage of the resettlement experience.

The fact is that the Manychanhs came close to being a model, or at least modal, family. According to a report heard on a local radio station on the very day I met passengers from Flight #50, I learned that the typical Indochinese family in the Bay Area was headed by a thirty-six-year-old ethnic Chinese, a spouse of thirty-three, with three children and no usable skills. Kenh was three years older than the average and had one more child but otherwise he and his family filled the bill.

An interpreter at the airport introduced me to the Manychanhs, explaining that I was a writer who hoping to tell the story of the refugee experience and that they were one of several families I was interested in getting to know. They were confused and, for a time, I worried that they would think I was their sponsor and would then be disappointed later on. (Three days later, when I left them, it *was* difficult for all of us.) They agreed that I would be with them and together we all went through the acronymic mill—USPHS, INS, Customs, and off to ICM's Hamilton facility where we were met by N.T.N. (Nguyen T. Nguyen) of IRC.

Kenh spoke only fragments of English. What he did know was based on his ESL course in Phanat Nikom, the camp to which he had been moved from Ubon in the north of Thailand. (He had spent almost a year in Ubon, arriving there after having crossed the Mekong in a small boat to "get away from the Communists and the discrimination against Chinese people.") Mostly, he and I talked through interpreters—first a Chinese-Lao, then a Chinese-Vietnamese, and then through an IRC caseworker Chu. (Ms. Chu had been born in China, raised in Vietnam, and received her university training in Taiwan.) During the first day I learned little about Kenh and his family and didn't press them. But I did stay with them until they were settled in Room 805 at Hamilton.

The next day the Manychanhs—and a number of others—were bused to downtown San Francisco and dropped at the International Institute, an affiliate of the American Council of Nationalities Service, a VOLAG located on Van Ness Boulevard. I was there to meet the bus and to go with the Manychanhs to the IRC office three blocks away.

Once there the Manychanhs were introduced to Li, their caseworker, who spoke to them in Mandarin. She was most efficient—both hard and firm. From the local IRC director, Don Climent, I learned that those in his office believed that refugees must learn to stand on their own feet as soon as possible, to become independent, not dependent.

Li followed what I later learned was a standard procedure. Documents are checked. Several are kept and the I-94 forms are returned to the head of the household. Kenh put them in his pocket, a minor but significant *rite de passage*. There was no more need for the ICM bag although it was not discarded. Kenh was then given a promissory note for money that would be advanced to him from IRC. He was told that an apartment had been rented for his family, that the first month's rent and key money had already been paid, and that he would be given $90 for groceries for the first week and $80 for the second until welfare payments could begin, or he had employment. He was handed the first check for $90 and sent off to cash it in a nearby bank using his precious I-94 as an I.D. I tagged along. (I thought to myself, "What an introduction to the U.S. The first non-refugee-connected place that is seen is a bank!")

He followed instructions, went up to a bank officer, had the check approved, stood in line at the teller window, got his money, counted it, and we went back to the IRC office to wait for a ride to the new apartment.

While waiting, I had a chance to question Kenh further. It was then that

I learned a bit more about his background, his life in Khampassak, Laos, his attitude toward the Communist regime—"a government of liars," his escape by paying a fisherman to row his family across the Mekong River, and his stay in the UNHCR-administered refugee camp at Ubon.

Prior to his flight from Laos, Kenh said he had no notion of going to America or any place else in particular. He said he just wanted to get away from Communist persecution and ethnic discrimination, "to live free." While he had few ideas about the United States, he was positive about what Americans had done in Laos. "Good things," he said. "They were kind people." Once in Ubon he said he heard more about America from others in the camp and soon decided to apply for resettlement because, he said, "Of all the places I thought America is best." He told the UN authorities, who put him in touch with American caseworkers from the JVA/Bangkok. Eventually he went through the process previously described and, once cleared by the State Department and INSed, was moved to Phanat Nikom. Kenh said that once he and his wife decided to apply for resettlement they spent many days going to the board at the office in Ubon to see if they were on the list. Asked what else they did there he smiled and said, simply, "Nothing."

In Phanat Nikom things were different. He studied—or tried to study— English with American teachers and had some cultural orientation ("Very practical things," he said, "like how to use a toilet.") Yinh also took the same courses. Kenh went for four hours each morning; she in the afternoon. (My impression was that they learned very little English, and very little about what to expect in America.) They received no occupational training.

After three months the course of study was ended and Kenh was told to watch for his number. Finally, he saw it on the board.

"How did you feel?" I asked through Li.

"Good," he said. "We were going to America. But we still were anxious. Not sure when we would go or how. The next thing that happened was that we were moved across the road [to a holding center]. Finally, after several days we were told to pack up again. We boarded buses and were taken to Bangkok. Then I knew it was going to happen."

"And the flight," I asked, "what about that?"

"It was long, very long."

"Were people excited?"

Li, the caseworker-interpreter, explained to me that he didn't know what I meant but that the people were numb and quiet.

Finally I asked Kenh what he wanted to do. He told me that was a hard question. He had virtually no English skills. Still, he hoped to find work, any work, but especially in a factory. Perhaps he could be a tailor for he could sew, too, like Yinh, and had done so before.

"And the children?"

"School. Then they will decide. But as much education as they can get. That is very important."

As the informal interview terminated, Li asked Kenh if he would be inerested in having the children enroll in a summer day care program at the downtown YMCA, recently established for six- to sixteen-year-old recent arrivals from Southeast Asia. He was interested but hesitant. It would cost 50¢ per child per week. We tried to explain that this was an incredible deal but he wanted time to think it over. Since there were only seventy-five places and already many applicants, time was of the essence. But he couldn't be pushed. Then, after thinking for a few minutes, he made his decision, to wait twenty-four hours. The next day he said he had thought it over again and did want to enroll the children. It was too late, all the spaces had been filled. (Introduction to American values: "He who hesitates is lost.")

At last a Vietnamese paraprofessional worker, who, like the family, was also of Chinese background, came back to the office and the seven of us and all of the Manychanhs' possessions—including bedding and kitchen utensils supplied by the IRC—were piled into his car for a short trip to the apartment on Jones Street in the depressed and depressing "Tenderloin" area, a place long inhabited by many poor and dispossessed people, now including a number of Indochinese refugees. Still, it was to be a home.

We carried the baggage into the building through a door which Kenh unlocked with the key he had been given, his *own* key, took the elevator to the sixth floor, walked down the hall and waited while, again, Kenh opened the door. Everyone was eager to see the place. It was a large, bright, somewhat shabby unfurnished room with two closets, a bathroom and a small kitchen. Not much for six people. But it was theirs. The furniture, beds and tables and chairs, was due in an hour but Kenh couldn't wait. He moved several suitcases and bigger bundles into a big closet, unpacked a large, square Laotian mat, spread it out, and tossed four of the new pillows on it. As if on cue, the children all kicked off their shoes, crawled over the mat and promptly fell asleep. Yinh smiled shyly. Kenh looked at me and at the interpreter and at the neighbors, a Chinese-Vietnamese family from downstairs, who came up to help. He smiled too. (The neighbors had arrived fifteen months before from a camp in Malaysia. They, too, were sponsored by the IRC. Their seven-year-old bilingual son proved to be a most useful additional interpreter for us all, speaking with equal fluency in English and Chinese.)

The Manychanhs were settled in and it was almost time for me to leave. But Kenh said he wanted to buy some food and I decided to go with him. As we were leaving, his new neighbor told him not to bother, that he and his wife would give the Manychanhs supper. Kenh was obviously touched by the gesture but still seemed eager to go out to bring something back. So we went. He bought rice, noodles, soup, eggs, and a bit of fruit. I walked him back home. We got there just as the furniture truck pulled up. Everyone helped to move things in. And I took my leave.

It had been but thirty-six hours since I first spotted the family whose "T (for Thailand) number" written across the ICM bag was 152902. They were no longer a number to me. In fact, I don't remember seeing the bag anywhere around the apartment. That was already part of the distant past. Part of yesterday.

In the Eye of the Storm

In recounting what I had observed to refugee workers in the Bay Area and in Seattle, San Diego, New Orleans, and Boston, and in following other families through the period of initial resettlement, I learned that the Manychanhs' experiences those first days were quite typical, with one exception. It is usually the case that American families, often representatives of church groups or other sponsoring organizations, provide the sort of welcome the Manychanhs' Chinese neighbors offered.

What I was also to learn was that the seemingly easy and relatively painless entry is very deceptive. Refugees undergo an experience much like flying through a hurricane. They enter on one side, are buffeted first by home-grown political cadres or foreign occupiers and then by international bureaucrats and resettlement officers, are shunted around the countryside, moved first hundreds, then thousands, of miles, then, finally, find their safe haven, a place of refuge—a flat in the Rainier Valley of Seattle, a tiny apartment in Boston's Chinatown, or a few rooms on Jones Street in San Francisco—that is, a haven in the eye of the storm.

But they still have to go through much more turbulence to get to the other side. For the Manychanhs, the third stage was to start the day after I left, their third day in America, with meetings with the caseworkers, bureaucrats in the social security office, the welfare department, and the employment office.

I returned to San Francisco two times in the few months after I first met the Manychanhs and visited with them. I was made aware that, like so many others, they were having a difficult time but were beginning to find themselves. One source of solace for them was being found in Chinatown where the children were taken to "after-school school" while Kenh waited outside. Yinh had found a job and was starting to get her bearings.

Agents of Acculturation

The rescue, aid, and resettlement of refugees (as noted in the essay "Tempest-Tost") has always been subject to the vagaries and vicissitudes of politics, with the quality of mercy often seeming to depend on judgments of governments in the calculus of international and domestic affairs. American refugee policy is a classic case in point. Much has already been written about the lack of responsiveness to the pleas of Nazism victims to permit them to find asylum in this country in the 1930s and to the cold shoulder given so many because, it was said, it wasn't in the national interest. In recent years, Cold War concerns have dominated a policy which, while far more generous than it was in the 1930s and the dark days of World War II, has been characterized by a distinctive bias favoring assistance to "those fleeing communism." (Indeed, from 1952 to 1980 that was the principal definition of a refugee in American law.) None can gainsay the fact that our policies and practices have been biased nor that refugee workers have often become unwitting partners in a very selective process that many have decried and worked to change. And yet it must be said that those same refugee workers are the unsung heroes to the hundreds of thousands of people forced to flee their homelands, cared for in camps from the borders of Kampuchea to the Khyber Pass, and, however unfair the selection process, assisted in coming to this country. Indeed, the fact that the refugees from Indochina—and many other parts of the world—do find protection, care, succor, and, eventually, new homes in the United States is in no small measure due to the often chaotic but somehow coordinated efforts of a number of government departments and voluntary agencies.

While often at loggerheads over policy or program, there is common concern of those in operations. Individuals at every level will tell you (told me) that their main raison d'être is protecting victims and facilitating movement. And, by and large, it works.

Being committed to doing good, of course, is hardly the be all or end all. Nor are the inevitable bureaucratic snafus which often slow down and sometimes derail the process at crucial moments. There are significant problems in preparing people for new lives. One of the thorniest is that there seems to be too little preparation for refugees for what to expect in the United States. Part of that undoubtedly is attributable to the fact that there is almost no way to convey the experience of living here as opposed to what they knew at home and in the refugee camps. Still, I found that those caseworkers in Southeast Asia who seem most effective are those who have spent time helping to resettle people in the United States *before* going into the field. It isn't that those without such experience do not do their jobs adequately. They do. They are usually quite compassionate and extremely sympathetic. But in trying to deal with the initial struggle of the refugees here, they are at a decided disadvantage. This is especially true of those hired not to process refugees but to teach them, that is, the ESL and cultural orientation teachers. Unlike many of the caseworkers, they often seemed too far removed from the nitty-gritty concerns of the refugees. (Many seemed aware of this and were rethinking the programs.)

It should be mentioned that the local crew who receive the refugees and send them onward and the agency personnel (at least those in the local vo-lag office in San Francisco) are to be commended for their skills—and their empathy. Many of the workers I met have been involved in various parts of the overall program in the United States and in Southeast Asia (a number of them are Indochinese themselves) and that makes a big difference.

While the final test is how the refugees themselves fare, the burden can be eased by dedicated and skilled workers. But even they can only vicar-iously enter the minds and hearts of those who have given up much to come to the United States and to start over. Acculturation is a long and dif-ficult process. It takes many years of immersion in the new society and many setbacks before one can reconcile the old world and the new and be-come something familiar to many of us in this nation, a hyphenated Amer-ican.

The Once and Would-Be King

N ORODOM SIHANOUK is a man for all seasons. But he is no Thomas More. A consummate political, Sihanouk has kept his head and, according to his critics, his reputation as the "Chameleon of Cambodia." Those less inclined to cynicism claim that, owing to his ancestry and his patriotic fervor, he is the true embodiment of the Khmer nation. Whatever the case, he is a survivor.

The Saigon- and Paris-educated prince ruled France's colonial dominion as King from 1941 until his abdication in 1955. In the government of newly independent Cambodia, the prince became Prime Minister and Minister for Foreign Affairs in a coalition government. He maintained those two posts until 1957. Three years later he was restored to power as Head of State. Seeming to grow increasingly antipathetic to his former friends in the West, in the early 1960s Sihanouk terminated all U.S. aid projects and began to take a decidedly anti-American stance. By 1973 his concern about the treachery of those in the "U.S. of America" was spelled out in a book *My War with the CIA*. Yet many close observers claim that the Prince never fully abandoned the belief that the United States itself would provide the shield that would ultimately protect Cambodia from its traditional enemy to the east, Vietnam.

The rule of America's man in Phnom Penh, Lon Nol, was short-lived. After the fall of Saigon and the simultaneous collapse of the anti-communist government in Cambodia, a Royal Government of National Unity was formed. Sihanouk was restored as Chief of State. Publicly it was touted as a broad-based coalition. The reality was quite different. This time the center could not hold. Sihanouk was forced to resign in 1976 and departed the country. He moved to France, to China, and to North Korea. From such varied bases of operation, the prince maintained contact with other exiled Cambodians and sought the assistance of a broad spectrum of gov-

*Originally published as "Norodom Sihanouk of Cambodia: [An Interview with] The Once and Would-Be-King," in *Migration Today*, vol. XIII, no. 2, 1985, pp. 13–17.

ernments, those of both right and left, whose common cause was opposition to the victorious Vietnamese.

National elections were held on March 2, 1976 and the Khmer Rouge, lead by Pol Pot, took over. After a series of purges and the elimination of all potential rivals, Pol Pot established under the direction of his reign. It proved to be a reign of terror that officially lasted until December 1979 when, with the support of Vietnamese forces, a new socialist regime was established under the titular authority of Heng Samrin. The country was renamed the Democratic People's Republic of Kampuchea.

The general policies carried out by Khmer Rouge cadres decimated the population and eliminated a substantial percentage of the old elite and the newer middle class. Moreover, new measures failed to maintain even a modicum of agricultural productivity or any other form of economic viability. Thousands of half-starved, desperate men, women, and children sought sanctuary across the frontier in Thailand. With the collapse of Pol Pot's government, thousands more—Khmer Rouge soldiers and sympathizers—also fled the country. The borderlands became a landscape filled with refugees of various factions and the site of a gigantic relief effort. It remains both to this day, although several hundred thousand Khmer have been resettled in western nations, well over 100,000 of them in the United States alone.

Sihanouk, no longer king nor chief of state but still prince by inheritance, once again attempted to use his traditional station to reestablish his authority. He was also used by those who felt that his presence in any sort of government-in-exile might provide legitimacy. This crazy-quilt tripartite coalition was constructed consisting of Sihanouk's old loyalists, members of the Khmer People's National Liberation Front under the leadership of the former Cambodian Premier Son Sann, and those who still claimed to be the rightful rulers, Pol Pot's Khmer Rouge. The latter maintains Cambodia's seat in the United Nations and, in the convoluted logic of "the enemy of my enemy is my friend"—in this case the People's Republic of Vietnam and its client, the DPRK, the United States government recognizes Pol Pot's non-residential regime, the coalition, and Prince Sihanouk who currently refers to himself as President of Cambodia. As such he is back in the graces of the West, many of whose own leaders see Sihanouk as the one stable factor in a highly volatile admixture of personalities and politics. Perhaps they are right. He, at least, thinks so and acts accordingly.

The charismatic prince spends much of his time traveling the world trying to rally support for the coalition's anti-Vietnamese platform, using MacArthurian "We-Shall-Return" rhetoric, especially in those places where large numbers of Khmer have found new homes. He does double duty, at once acting as the savior of his battered land and symbolic leader of all Khmer, regardless of party, whom, he claims are united in their hatred of the foreign occupiers and their Cambodian lackeys, and as a gracious spokesman for the less articulate refugees who wish to thank their hosts for providing solace and safety and the opportunity to reconstruct shattered lives. In both tasks, he has been quite successful.

Colloquy with the Prince

A few months ago, while in Southern California to visit a variety of refugee programs, I had the chance to meet with the prince. He had come to San Diego, he said, "to see my people." He was also to meet the press and to spend some time with a group of refugee workers and sponsors. Through the intervention of several acquaintances closely connected to the Khmer community in San Diego County, I was able to attend both the press conference and the session with the others. They were very similar.

In both meetings in perfect English the prince thanked the United States and the people of the area for what he called their unstinting support and kind assistance to those uprooted by the series of tragedies in his country. He went on to state his views of the current situation and the necessity for all to understand that the real enemy is not another faction in his admittedly fractious current coalition but the Vietnamese who have brought nothing but "further hardship and foreign hegemonism to Cambodia."

To better understand his arguments, I will turn to some of his own words, transcribed from tapes made during the meetings with Ben Moser, a sociologist who works with Cambodian refugees and had coordinated this particular event. Moser opened the discussion and introduced a couple who have sponsored a number of Cambodian refugees to the local heads of two of the four voluntary agencies involved in resettlement in San Diego; a psychotherapist, who has been providing counseling to Indochinese refugees since 1974; two sociologists, John Weeks and Rubén Rumbaut, both involved in the study of the resettlement and adaptation of Indochinese refugees and their reception in the U.S., and the writer.

Prince Sihanouk: May I avail myself to the opportunity to say how much I am grateful to you and the U.S. of America for generous and, if I may say so, affectionate hospitality given to so many Cambodian refugees here.

There are about 70,000 Cambodian refugees in the U.S. I am trying to meet as many of them as possible this year, after fulfilling my mission at the U.N. in the General Assembly, in my capacity as president of Cambodia. I am here in order to establish close contact with my compatriots here in California. In San Diego there aren't many Cambodians but today and tomorrow I am going to meet with many Cambodians coming from other towns and other parts of California, like San Francisco, Los Angeles, and so on. They feel very happy to here be here in the U.S., and they enjoy very much your hospitality, your attention, all the facilities you have given them, and in particular the fact that, their children are being well-educated. If I may say so, they are good American citizens and also will remain dedicated to Cambodia.

They are good patriots as Cambodians. They continue to have activities in favor of an independent Cambodia. They want their country to be liberated and they send money, medicine, to the populations of the zones of Cambodia. I am coming here in order to congratulate them and thank them for their good behavior vis-à-vis the host country, the United States of America, and vis-à-vis the former homeland of Cambodia. They are willing to contribute towards the liberation of Cambodia. Many of them, the young ones, too, would like to participate in the struggle against the Vietnamese in order to liberate the homeland. I had to tell them that they must, for the time being, stay here in order to prepare the younger generation of Cambodians to be able to rebuild the culture because we are a country which is destroyed by war. And, if one day we are lucky enough to become once again, a free and independent nation, we will need doctors, teachers, engineers, etc. So they will be very useful to Cambodia, the day Cambodia needs them. For the time being they must stay here. And they agree with me so far as my advisers are concerned.

The situation of our country remains very difficult but we are doing our best in order to break the present deadlock. What people call the "Cambodian problem" is not created by the Cambodians but by the Vietnamese, who, since 1979 occupied our country militarily. There are in Cambodia, 200,000 Vietnamese soldiers, whose activities are to prevent the Cambodian people from being free and Cambodia from being independent. Vietnam is willing to swallow our country physically, because there are now about 600,000 Vietnamese settlers coming from Vietnam in order to take our lands, to exploit our national resources, to Vietnamize our traditional culture, and so on. So, the situation in Cambodia is very difficult, but our people are very courageous and now there are more and more volunteers to fight back, and to participate in the struggle against the Vietnamese invaders.

We are a peace loving people, but peace without freedom is unacceptable. We cannot accept the Vietnamese *fait accompli* in Cambodia.

We are very fortunate in our endeavors to be supported very nobly by the U.S. of America and by the U.N. organization itself. Recently, exactly 110 countries which are members of the United Nations, and beginning with the U.S. of America voted in favor of the U.N. resolution on Cambodia. In the resolution it is said that; one, all foreign troops—that is to say, Vietnamese troops, must withdraw from Cambodia; two, the Cambodian people must become once again a sovereign people, and there will be general elections under U.N. supervision, enabling the Cambodian people to choose freely their leader, their government and their representatives, and their social and political system. The Cambodian people reject, definitely, Communism. They want to rebuild a nationalist and free and Western-style Cambodian democracy, with a free enterprise system. So the Cambodian people through general election could rebuild, remake such a Cambodia. And three, it is said that an international conference on Cambodia under the sponsor of the U.N. should take place with the participation of all concerned countries.

For the time being, Vietnam and the Soviet Union reject all U.N. resolutions on Cambodia because they want to remain in Cambodia, to use Cambodia as a base to threaten—a military base, a strategy base—the peace and security of free countries like Thailand, Singapore, Malaysia, and other countries which are being threatened by the Soviets and the Vietnamese and are supporting us really actively in order to enable us to get an international conference to solve the problem of Cambodia. I repeat, we are a peace loving people, we are not waging war for the sake of war, but in order to let the Vietnamese see that if Cambodia has no peace, they will have no peace because when a people is determined to fight for freedom, we cannot be wiped out. . . .

I am at your disposal to answer your questions.

Rose: In this period when you are waiting for the opportunity to reform your society, there are thousands of Cambodians scattered throughout the world. The refugees. Can you tell us how you see them faring in their exile? And can you say something of what they tell you of their problems here in America?

Prince Sihanouk: Each year, I see many Cambodian refugees in the states and in Western Europe. Each year I visit the reconquered zones inside Cambodia, but also outside Cambodia. I have to travel a lot as a leader of the Cambodian resistance, so I need to establish contact with governments, friendly governments and countries, as many as possible. And, on the other hand, I have to establish contacts with the many Cambodian refugees in friendly countries. There are 120,000 in Thailand, 70,000 in the U.S., and about 50,000 in France, and thousands and thousands in other countries like Canada, Australia, New Zealand, Malaysia, Singapore, the Philippines, Indonesia, even the People's Republic of China, and Hong Kong, and Macao, and Japan and so on. I see as many as possible, I try to establish contact with them.

I can tell you this: there is no complaint from them. It appears that all of them are very satisfied. You know as far as their accommodation in many countries is concerned, as far as their lives in those countries are concerned. I hear only praises from their mouths, only praise of the U.S. They love you; they admire the U.S. They tell me that they have a good life for them, a good education for their children, and that many American families give them facilities and protection, help, and so on. Only praises, no complaints. So I feel happy about it since it appears that they are happy. . . .

They feel very, very happy as guests of the host country. Not only here, but in France and in other Western European countries there are only praises.

In Thailand, the Thai people and government are very friendly to us. Very generous. But as you know, the burden in Thailand is very, very heavy. Thailand has to accommodate so many Indochinese refugees, not just the Cambodians, but Laotians and Vietnamese, because many Vietnamese flee from Vietnam. They flee every day. And Thailand has to give shelter to them, and the burden—the financial, economic, social burden—is getting heavier and heavier for Thailand. So, Thailand, on the one hand, and, on the other hand, the Cambodian refugees themselves, would like to see the rich countries take more and more refugees—Cambodian refugees—from refugee camps in Thailand. In those [Asian] countries I met Cambodian refugees. They told me that they would like to be allowed to, you know, establish themselves in countries like the U.S., France, and so on. But I know quite well that those rich and very friendly countries cannot accept them all. But already each year, you extend your hospitality to more and more refugees and I am very grateful to the U.S.

And, finally, may I say a few words about the mentality, the minds and hearts of my countrymen here. They are good, loving American citizens. They love their new homeland, America. But they continue, also at the same time, to be good Cambodian patriots and they send money, when they earn money here, to their compatriots in refugee camps inside Cambodia near Thailand—all along the frontier—there are more than three hundred thousand Cambodians we have to accommodate in the free zones near Thailand. They are not selfish; they are good patriots.

Rumbaut: I have a question that partly reflects my own personal experience. I came from Cuba as a refugee a little over twenty years ago, and I have seen a new generation of Cubans grow up here in the U.S. Many of the parents' generation continue to dream and to hope of the possibility of a free Cuba, and to return to Cuba in such an event. But a new generation of Cuban Americans have been born in the U.S. and have grown up in the U.S. during the past quarter-century. Now in our own research in the Cambodian community of refugees in the U.S., we have found that according to the U.S. government about 100,000 Cambodian refugees have been admitted to the U.S. already as of this year. And, in addition, we estimate that at least between ten and twenty thousand Cambodian children—perhaps more—have been born in the U.S already as of this year. In other words, the beginning of the new Cambodian-American generation is taking place. Now given your optimism about the isolation of Vietnam in the international community and the possibility of the liberation of Cambodia, perhaps later in this decade—in the 1980s, what do you think would be the response of this new generation of Cambodians in the U.S. with respect to

Cambodia? Do you think that they would have a conflict of loyalties, that they would be torn? You have said they have nothing but praise for the U.S., they are well received. Perhaps they like it so much they'll want to stay.

Prince Sihanouk: Thank you so much for your question, which is very important. May I tell you this very frankly. Nobody among those Cambodians—even the young Cambodians—dare to tell me that they would like to, you know, stay far away from home, stay here or stay in France.

Each time I ask: "Would you like to go back to Cambodia once we are liberated?" "Yes! Sure!" They tell me always. "Sure, sure. We are willing to go back." Not only the older generation, but the younger one. But I know that among the younger Cambodians there are, yes, a good number of them who think that they are not to go back. They would like to stay because they enjoy the American way of life, or the French way of life. . . . I know that. But I don't think that there is a problem because we Cambodians are determined, and we are willing to remain a very close friend of the U.S. of America.

I am not sure when we are going to be liberated. But in the long run I think that the Vietnamese will not be able to stay in Cambodia. When it happens we will have enough Cambodians and also aids from you and other countries—engineers and so on, to rebuild our own country.

You know, when I was head of the government I had some problems about jobs to be given to so many students. We built schools, colleges, universities. But after that we had to provide jobs. And as a developing—not developed country (in the Third World those countries are called developing countries, but there to be frank, "developing countries" is a euphemism). We are underdeveloped, so on the one hand we have more than enough intellectuals, on the other hand, not enough jobs for them. So, it is good that one part decided to stay in their new countries; we will have less problems as far as the job situation is concerned. So all right. They can stay. I don't worry about it. The ones who decided to go, they will be enough for Cambodia. We will have enough among the volunteers—the ones who, really, really want to go. And I assure you that we will get many doctors, nurses, teachers, engineers, and so on. I know them. They are very anxious to go back to Cambodia. Among them there are also those who are asking for permission for the honor to fight, to become soldiers. They remain highly patriotic. No, I don't worry. There will be one part who decide to stay; one part will decide to go home. I think it is a well-balanced situation.

I think it is good. It is good for the Cuban people themselves. It is a good thing to have links always with the U.S. and not to be cut off. If you decided to send all Cubans to Cuba once Castro disappeared, it is not good. Cambodians in France, and in the U.S., W. Germany, Holland, and so on, they are links—physical and also moral and spiritual links—uniting our countries.

Metcalf (from Church World Service, San Diego office): I understand the Asian countries' coalition has been endeavoring to try to facilitate a repatriation of many of those people—of your people—now in Thailand. Send them back into Cambodia. How do you feel? Do you support that effort to try to repatriate at this time?

Prince Sihanouk: You know, as I have told you, the burden of Thailand is very heavy. I understand the wish of Thailand to repatriate more and more Cambodians to Cambodia. But they (the refugees), on the one hand, want to be exiled to Europe or to America. And, on the other hand, they refuse to go to the occupied zones under the Vietnamese occupation. So, each time Thailand repatriates Cambodians, we, the coalition government, have to resettle them in the free zone we have under our control near the Thai border. So the problems of Thailand for us and for the international communities remain the same. In Thailand and in the free zones there are refugees. They need your help; they need humanitarian aids—food, medicine, and so on. And we have gotten more and more assistance from the international community to feed the population, to take care of them in the field of public health, education, and so on, so we are grateful to you and to all humanitarian relief agencies and to Thailand for such a solidarity with us. But there remains, you know, a problem. We still do not have enough food to feed them or enough medicine.

Palmer (a local citizen who, with his wife, has sponsored many Cambodian refugees): We hear of so many horrible things during the Pol Pot years. I can see certainly, the objection to the Vietnamese coming in, and the very strong feeling you have and your people do, about that. But, how do you see the Khmer Rouge fitting in to a new government?

Prince Sihanouk: The Prime Minister and his followers, myself and my followers, we would like to be separated from the Khmer Rouge. We would like to form a nationalist government without the Khmer Rouge. But how can we form a nationalist government outside the legal framework of Democratic Kampuchea because Democratic Kampuchea is the legal entity; it is still the full member of the U.N. If we don't accept the legality of Democratic Kampuchea, we cannot be recognized by the U.N., and if we are not recognized by the U.N., we might just protest against the Vietnamese in the streets, in front of the U.N. No, if we want to be helpful to Cambodia, we must have at our disposal the U.N. platform. We can speak out against the Vietnamese, and get legal and official support from the U.N. If we protest only in the streets of San Diego, or New York, we can not impress the Vietnamese—they are not so easily impressed. They must be isolated in the international arena, vis-à-vis international law.

The Khmer Rouge themselves, they are trying now to improve their behavior vis-à-vis their own people. I know that they have not changed completely. Their minds are communist, but they accepted to join us in the writing of a common political platform for the future of Cambodia. They accept our ideas of free world-style democracy. Even capitalism—free enterprise economics. They swear, they promise very solemnly, that they will abide by the tripartite coalition to make Cambodia a free-style democracy.

We can get rid of the Khmer Rouge on paper, but we cannot get rid of them on the ground since they are there. And we are not going to make a general fight with the Khmer Rouge. We have no means to kill them. Secondly, we must not try to wipe out one part of the Cambodian nation by more killings. The main problem is no more the Khmer Rouge problem, but to get rid of the Vietnamese in Cambodia. We want the Vietnamese to go home. And so long as they are not willing to go, we have to unite as patriots to fight the Vietnamese. And the U.S. of America, herself, she chose to vote for the Khmer Rouge in the years 1979, 1980, 1981. Why did the U.S. of America vote for the Khmer Rouge at the U.N.? Because, no, you did not like the Khmer Rouge, but you had to prevent the Vietnamese from swallowing Kampuchea.

Postscript

Prince Sihanouk stayed to answer a few other questions. Then, as we took our leave, he clasped our hands warmly and spoke a few words of thanks to each of us.

He was as charming, as careful, and, in certain ways, as crafty as I had been led to believe from the many press accounts and lengthier assessments I had read over the years.

Shortly after the departure of our modest entourage, Prince Sihanouk met with his people; first, with a select group of ardent supporters, then with a much larger one—which included his followers and others who expressed very ambivalent feelings about him and his willingness to sit down with, even to publicly support, the Khmer Rouge.

The next evening Norodom Sihanouk was a guest of honor at a Cambodian rally and banquet. Hundreds attended and paid homage to their once and—at least to some—future king. An accomplished poet and musician as well as statesman, he acknowledged their warm welcome and gestures of patriotic fidelity with words and songs. He told them that they had to remain steadfast in the firm belief that someday soon Kampuchea would be free again. He, Norodom Sihanouk, would lead them from their diaspora back to their rightful homes.

For that one evening, at least, most seemed to believe it.

P.P.S. In 1985 Norodom Sihanouk became the King of Cambodia once again.

The Cantonese Connection

―――――

I

A N UNEXPECTED fringe benefit of a three-day delay in Guangzhou (the city most Westerners still call Canton) on a recent trip to China [in 1986] gave me a chance to observe a phenomenon that seemed at once un-usual and familiar. It was the interviewing and processing of visa applicants at the U.S. Consulate.

Those who came to the office, almost hidden away in a labyrinthine warren alongside a beauty parlor and several restaurants in a hotel complex several miles from the more centrally located, pre-1949 consular mansion, were not just students seeking temporary admission as I expected. They were would-be immigrants from southern China and refugees from Viet-nam, a strange mix in this strange old/new world.

I was curious to learn more. After meeting a group of American foreign service officers (many on their first tour of duty) and their superiors, and after getting permission from the chief of the section, I managed to do so.

My principal guide was David Kornbluth, an historian of China, a law-yer, and at the time of my visit, deputy head of the consular section. He had attended a lecture I had given on the then-recent waves of East and Southeast Asians in America. Afterward, he asked me if I would like to see what they (or at least a small sampling of them) looked like before embark-ing to the United States. I replied enthusiastically, indicating that most of my field experience with visa sections and INS offices in Asia had been limited to refugee cases. He smiled and said, "But we have refugee cases, too."

They were some of the thousands of ethnic Chinese who had been leav-ing the northern part of reunited Vietnam since the late nineteen seventies and early eighties. Most were "boat people" who hoped to make it safely to Hong Kong or Macao. The majority of them did get to one of these ports. Some did not. Owing to difficulties on board the overloaded vessels or un-favorable winds, the unlucky ones got no farther than Hainan Island or

*Originally published in *Migration World* vol. xiv, no. 4, 1987, 24–28.

were forced to land on the People's Republic of China mainland. Others walked out of Vietnam, crossing the northern frontier into China.

To an outsider it seems truly ironic that those fleeing communism would find safe haven in the world's largest people's republic; yet they did. Vietnam's Chinese were welcomed openly in part no doubt because of the strained relations between the two former allies, Vietnam and the PRC, but also because, as a Chinese friend told me, "When it comes to China, blood is thicker than politics, especially where Overseas Chinese are concerned. These are *our* people."

Still, the fact remains that, however they were viewed by the Chinese, few of the *Viet Hoa* left Vietnam hoping to settle on the soil of their putative motherland. This was not what they bargained for with the boat captains who promised to take them to some waystation en route to the United States or Canada. They had gotten there by fluke or necessity.

II

The Chinese authorities must have been aware of their true intentions. While they welcomed them with equanimity for the reasons mentioned, I wondered how they would deal with these "reluctant returnees." The answer was not hard to come by.

Despite the peculiarity of their circumstances, the refugees were given a proper place in their unintended "country of first asylum," provided with papers, and assigned to units just like others. By all apparent evidence, they were treated well. But, even for those who had strong cultural ties to if not political sympathies with the people of China, life in the PRC was (and is) not easy and adaptation to the regimentation of the socialist state is especially hard for those coming from lands where they had lived quite independent lives apart from the mainstream of their society, and where, often as prototypical capitalists, they has served in a variety of capacities as storekeepers and bookkeepers, small time merchants and international tradesmen, physicians and teachers.

Separation from relatives was even more difficult for many to bear than adapting to the social and political environment of the PRC. They wanted to be reunited with family members already resettled across the Pacific. And since the Chinese authorities did not prevent them from trying, this is what invariably led them to a large room in the Guangzhou's Dong Fang Hotel where they joined other petitioners quietly seated under an American flag, anxiously waiting to discuss their claims with a consular officer.

Bona fide refugees bound for America, in China as elsewhere, are treated differently from other potential immigrants, including those basing their claim to acceptance on family reunion. They get to jump the queue and to have their cases heard out of order.

"Regular" applicants can also apply for family reunion but the process is long though not terribly complicated. As David Kornbluth reminded me, in China as elsewhere:

> [Aside from refugees], there are two categories of immigrants. Those subject to the numerical limitation of 20,000 per year from each sovereign state [established by the Immigration Act of 1965] and those not subject to numerical limitation. Spouses, minor children, and parents of United States citizens (called "IRs" for immediate relatives) are admitted without limitation. Those subject to limitation are divided into six categories, P-1 through P-6, which include unmarried adult children of U.S., citizens (P-1), spouses and unmarried children of lawful permanent residents of the U.S., the green card holders (P-2), persons of distinguished merit and ability who have offers of employment in the U.S. and whose employment will not harm wages or working conditions of American workers (P-3), married adult children of U.S. citizens (P-4), siblings of U.S. citizens (P-5) and skilled and unskilled workers who have offers of employment in the U.S. (P-6). A state's allotment of 20,000 visas is allocated according to a system of percentages.

Invariably, there are more applicants in the various preference categories than can be accommodated in any given year. They are backlogged and a system of priority dates is used to determine the order in which applicants will be permitted to go. Worldwide, the most crowded category is P-5, siblings. Commenting on this rather universal phenomenon, Kornbluth said:

> In China at present [June 1986] only persons whose petitions were filed before July 1980 may apply for visas. The cut-off date, as it is called, is changed monthly. It advances more or less quickly depending on the preference category. In the case of "China P-5" it advances approximately 10 days every month. This means that the Chinese whose claim to immigration benefits is based on having a U.S. citizen brother will wait for years before becoming eligible to apply for a visa. For persons born in Hong Kong, the wait will be more than 10 years in the fifth preference. Other categories have different waiting periods. For example, the August cut-off date for "China P-2" (spouses and kids of green card holders) is May 20, 1985. This means that Chinese in that category need wait only a year to apply.

Once a petitioner is eligible, an application may be filed. Affidavits providing the veracity of claims such as family connections need to be prepared. However, since it is known that, in most cases, the building of the file can be accomplished within a relatively brief span of time, the Consular Affairs Bureau sets qualifying dates. (Like the cut-off dates mentioned by Kornbluth, these too are constantly being revised.) The qualifying dates are used by the consular officers to determine when to advise the applicant who has been waiting that he or she should prepare the application and how and where to obtain the necessary documents.

According to Kornbluth, the qualifying dates are usually about six months ahead of the cut-off dates. They allow him and his colleagues to use the waiting time to build the case file.

Eventually, the applicants, with whom the consular officer has maintained contact, are notified. They return to the nearest U.S. Consulate or Embassy on a specified day and, with a case officer, review all documents, including health records. If all is in order, they are approved and can leave on the next available transport.

While, for most the application process ends on the day of the interview, for a significant number it does not. As Kornbluth and several of his colleagues pointed out to me, it is not infrequently that applications are denied because the petitioners are not able to adequately document the relationship claimed in one of the family-reunion categories, that is, all, save P-2.

In the course of my observations, I witnessed one outright rejection and several "holds." The latter pertains to those told they must obtain further evidence of their claims.

Of the family reunion cases I managed to sit in on the brief period I was in Guangzhou, two may give a sense of similarities and differences in the manner of treating refugees and immigrants.

III

The first case was one of a Sino Vietnamese whose family had fled from Vietnam in 1980, bribing their way out of the country and "booking" passage on a leaky coaster. Luckier than some, they made the trip to Hong Kong without anything untoward occurring. After processing in the Crown Colony and a lengthy stay in one of the six refugee centers in the city, they were resettled on the West Coast of the United States through the combined efforts of governmental agencies and voluntary agencies, specifically involved in the rescue and resettlement of refugees.

Several years later other family members sought to join their relatives and followed the path they knew their kin had taken. They found it more difficult to get out of Vietnam, and once at sea (on a much smaller craft), had a far more harrowing, if briefer, voyage. They only got as far as Hainan Island where the Chinese authorities first interned them and then moved them to the mainland where they were eventually given legal status owing to something akin to Israel's "law of return." In time they learned it was possible to be considered for reunion with those who had preceded them but that they would have to prove that they were, indeed, close relatives. The consulate in Guangzhou was the nearest point of contact with American authorities and it was there that they went to obtain information and the necessary forms.

Once they had sufficient material to establish the veracity of their claim, they were able to ask for permission to enter the United States as refugees themselves, refugees with immediate relatives in the United States, third in the list of *refugee* preference categories. (First, is a former employee of the U.S. government during the war in Vietnam; second, is a former member of the South Vietnamese army or a member of government of the Republic of Vietnam.) Like other refugees, their cases were handled by intermediaries, members of the American Council of Voluntary Agencies' Migration Committee, who contact voluntary agencies that handled the original arrivals.

Once approved, the Chinese residing refugees were then to be permitted to come to the United States where they would receive a variety of benefits under the Refugee Act of 1980.

IV

For the regular immigrants, including those who had close relatives in the United States, the situation is a bit different.

Consider another case whose hearing I sat in on in David Kornbluth's office. There were three applicants: two, husband and wife, were fairly elderly farmers; the other was their seventeen-year-old daughter, the youngest of six. Five years before they had started the process of trying to join the husband's youngest brother in New Jersey where he and his wife, now American citizens, had been living for a number of years and where they had raised a family of their own.

The day for decision had finally come and the three applicants were finally ushered into the room where their papers were thoroughly reviewed. In addition to the necessary affidavits, in the case file were letters written in Chinese which Kornbluth perused. They were presented by the husband to indicate that he and his brother had maintained contact over many years. After perusing the material and asking a few questions of each person, they were told they were acceptable. The husband and daughter signed their names; the wife, illiterate, made a thumbprint.

I asked Kornbluth what they would do in America. He said that, while clearly eligible, it was doubtful they would work. Instead, they would be cared for by their relatives who, it was clear from the record, had the necessary assets. They might stay on in the country but they might do as many others had done: help their younger offspring get to the States, and, then return to China, to their farming area, to their real home. "And what of the daughter?" I asked. Kornbluth said she would doubtless become a citizen at the first opportunity and a productive one at that.

V

The difference between the two cases is that the first would receive assistance from societal institutions specifically geared to working with refugees. The second would have to depend on the promised support of family members.

Surely not all cases are so clear cut nor have such a satisfactory solution. I witnessed difficulties in getting at the evidence of claims of family connections; I witnessed the rejection of applications. And I noted, with a sense of compassion, the anguished expressions of some of the officers as they made tough, negative decisions.

But what struck me most about what I was privileged to observe was how much like other consular offices the one in Guangzhou seemed. It wasn't until I moved back outside that I was brought back to the absurdity of it all. Here I was in the People's Republic of China—a place that not so long ago was viewed by a U.S. president as *the* Evil Empire, a place that only recently had had to cope with the escape of thousands of its own peoples who sought asylum in the other lands, now supporting, or at least, hardly impeding, the lawful movement of people, both through and from its soil to go to America.

What a world!

In Whom They Trust

"TRUST" is an interesting word. It has a number of connotations, some of which suggests a particular kind of symbiotic relationship between two or more parties. In popular parlance, for example, the word is frequently used to mean reliance on or faith in others. But there is another common way in which it is rendered, expressing an obligation or responsibility imposed on one in whom authority is placed—as "in a position of trust." In the first of the two definitions the emphasis might be said to be on the "weaker" party, the one in need of guidance or assistance or protection. In the second it is on the "stronger" one, the person or group in whom the dependent ones are expected or required to place their faith and confidence. The relationship between refugees and those who care for them illustrates a classic case of such dependency.

Wherever they may find themselves, refugees—weakened by the circumstances that cause their uprooting, suffering from chaotic and, often, anomic conditions in camps or other temporary quarters, frequently disoriented, confused, and alienated in the most literal sense of the term—are almost invariably dependent upon others for their immediate and, in many cases, long-term survival. Sometimes those others are strangers, true Samaritans. Sometimes they are kith and kin, co-religionists or compatriots, political allies, or personal friends. Compassion and empathy with the plight of the dispossessed may mitigate but can never entirely eliminate the nature of the dependency between the victims and those on whom they must rely for care, safety, and succor. That much we know about these relationships.

We know why refugees put their trust in others. They have to. But why do those others risk their lives—or, in the case of refugee workers, spend their lives—aiding the uprooted? We are only beginning to understand

*A version of this chapter was originally prepared for a symposium on "Trust and the Refugee Experience" sponsored by the United Nations University and held in Bergen, Norway, June 11–13, 1992. The section of it summarizing the mail survey appeared, in different form, under the title "The Business of Caring: Refugee Workers and Voluntary Agencies," in *Refugee Reports*, vol. 4, no. 2, 1983, 1–6.

this as the attention of some researchers begins to consider the sociology and psychology of altruism in specific regard to refugees.

To illustrate this let me offer a case in point.

Getting to Know Tante Toos

My Dutch wife, Hedy, lived the life of Anne Frank. For nearly four years she and her sister Betsy were hidden in the basement of a liquor shop in the western part of Amsterdam.[1] The proprietress, Cato Koolhaas Revers-Dewitt, known to the children as Tante Toos (Aunt Toos), had once worked in their father's bakery. That was all they knew of the Christian woman who risked everything to provide asylum for them and for their mother (who died in hiding in 1943) from the time their father was arrested and taken away to Auschwitz until Holland was liberated in 1945.

A lack of detailed knowledge about those who offered refuge, care, and succor to Jewish and other victims of Nazism is not unique. Even those who benefited from such life-saving acts, like most of those well outside the zone of persecution, were only vaguely aware of the life histories and personal motivations of the rescuers. Recently, a book about people like Tante Toos provided some insights into who they were and why they did what they did.[2]

Sociologist Samuel Oliner, a Holocaust survivor who was aided and protected by a Polish Christian woman in his native land; Oliner's wife, Pearl, a professor of education; and a team of fellow social scientists interviewed 406 "rescuers" and a roughly matched (for age, gender, education and geographic residence during the war) sample of 126 "non-rescuers." Some of those in the latter category turned out to have been active in resistance movements but had not been directly involved in saving Jews. That special attribute, *saving Jews*, plus voluntary involvement in high-risk activities unaccompanied by external rewards, were the criteria used by the Oliners to define their "rescuers."

An elaborate six-part questionnaire was used to elicit background information, patterns of social interaction, political activities, and opinions on a number of relevant subjects and measures of such personal characteristics as social responsibility, empathy, and self-esteem from individuals who were involved in one or more of four types of clandestine activity on behalf of Jewish victims. These were: helping them to sustain life as they were being systematically stripped of their rights; aiding their escape from camps and prisons; smuggling them out of Germany or the occupied countries; and, especially, providing sanctuary and sustenance to those who lived underground in the rescuers' own lands.

In addition to profiling the rescuers and those who might have helped but didn't, the authors sought answers to the following questions: Were the actions of the rescuers the result of particular facilitating circumstances? If so, what were those circumstances? Was their involvement a matter of personal proclivities, that is, of particular values, attitudes, and character traits? If so, what kind? (They did not ask, nor did they attempt to answer, such epistemological questions as those relating to the reliability of hindsight, a special problem since most of the respondents were recalling events that took place 50 years earlier.)

Highly varied conditions were described in answers to the queries about the circumstances of the key action under their consideration. While all rescuers were predefined as "altruists" (95 percent of their names having been obtained from the lists of "Righteous Christians" in Yad Vashem, the Holocaust Memorial Archives in Jerusalem), the authors point out that there were some clearly identifiable variations on the theme of Samaritanism. In their conclusions, the Oliners suggested several reasons for the action on the part of the rescuers.[3]

Some fell into a category of those given to highly personalized "empathetic responses." "There but for the grace of God. . . ."

Others were said to have acted according to a norm of collective obligation, often leading to group action. "It was not personal, individual activity. . . . I had orders from the [political] organization."

There were those who followed an important principle, in this instance, an ethic of caring. Illustrating this type, the Oliners quote from a Dutch rescuer whose statement begins with the comment that "It's not because I have an altruistic personality; it's because I am an obedient Christian. I know that that is the reason why I did it. What good is it to say you love your neighbor if you don't help them? . . . We could not let those people go to their doom."[4]

Still others offered less precise explanations for why they did what they did.

From the Oliners' study of those who aided Jewish victims in France, Germany, Italy, Poland, and the Netherlands, it was possible for them to delineate four, admittedly overlapping, principal motivations of persons involved in helping such hiders—or *onderduikers* as they were known in Dutch—as my wife and her sister. They did what they did for *religious, political, personal,* and, sometimes, for *economic* reasons. The last category refers to those who were paid to assist others. (Despite their own "operational definition" of rescuers, which seemed to preclude inclusion of such individuals, like others who studied the matter, the Oliners found that even in their representative sample there were those who took money.)[5]

Working with Refugees

Hedy Cohen and her sister Betsy came to America in 1947. Their resettlement was facilitated by the "JDC," the American Jewish Joint Distribution Committee, a private voluntary agency dedicated to "rescue, relief, and reconstruction" and, until the Hebrew Immigrant Aid Society took over some of its functions, to the resettlement of refugees.

Sometime in 1947, after nearly two years of searching for any family survivors, an aunt and uncle who had managed to get to the United States from Vienna in 1939, finally made contact with the children left behind in Holland and arranged for their resettlement in this country. A JDC case worker arranged for the movement of the Cohen sisters to the United States. She (or someone from her office) took them from Amsterdam to Marseille where they were put aboard a Greek transport ship carrying mostly French war orphans to America. When the ship arrived in New York harbor, American workers received them and assisted them in joining their relatives, who became their guardians and their new parents.

As in the case of "Tante Toos," neither my wife or her sister—nor for that matter, her aunt and uncle, knew very much about those who arranged their departure, handled their emigration, or assisted in their resettlement. It is an ignorance shared by many other former refugees. Despite increasing publicity about the activities of rescuers and others involved in such actions after the war, the general public was equally uninformed. At best they may know something of what such people do but little about who they are or why they do it.

This lack of information was something that had interested me for some time, doubtlessly stimulated by my wife's experiences and those of many friends and colleagues who were World War II refugees. But involvement with others aspects of migration and settlement kept distracting me from undertaking anything more than a very cursory inquiry into the general issue; and this was in conjunction with my long-time interest in race and ethnicity in American society.

The fall of Saigon in 1975 and the airlifting of some 100,000 Vietnamese escapees followed several years later by the exodus of hundreds of thousands of "boat people" and with the genocide in Cambodia were the main catalysts for me to stop procrastinating. By that time there was considerable media coverage of the situation in Southeast Asia and many comparisons were being made to the relative openness of U.S. policy toward these and other "exiles from Communism" (Hungarians in 1956, Czechs in 1968, Cubans, and Soviet Jews as well as the Indochinese more recently) to the difficulties so many "exiles from Nazism" had in entering this country. While already concerned with this aspect of overall immigration policy (see the chapter "Tempest-Tost"), it was time to begin my own investigation.

Because one of my personal interests had long been the plight of Jewish intellectuals in Europe in the 1930s, their impact on American culture, and the role of such agencies as the International Rescue Committee in rescuing many of them, it seemed fitting to begin by looking at the experiences of targeted Vietnamese artists and scholars and their movement to the United States. It proved a false start for I quickly learned that, as one informant bluntly put it, "By and large, France got the intellectuals; we got the generals!"

Chastened but undaunted, I began again, broadening the scope while focusing less on the refugees and more on those in whom they put their trust. It turned out that they were about to become involved in the largest flow of refugees in American history, with nearly one million Indochinese in the United States being admitted to this country between 1975 and 1990.

With the backing of several acquaintances willing to endorse the project, contact was made with several key figures, including Charles Sternberg, the Executive Director of the International Rescue Committee, one of the two agencies I had heard about. I quickly learned that the IRC, so important in the 1930s had, over the ensuing decades, become an agency deeply involved in a wide range of rescue and resettlement situations. With Sternberg's guidance and that of several others willing to serve as my "sponsors," interviews were conducted with a number of government officials and with others employed in private organizations (known as "volags" for independent, voluntary agencies) like the IRC, some with equally long histories of assisting specific groups of refugees, others established much more recently. While the volags continued to be classified as "NGOs" (non-governmental agencies) the term has become a bit of a misnomer. Although still dependent on charitable contributions raised in annual campaigns and supplemental ones for special causes, many also receive considerable subventions from the federal government in the form of contracts to help in the processing and resettling of legally defined refugees. Moreover, those who work for volags are usually paid for their efforts and sometimes known by the oxymoron as "paid volunteers."

What began as something akin to a piece of investigative journalism began turning into a much larger look into the multilayered system that had developed to address the needs of the dispossessed. My "study" (as I began to think of it) was to have three phases. The first, in 1980–1982 was devoted to travel and reconnaissance, getting to know the makers and implementers of Amerian refugee resettlement policy and, as much as possible, to see them in action. The second and briefest phase occured in 1983. It involved conducting a mail survey of refugee workers who worked for the fourteen voluntary agencies directly involved in the resettlement of Indochinese and the members of several other refugee populations, the largest of the "others" being from Cuba and the U.S.S.R. The third, which, in many ways is still on-going, is a series of portraits of the likes of Charles Sternberg and other leaders of the principal volags actively involved in the rescue and resettlement of refugees throughout the 1970s and 1980s, and a selected group of movers and shakers, in both the private and public sector, also involved in the field. [N.B. The lives of eight such leaders are described in the next chapter.]

In the course of preparation for field work, a review of the literatures on forced migration and the politics of exile turned up many interesting studies and reports but few provided clues to the things I wanted to know most about: the development of American refugee policies, the role of voluntary agencies, or the sorts of individuals who were drawn into the field. [6] The dearth of such material proved to be a goal if not a blessing for it forced me to make up my own questions and pursue my own muse.

The Altruistic Personality was not published until I was well into my research. When I read it, I was struck by how much my preliminary findings on the motivations of those who aid the dispossessed generally corroborated those of the Oliners' despite the fact that my attention was mainly centered on those *professionally* involved in the rescue and resettlement of refugees and theirs was on those who were decidely *non-professional*.[7] They were individuals who had volunteered to risk their lives to save others.

The Business of Caring

In the minds of many far removed from the venues of their principal activities, those Americans known to work with refugees have been viewed in both public and private circles as selfless caregivers, modern-day Samaritans. Such a characterization, which parrallels the growth of television coverage of international news, especially since the time of the war in Vietnam, has had an important not-so-latent function. It has aroused general concern, sympathy, and considerable financial support of agencies primarily concerned with the plight of refugees. Moreover, largely as a result of such problems, a small but significant part of the public has been moved to go beyond the writing of checks or depositing used clothes by the graphic appeals of agencies and organizations dedicated to "rescue, relief and resettlement." Quite a number have responded favorably to encouragement to volunteer in local church or agency-led programs or to "go overseas" themselves. For some, both sorts of action have been but first steps leading to careers as refugee workers. Individually and, in many ways, collectively, in the United States (and, to some extent, in the U.K. and several other countries of western Europe), refugee work has become something akin to social work, the classic example of a case study in the professionalization of volunteerism.[8]

That refugee work was undergoing the same metamorphisis in the 1980s would have been quite obvious to anyone who followed it closely during that decade. While I have not systematically gone back to reinterview all of those first met in 1980–1982, many with whom I have kept in contact have described the process which, even to those directly involved, has, as one person put it, "been a transformative experience" though he wasn't sure he liked it. "In ten years we have gone from a fly-by-the-seats-of-our-pants operation to a highly bureaucratized business, albeit," he added as an afterthought, "still a humanitarian one. We still care."

And they do. Yet, when asked to describe experiences in the field, many refugee workers to whom I spoke also reported that they soon learned that caring—or "caregiving"—was only part of what they do. One doesn't have to spend much time in a volag to learn that refugee flows are generated by political conditions and that refugee work often means being some sort of link in a larger political chain.

Commentators such as Teresa Hayter and Catherine Wilson,[9] Barbara Harrell-Bond,[10] and Myles Harris[11] and others have written about how easily the organizations that employ refugee workers, the so-called humanitarian regimes can exploit the situation of dependency and the naiveté of those recruited to assist them. Their studies and assessments raise important questions about a range of issues relating to the matter of "imposing aid." Others, more concerned (as I am here) with the more specific matters of rescue and resettlement, point to its highly politicized and often selective character, referred to by Gilburt Loescher and John Scanlan by the hardly felicitous couplet "calculated kindness."[12]

I, too, found that in carrying out their tasks, refugee workers may become—by cooptation or intention—implementers of policies established by others: international bodies, specific governments, and the often chartered agencies for which they work. In this they are quite different from Tante Toos and others like her who function as outlaws themselves, acting in subversion of the rules of behavior within their own societies. The very nature of the activities of regular refugee workers, even at a very low level in the organizational structure of a particular agency, means not only being a part of a larger geopolitical struggle but being accorded varying degrees of direct power over the lives of refugees. Working with refugees is, in fact, political at every level.

Early in the process of socialization refugee resettlement workers learn that they are not merely to be caregivers, or caretakers (like those in relief work), responsible for establishing and maintaining facilities for short- and, sometimes, long-term assistance. They find they must often temper humanitarian tendencies to meet the exigencies of the situations in which they find themselves. Thus [as already illustrated in the chapter "Caretakers, Gatekeepers . . ."] they are sometimes called upon to be "gatekeepers" who determine or help to determine who shall receive what food, clothing, housing, etc. and, in some instances, to prepare the background files on those who may be resettled, and to assist in determining where they might go. More often they are expected to serve as "guides," providing instruction, cultural orientation, and, on occasion, political or religious indoctrination, and as "go-betweens" who serve as liaisons, even brokers, among various internal factions and between the refugee community and the outside. While the desire to aid the uprooted may be based on the best and purest of motives, its exercise, at least for those who carry out policies that provide resettlement services as well as relief, generally involves engaging in a highly instrumental enterprise. *Yet, even when made more fully aware of their often compromised situation, refugee workers continue to believe that they are remaining true to what, to them, is a primary mission, helping the subjects of their trust.* Such a view is summed up in the following statements.

> I work with refugees. My business is caring. I can't say it's just a job, or just a profession, or a calling. Working with refugees is all those things—an underpaid job, an unrecognized profession, and . . . well, how do you explain to somebody that you do what you do because, well, somebody has to do it. After all, we are supposed to be our brothers' keepers.

The person who made these remarks works for a voluntary agency in Portland, Oregon. Her five-sentence response to a query about how she would define what she does captured the flavor of the experience, reflected some personal values, and offered gut reactions to probing questions. In speaking to people like this woman, a considerable amount of earnest candor and general eagerness to share thoughts and feelings and opinions was constantly revealed. Such openness may be because those spoken and written to took to heart the fact that the interest was in them as much as with those with whom they worked in contrast to most studies relating to refugee matters. (Those tend to be focused on particular issues: root causes, patterns of escape, modes of adaptation, schemes for repatriation, local integration, or third country resettlement. The agencies involved in relief or resettlement only occasionally have been the subject of investigation and analysis.)[13]

Even those interviewed were often somewhat startled by this emphasis. Often at the end of a lengthy session, the person to whom I was speaking would state that he or she had been surprised that it was their personal views that were of particular interest to me.

> Usually the people who come to talk to us want to know about the refugees—their health, their welfare. They want quantification. They see us as functionaries, faceless functionaries—as faceless as they see the refugees themselves! The only difference is that the refugees are the statistics and we are supposed to be the statisticians.

Another commented that:

> We are constantly trying to remind ourselves that every refugee, and there are now over 15,000 in this camp alone, is an individual. It isn't easy. There is so much to do. So many to care for. There is the danger that we will not make distinctions among them. An equal danger is that we will. . . . and we will begin to play favorites.

First Encounters

Once my "bona fides" had been established, the field work began. The "reconnaissance" interviews were conducted in Geneva and in Southeast Asia with representives of international bodies including the United Nations

High Commission for Refugees and with policymakers, program administrators, and refugee workers in government offices in Washington and in
the headquarters of the principal volags there and in New York City, in regional offices throughout the United States and in refugee camps and
processing centers in Hong Kong, Indonesia, Macao, Malaysia, the Philippines, Singapore, Thailand. I also spent time, mainly for comparative purposes, in processing centers in Austria and Italy and American cities where
refugees, mostly from Cuba, Indochina, the Soviet Union, and Ethiopia
were also being resettled. And I spoke to a number of refugees.

The purpose was to get to know a fairly representative sampling of
those in the resettlement chain: from the highest ranking heads of agencies
with multimillion dollar budgets and huge government contracts to those
on the front line, quite literally "in the trenches."[14] Three trips to Southeast Asia within the two-year period helped to get a sense of the process—
protection, assistance, selection, admission, movement, resettlement,
adaptation, and attempts at integration—as well as to get to know the
players.

In loosely structured interviews those who carried out American refugee resettlement policies were asked mainly about what they did, how they
did it, and what they thought about their work. From the start I realized
that, almost invariably, discussions of these matters included unsolicited
commentaries on their backgrounds and motives. These remarks were
frequently augmented with personal anecdotes, sometimes prompted by a
gentle prod: "That's interesting. Tell me more." Often such encouragement was unnecessary. I had become a sounding board and many seemed
to welcome a chance to talk about their work and themselves.

While the principal emphasis of the investigation was to get a clear picture of the practices and perspectives of those who set policies and those
who carry them out rather than reactions of the refugees, the "clients," as
some were wont to call them, could not be ignored. But getting to them,
even in a limited way given the barriers of culture and language and the severe constraints of time, was a far more difficult task. Nevertheless, in the
beginning of my odyssey, I made it a point to seek out and talk, through interpreters, to refugees, frequently choosing them at random. It was not
very satisfactory. Then I discovered what I thought was a solution.

Many of the volag personnel I met turned out to be refugees themselves. For me they seemed ideal informants, being or having been on both
sides of the "trust" dichotomy: those in need *and* agents of assistance. They
were most helpful. But they were also sometimes quite wary. This, it
turned out, was due to the fact that others saw them as key informants, too.

Many *refugee*-refugee workers, especially those who were ethnic Chinese, Vietnamese, Laotian, Hmong, or Cambodian, were considered by
some of their volag colleagues as useful messengers. They could provide
information, including the "regs," regulations that had to be followed, to
their respective communities. For their part, refugees languishing in

camps often saw compatriots who worked in the volags not only as representatives from the agencies but as *their* advocates.

Not a few refugee-refugee workers reported finding themselves caught
in a double-bind, reluctant, as several put it, "to be the agents or the eyes
and ears of the authorities," but equally concerned about presuming to
speak for others when this was not their assigned role.[15] In fact, being both
a part of the system and apart from it, they represented an interesting example of what sociologists' called "marginal men." Their marginality, living in and on the edges of different worlds, gave them some distinct
advantages but it also exacerbated their own problems of membership and
identity, a commonly acknowledged situation by those who study refugee
populations, especially, those who are better educated among them.

Of course, not all refugees workers, or even most, are refugees. Many of
those I met in the early days of the study, like almost all of the older ones
had limited contact with refugees and no specific training in working with
dispossessed populations, though a few had degrees in social work. However, a surprising a number had some previous experience in "care-giving,"
often on a voluntary basis through church or synagogue groups or service
organizations in colleges and universities. And, overseas, many of those
called "local hires," expatriate Americans, had been Peace Corps or Vista
volunteers.

While some reported having started to work with refugees as true volunteers, usually through church-sponsored programs, far more began as
contracted workers, hired for a particular time period. A significant number of regional directors and assistant directors reported that, after a six- or
nine- or twelve-month tour they had decided to extend their contracts. Often in that second period they were given more responsibility. This was
especially true of those on the front lines overseas but it also occurred with
some regularity in domestic resettlement settings. As one district manager
put it, "If you can take it and not burn out, you can become quite expert at
what you are doing in a very short period of time." Said another, "If you're
sharp, well-organized and pay attention to what is going on, you can become a manager in a very short period of time." Others described the process of climbing the organizational ladder with rungs labeled "Case
Manager," "Section Head," "Regional Coordinator," etc., some saying
they hoped to go on to reach the very top of an agency.

The rank-and-file workers interviewed in the field, in particular the
younger ones, frequently allowed as to how, as they were given more and
more responsibilities, they ceased to have a sense of being "amateur do-
gooders." One wag said "Now I'm a professional do-gooder!" Another put
it in more processual terms, confirming an early assumption, "It's like being 'professionalized' on the job."

Attitudes and Opinions

To augment the reconnaissance interviews and site visits carried out in the United States and abroad in 1980, 1981, and in early 1982, 2,000 questionnaires with 28 questions dealing with the backgrounds, training, work experiences, perceptions, criticisms, and recommendations of refugee workers were sent to the executive directors of each of the American volags involved in resettlement in March 1982. The directors, who received multiple copies of the questionnaires based on a prorated basis, depending on the reported size of their staffs, were asked to distribute them to all workers at every level. By August 15, 1982 responses were received from 448 individuals.[16] (A follow-up brought in 47 more over the period of nearly a full calender year.)

The results of the survey provided a good deal of useful information about the rewards and frustrations of refugee work, recommendations for improving services to refugees and for improving their own situations, and commentaries on the personality traits and training that the respondents' thought would make the best refugee workers.

As a cohort, those who filled out and returned the questionnaires range in age from the late teens to the early seventies; two-thirds were middle-aged, forty to sixty. Forty percent of the overall group was foreign born and two out of three of that large minority said they were, or had been, refugees themselves. Reflecting the period of the survey, among this group of refugee-refugee workers, nearly half were from Indochina. Most of the rest were of European background.

Most of those who returned the questionnaires were highly educated. Almost all had at least a Bachelor's degree or its equivalent; slightly more than half of them had majored or concentrated in one of the social sciences and many had graduate degrees. A third of the overall group were trained social workers. Sixteen percent said they had higher degrees, mostly M.A.s in education or counseling or in nursing. Twelve percent were members of the clergy; a few were lawyers and some had Ph.D.s in sociology, political science, psychology, and public policy. There were many (including the vast majority of the refugee-refugee workers) who had higher degrees in fields completely unrelated to their then-present occupations. The last finding corroborated what was suggested in the preliminary round of interviews.

Thirty-eight percent of those who were willing to specify (462 of the augmented base of 495) said their annual income [in 1981] was between $10–15,000; 26 percent said it was $15-20,000; 14 percent said it was higher than $20,000. Some complained about their incomes; but many others, if they said anything at all, indicated that while they would like more money, it was not the reason they do what they do. "After all," said one respondent, "He who does God's work gets God's pay."

There was a "return bias" which may have been simply an artifact of the manner in which the schedules were distributed or the difficulty in getting responses from the most remote areas where, more likely than not, many of the lowest ranking workers in the volags' table of organization were often carrying out their duties. In any case, most of those who responded were of fairly high status in their organizations. Included were some of the executive directors themselves and other headquartered officials, regional coordinators, and field supervisors. One in four of the overall group described him or herself as a "case worker" or "case manager" or "resettlement worker," all somewhat ambiguous titles but clearly a notch down from the program administration. Almost all of those who indicated that they were then in supervisory capacities or senior administrators presented evidence that they had come up through the ranks. Most had had considerable field experience in this country or overseas (and many had both). In addition, nearly a third of those who filled out and returned questionnaires had been members of the Peace Corps or had been Vista volunteers.

While some of the respondents appeared to have had the same difficulties in defining themselves as had the woman from Portland quoted earlier, many seemed to be able to specify what they were doing as either a "Job" or a "Profession" or a "Calling." These self-selected descriptors (from a simple checklist asking which term best described a person's view of what they did) proved to be critical.[17]

Twelve of the respondents checked more than one category and twenty-eight did not answer the question at all but, of those who did make the requested arbitrary choice, one in three checked "Calling," one in in four, "Profession," and one in five checked the box next to "Job." Not surprisingly, compared to those in non-sectarian agencies, far more of those in the religiously based volags checked "Calling." One of the many in the last subset who added a comment wrote that "I see my work as minister and missionary as a calling and refugee work is a continuation of that." Another, a lay person working in a different religiously affiliated Protestant agency said "I am doing the Lord's work; that is my calling."

Many of the American volags (like the American Jewish Joint Distribution Committee, mentioned above) are religiously based. The oldest, founded in 1880, is the Hebrew Immigrant Aid Society (known as HIAS); the largest, the Migration and Refugee Service of the U.S. Catholic Conference. Others with religious connections are the Church World Service's refugee program; the Lutheran Immigration and Refugee Service; the evangelical World Relief; the Presiding Bishops' Fund of the Episcopal Church; and a Buddhist organization. Two of the volags, the Tolstoy Foundation and the American Fund for Czechoslovakian Refugees, were both founded to serve the needs of particular "nationality" groups: white Russian emigrés and Czech refugees from the Communist takeover in 1948, respectively. Finally, there are two that are strictly non-sectarian, the International Rescue Committee and the American Council of Nationalities Services. The latter, orginally an offshoot of the YWCA, is, today, a conglomerate organization of Traveler's Aid offices, International Institutes, the closest thing to modern-day settlement houses providing all sorts of services to newcomers in many major cities, and the U.S. Committee on Refugees, an advocacy and information group that conducts research and publishes occasional papers and the annual *World Refugee Survey.*

Despite the fact that the majority of the volags are in some way connected to particular religious groups, even among them only a minority of those who work for such agencies claim their activities are based on a "calling." While such individuals are most evident in the Protestant-sponsored organizations, especially LIRS and World Relief, many others, in such agencies as HIAS and the Catholic Migration Services of USCC, and most of those in the non-sectarian ones, saw themselves as professional. Part of this may be a function of the fact that most Protestant agencies favor "congregation-based" resettlement practices rather than "case management," the former stressing hands-on community involvement, the latter a more formal relationship between the refugee worker and the "client."

Each system has its advocates and its detractors. Those who support the more communal approach claim that it fosters selfless service to one's fellow man (or woman) by the care-givers and a sense of familial attachment to the newcomers. Those who are critical say that it works only when there are no serious problems for which the host church or other group is ill-prepared to cope. Moreover, many add, even the warmest of welcomes, if overdone, may inadvertently contribute to long-term dependency.

Promotors of the "case management" approach think it is better to have trained people work with refugees, especially in the early stages of their re-settlement. They contend that such workers are usually better suited to deal with the inevitable stresses of dislocation and with the problems of adaptation in the new environment. Those volags whose workers favor case management are more likely than the others to provide other services such as cultural orientation, ESL, and job training.

"It seems to me that it all depends on [the] worker's position, salary and religion, whether the work is seen as a job, calling or profession." The "Professional" woman who said that was right on target. How refugee workers among the respondents identified themselves was indeed highly correlated with status, salary, and the degree of religiosity, the latter measured by a scale based on four questions: belief, affiliation, participation in activities, frequency of attendance at religious services.

The self-chosen labels proved to be directly related to attitudes, complaints, and suggestions. And they were found to serve as useful ex post facto "predictors" of how refugee workers fared in doing their work.

Those defining their work as a "Calling" were the highest scorers on a scale measuring "a tolerance for ambiguity" and far less critical than others of rules and regulations than the "Professionals." The members of the latter group were, however, hardly homogeneous in their own opinions.

Some were ever ready to compare the ordered chaos of refugee work to other situations with which they were familiar, sometimes positively, sometimes unfavorably. Moreover, here, more than anywhere else, the self-styled professionals were wont to make comparisons of how the different refugee agencies function. Not a few described a particular volag (not necessarily their own) as "a truly professional organization" and another as "an amateur show."

Those who saw their work mainly as a job, whether refugees themselves or not (and a disproportionately large percentage in this subgroup were former refugees), seemed most uninhibited in expressing their displeasure at everything from the notoriously poor pay to the bureaucratic mazes through which they, and their clients, have to wend their ways day after day.

How much these attitudes and opinions had to do with early socialization was somewhat difficult to determine, although answers to questions about how they came to work with refugees did provide some limited clues. The respondents suggested that many factors bring people into the field. These ranged, they said, from those seeking to help specific groups owing to a sense of personal or political involvement to more universalistic motives expressed especially but not exclusively by those who see what they are doing as a calling to a pragmatic desire to use academic and professional skills in a meaningful and rewarding way to a good way to make a bit of money while "doing good."

Looking over the responses again and again, and reading numerous marginal comments, it became quite clear that there was considerable evidence in the data to suggest that individuals working for American refugee agencies in the 1980s actually fit into one or another of the categories Sam and Pearl Oliner had used in their study of "rescuers" of Jewish victims of Nazism.[18] Those who answered the questionnaires mailed in 1982 also seem to do what they do for *personal, religious, political,* or *economic* reasons.

Here are several commentaries written by respondents to explain how they came to join the agencies for which they were working at the time of the survey.

> I had been a victim of Hitler. I knew what it meant to be a refugee. I wanted to do something to help others who had suffered as we had. Somehow I was especially drawn to the Cambodians. I began as a volunteer and eventually became a paid worker. Now I am working mainly with Soviet Jews."

> A friend of mine was working with the Hmong and I was intrigued, especially since I hadn't heard much about these mountain people since I was a gung-ho super-patriot in the early sixties. I remembered their part in the war and realized that maybe they now thought they'd backed the wrong side . . . in a sense I guess they did for here they are, a long, long way from home. What can I say. It is to me a ministry. I must help the helpless wherever I can. Whoever they are."

> I was in Bangkok looking for work and heard that the JVA [Joint Voluntary Agency, the volag contracted to gather biodata and prepare potentially reset-

tleable refugees for screening by the U.S Immigration and Naturalization Service] needed people. I didn't know what the JVA was but found out it was

the agency that helped process refugees. I thought that might be interesting work. . . . They hired me and I worked in the Lao section mainly because I knew some Thai I suppose [N.B. The languages are similar]. In any event, I found it most satisfying. I was hooked. And here [at a refugee agency in downtown Seattle] I am!

The last person to "speak," a registered nurse, added, "I had also been upset with the Vietnam War and the bombing of Cambodia." This sort of double-commitment, a way to use professional skills in a personally relevant manner is rather typical of many, including those, like the commentator, who see themselves primarily as professionals.

Refugee workers heard from in the mail survey echoed sentiments expressed by many who had been interviewed earlier. They, too, indicated that, while many factors contributed to their entering the field, several stood out in rather bold relief: ethical proclivities toward altruistic ventures, ideological concerns, personal experiences and involvements, and happenstance.

In response to one of many open-ended questions—"What would you say are the greatest problems you encounter in your work?"—four related issues were the most frequently mentioned: confusion about work regulations and welfare practices; language and cultural barriers; the public's negative attitudes toward refugees, often described as a form of "racism"; and the poor job market and lack of opportunity for many refugees who are able, ready, and eager to work. "Bureaucracy," "corruption," and "the welfare system in general" were also frequently cited as problematic.

Finally, all were also asked about rewards. Most, clearly reflecting what Morton Hunt noted in his summary of research on altruism, wrote of the satisfaction of helping others. It was a personal rather than a political or monetary pay-off that seemed to have the highest priority. [19]

All Players on Stage

In the spring of 1983, a conference on "Working with Refugees" was held at Smith College in Northampton, Massachusetts. With the support of the Weatherhead, Rockefeller, and Exxon Educational Foundations, it was possible for me to assemble some sixty refugee workers including a retired Deputy High Commissioner at UNHCR, high-ranking State, Justice, and Health and Human Services Department officials, active and retired foreign service officers, representatives of most of the Joint Voluntary Agencies affiliated with the U.S. embassies in the countries surrounding Vietnam, Laos, and Cambodia, heads of regional and local refugee agencies, resettlement officers and relief workers, advocates for refugees, including those from lawyers' groups, politicians, leaders of refugee communities, and the director of a number of the major volags. In addition, several social scientists also engaged in the study of refugee policy were also in attendance. Almost all the guests were persons I had met and many were those I had interviewed about their work either in this country or abroad. Some were respondents to the mailed questionnaires who had volunteered to sign their names when asked to be included in follow-up activities.

Over a three-day period discussions were held on the role of the refugee worker in the protection and assistance of those seeking asylum; in the process of selection and admission to third countries; on patterns of resettlement and policies relating to facilitating adaptation and acculturation.[20] While the focus of this unique and, it turned out, quite unprecedented, gathering was on issues relating to working with refugees, a latent function proved to be a display of personalities. I was especially intrigued by seeing those I had gotten to know on a one-on-one basis interact with one another, with those at their own level and those above, and sometimes, way below them, too.

They not only compared notes, shared experiences, and played refugee-worker geography ("Do you know so and so? He used to be in Thailand but has recently moved to the Sudan? No, he's no longer with . . . but seems quite pleased with his new appointment as. . . .") but also talked in very personal terms to one another and to me about reactions to particular situations.

Hearing such conversations emboldened me to take the occasion to begin asking a number of those assembled about how they got into the field. The stories told by some of the volag leaders were among the most interesting. Before they left Northampton to return to their duties, I asked if they would be willing to participate in what became the last phase in the study. All agreed.

The lengthy interviewing began within six months of the Smith College meeting and continues to this day. From the start, those leaders of agencies, government officials, and key figures in supporting the cause of refugees, whose personal stories were elicited, were not only willing and eager to talk about their work but also about themselves.

From the "biodata" (to use a word in their own newspeak) gathered and from the anecdotes they related, their life stories not only complemented and fleshed out the findings of the general interviews and the results of the mail questionnaire but offered the possibility of a quite separate contribution to the sociology of knowledge about leadership, altruism, and those in whom so many are asked to place their trust.

The Vicars of the Volags

Observing, interacting with, and talking to these leaders at meetings, over-seas or in their offices in Washington, D.C., or on Park Avenue South or Broadway, in New York City, theatrical metaphors kept coming to mind. They seemed an intrepid if highly idiosyncratic troop who, though frequently expected to act together (and often joined by a Greek chorus of supporters who admonish others to help in their work with the dispossessed), are not really en-semble players. Each is a veteran actor; each a star. Some are quite vain; others more self-effacing; but all seem quite sure of themselves. They are "the Vicars of the Volags."

T HESE WORDS were jotted down in my notebook one summer day as I stopped to take stock of the remarkable individuals I had been inter-acting with on and off for the better part of a decade. They were the exec-utive directors of the major voluntary agencies working with refugees during the crucial period from the fall of Saigon through the enactment of the Refugee Reform Act of 1980 (which provided a new definition of "ref-ugee," one that finally was in line with United Nations protocol as well as considerable assistance to refugees and refugee agencies in the form of en-titlements in the first instance and contracts in the second) to the time when immigration (and, by inference, refugee policy) had once again be-come the subject of national debate in 1996.

I had become acquainted with many of these men and women in the course of research on the making and implementing of U.S. refugee policy and, more specifically, on the refugee workers themselves. Of course, be-coming acquainted and getting to know people are two different things. As

*The first phase of this project was funded in part by travel stipends from the Weather-head Foundation for research in Southeast Asia, Europe, and the United States and by a study grant from the Rockefeller Foundation for a year at Harvard University. The Exxon Educational Foundation provided some support for the second and third phases and for a se-ries of conferences focused on the subject of "Working with Refugees." A Jean Picker Fel-lowship at Smith College in 1991–1992 allowed for some release time and travel monies to continue gathering material for the last phase of the project. The contributions of the three foundations and the Jean Picker Fund are gratefully acknowledged.

I became more interested in the personal lives and professional social-ization experiences of refugee workers, I became more determined to learn more about those who were the most visible and, despite the fact that their agencies all had boards of directors with chairs and committees and rules of procedure, they were the energizers that gave life to the programs, the real movers and shakers.

Here I introduce the senior cadre, eight of the twenty-two individuals I interviewed at length. The others' stories are still to be told.

I begin with the oldest, the late Dr. Jan Papanek, who was ninety years old when I last interviewed him. My portrait of Papanek is offered in the present time, for this is how I see him and his colleagues. Living, breath-ing, thinking, railing against injustice, acting.

The Diplomat

Jan Papanek is a tall, thin, ninety-year-old former Czech diplomat. Sitting erect, almost regal, in his unpretentious office on New York's Broadway, dressed in a suit that was obviously styled many years earlier, he spoke at length about his long involvement with the struggles of his homeland, his affection for the Masaryks, his hatred of fascists and communists, and his nearly seventy years of aiding his compatriots and others.

Asked when he first got involved with refugees—and how—he said, "Well, let me see." Then, fingering a silver-headed cane and staring off into space. . . . "I was in the Austro-Hungarian army. A sublieutenant. It was during the war. 1917." He explained that those first refugees he as-sisted were people who had been dispersed and were trying to return to what was not yet an independent country, Czechoslovakia.

Papanek, who came from a very wealthy and prominent family, was a student in Paris from 1919 to 1922. Immediately thereafter he entered the Czech diplomatic service. He also worked with those escaping from the Bolsheviks in the 1920s. The latter "jobs," he said, were, at first, incidental to his work as a steadily rising diplomat stationed in various parts of Eu-rope and in the United States. He eventually became a Czech delegate to the United Nations, particularly interested in social matters. He partic-ipated in the creation of the Children's Fund and a number of other insti-tutions that were established during the period from the founding of the United Nations to 1948 when the communists took over his country. It was at that time that the American Fund for Czechoslovakian Refugees [to become known as AFCR] was born.

"Fund," it seems, was a bit of a euphemism.

"Where did the money come from?" I asked.

"We had no funds."

"So you did it yourself?"

"Yes, and then we began to receive help, certain friends . . . but we did have a sort of reserve, money collected—hundreds of thousands of dollars, money kept here when the communists took over. . . . In fact, they [the new Czechoslovak government] sued me in the Supreme Court of New York."

They lost the case. The money was assigned by the court to the new organization, the AFCR. The Diplomat, then still a member of the United Nations, shuttled between New York and Paris until he left his post in 1951 and began to work, full time, on refugee matters.

The AFCR, while established mainly for the benefit of Czech refugees in 1948, was extremely useful in placing those who fled their homeland after the failed revolt in 1968 and some who belonged to Charter 77. It has also assisted Ugandan Asians, Indochinese, Ethiopians, and many others. With offices throughout the United States and in various parts of the world, it has helped to resettle nearly 200,000 refugees worldwide.

The Director

Gaynor Jacobson, for many years the Executive Vice President of HIAS, the Hebrew Immigrant Aid Society, has been described as "the very model of a modern social worker," the sort that students are encouraged to emulate. "He is cool-headed and even-handed, professional and compassionate—and passionate, too, especially when expressing outrage at the terrible things human beings can vest upon their fellows."

Jacobson had always wanted to be a social worker, a profession for which he was trained in his hometown of Buffalo, New York. He moved to Rochester in 1937 to become a case worker in the Jewish Family Agency where, as the new Executive Director, he and a colleague organized a program for German and Austrian refugees. That setting was a sort of launching pad.

After seven years in Rochester, Jacobson went overseas, to Italy, to be one of the two people in charge of a program run by the American Jewish Joint Distribution Committee. Their assignment was to help get Jews out from behind the lines in Italy—which were then just beyond Florence. They worked with a team from the Palestine Brigade and with a group of American and British Quakers and a Jewish Relief unit from London.

During and after the war, Gaynor Jacobson was Program Director with the American Jewish Joint Distribution Committee, serving in a number of countries in Europe and, for a time, in South America as well as Morocco before becoming head of the European Office of the HIAS, the oldest of all the American volags. Although HIAS also serves several other refugee populations (such as those from Vietnam and Cambodia), the organization, which works with NYANA, the New York Association for New Americans, and other local Jewish service agencies in the United States and many others abroad, remains the principal American agency supporting the resettlement of Jews.

Throughout his long career, Jacobson had seen, at first hand, the suffering of many. He still rails against the atrocities he witnessed. In interviews with him he described various particularly poignant occasions. For example, speaking of his work in Bari, Italy toward the end of the war: "We Jewish agencies together had managed to get from the British 900 certificates to send people off on a kind of liberty ship from Bari to Palestine. Legally. Nine hundred survivors! And the war was still on. . . . The lines were then just beyond Florence and we took out Jews, men and women and children. We assembled them; got the documents in order." Then, the still-seething anger of the genial man sitting before me in a colorful warm-up suit and running shoes, was clearly apparent as his jaw tightened and he said:

> I was already overwhelmed with the sense of tragedy I heard about, knew about, but [when] you talk to a man whose wife and children were burned at Auschwitz, a child whose parents had gone to their deaths, a woman whose whole family. . . . And people still wouldn't believe it. There were those, like some of the Quakers who were so kind and so helpful but who pooh-poohed these stories and said "How could you be so naive as to believe this? No human being could do the things these people say. Couldn't you tell that they were brainwashed, and that they were doing the same thing, telling the same kinds of things that the people did about Belgians in the First World War?" [Long pause] But, then, they, too, learned the horrid truth, as more of the remnants began coming out of the mountains, out from Auschwitz.

HIAS's long-time director related other stories and described his various moves and activities, including experiences in Czechoslovakia working with others who had survived the Holocaust and were passing through the countries of Eastern Europe just coming under communist control and still very much in postwar turmoil. Contacts were crucial. Jan Masaryk, the Czech foreign minister and son of the great Czech leader, proved to be a key figure in aiding the HIAS representative in finding safe passage for 200,000 Jews.

Jacobson spent time in Budapest (where he was temporarily jailed for his allegedly illegal activities), then worked in Vienna and continued traveling throughout Eastern Europe with one goal in mind. In his words: "Get them out!"

He finally went back to the States, to Philadelphia, first as head of the Jewish Child Care Association, then as Director of the American Technion Society. But after only three years, he was back in Europe, this time as head of the European Office of HIAS. He also spent periods of time as a HIAS regional director in Buenos Aires, Rio, Paris, Morocco, and Geneva, the European Headquarters. In the late 1960s he assumed the executive vice presidency (actually the directorship) of HIAS in New York City.

The Vicar General

John McCarthy is a red-faced, white-haired, and solidly built Irish-American. The first time I sought him out was at a meeting in Geneva. Not knowing what he looked like, I asked a colleague who described him as someone who is a dead-ringer for Jimmy Cagney. He is. He looks like him, sounds like him, and sometimes, when his ire is up, may be expected to blurt out, "You, you dirty rat," but he doesn't. He is given more to orations than to outbursts. He is an intellectual and a very political man.

McCarthy was born on the Lower East Side of New York, educated at local and Washington universities where he obtained a master's in social work, a bachelor of laws degree, and a Ph.D. in psychology in the late 1930s and early 1940s. A devout and devoted member of his church, McCarthy is proud of the many rewards he has been given for his human-itarian activities, especially the designation by John Paul II as a Knight of the Papal Order of St. Gregory. It was one of many he received for his ref-ugee work which goes back five decades.

McCarthy helped to develop and later headed the Migration and Refu-gee Service of the U.S. Catholic Conference and its international counter-part, the International Catholic Migration Commission. During his long tenure, the USCC became the largest refugee agency in the country and the most bureaucratic, something like the church from whose members come its main private support. Long involved in refugee programs, assist-ing victims of Nazism, Hungarians, Czechs, Poles, Cubans, and Haitians, like most other agencies, the biggest effort of all has gone into the resettle-ment of Indochinese refugees. Of all the volags, the USCC carried the largest caseload.

According to McCarthy, much of his agency's success is due to his faith in and appreciation for the diocesan structure of his church. "If I can get the top domino to drop," he said with a gleeful grin, "everything happens . . . A formal structure is a great thing. . . . When the Vietnamese crisis came up, I spoke to the Bishop and said 'We've got to do something about this.' He wrote his fellow bishops who wrote to their pastors. We estab-lished about 190 offices in two days."

While some of John McCarthy's critics say he is Napoleonic, he would say that good refugee resettlement policy requires a clear table of organiza-tion so that "things can be done almost automatically by people doing the same thing for years," "the structure is not enough," he would also say, and has said, "the real key is the commitment, and the compassion, of the refu-gee workers."

"They're not trained professionals but, like me, they're hooked. It's like a drug. It's a kind of self-aggrandizement that you can do something for someone else and it's so positive." He went on to say, "You're not casting bread on the water. You're putting bread in mouths, so to speak. And it does work. We can resettle anybody, anywhere, any time."

He means it. This vicar never thought that his agency was bound only to serve Catholics in trouble.

"I really think that by helping people, the basic norm of all religions is served. In fact, not only do we serve all in need, [but] I have a very strict

rule: I don't know the religion of those I help. And though we are resettling through church structures, we do not proselytize. For example, down
in Beaumont, Texas, after the refugees arrived, the first church—built with
our money—was a Buddhist temple."

Other groups, he suggests, do not adhere to such universalistic principles and see their mission not only as saving people but saving souls and
bringing them into the fold. Still, when asked why he doesn't advocate the
consolidation of all the volags into one super agency called, say, "The
American Refugee Service," he has an interesting response. "The church,"
he claims, "can appeal with special forcefulness to its members, admonish-
ing them to do their Catholic duty. It is a way of learning what your religion is all about, about the commitment of faith. After all, this is the only
reason for a church. 'Bringing to life,' as we say. That's what it's all about."

The Godfather

Charles Sternberg, known to everyone as "Carel," is less a Vicar General
in the mold of John McCarthy than the Godfather of an agency run
through the personal connections he has and the loyal following of his regional captains. The small and bespectacled Czech-born former publicist
for 20th Century Fox in Prague looks like the stereotype of a Middle-Eu-
ropean professor.

Sternberg left his home city as a refugee and moved to Paris in 1940.
There he became the unofficial representative of what was then known as
the International Relief Association (IRC), one of the two forerunners of
the International Rescue Committee. (The other was the Emergency Rescue Committee.)

"It wasn't a paid position. It wasn't really a job," he said, reminiscing at
the prompting of the questioner—but it was the beginning of a career.

Sternberg went further into exile, leaving France early in 1942 for the
United States. After serving in the American army, the IRC asked him to
return to Europe to work with CRALOG, the Council of Relief Agencies
Licensed for Operations in Germany. In Germany, the Committee
worked closely with a counterpart agency, the relief arm of the German
Social Democrats, which was assisting people coming out of the concentration camps. Sternberg was there a year, then, in March of 1947, he came
back to the United States and started work in the New York office of the
IRC as a case worker in the Resettlement Department. The principal
clients in those days were a special group of displaced persons, political exiles from Nazism.

In fact, the agency that he was eventually to direct until his retirement
several years ago, has long been the most political of the volags. From the
beginning, as Aaron Levenstein, author of a history of the IRC put it, "the
Committee's mission was not only humanitarian in the Judeo-Christian
tradition but also political in the broadest democratic sense."[1] It has been

especially devoted to aiding the victims of totalitarianism—right and left, especially, but not exclusively, refugee intellectuals. That orientation, set forth during the early days of the Nazi-era, continued after the end of the Second World War.

The first great post-war test came with the Soviet occupation of Hungary in 1956. "Then," Sternberg noted, "as before, the people with the political faces tended to find us because of our focus and concerns."

In those days, the IRC's New York office, staffed almost entirely by European refugees, was very busy. He noted that "the Hungarian escape was the most popular refugee situation in the United States. Everybody wanted to touch a Hungarian freedom fighter. . . . the only time I remember the people standing in the street cheering refugees. . . . All over the country they were saying, 'Can't we do something?'"

The IRC staff thought they could and resettlement offices began to be established on an ad hoc basis in various parts of the country. It was "a straight volunteer operation, with no strings to anything—not a church, not a political party, nothing. Most [of the volunteers] were professional people (doctors, lawyers, engineers) while their wives were self-confident, energetic, decent people. They were similar, in many ways, to those now getting involved in getting Salvadorans into churches."

Over and over, as Carel Sternberg spoke of crises that required the services of agencies like the IRC, the genial Godfather mentioned what he called "the altruism of many middle-class Americans" and the gratitude of those they helped.

His agency began to take new form in the 1960s as the regional offices became somewhat more formal in its organization. Still, "potential refugee workers seemed drawn to the IRC because they liked the flexibility, the lack of structure, the closeness."

Sternberg and the IRC's long-time board chairman, Leo Cherne, were the moving forces behind one operation after another. The Committee was in Vietnam right after the partitioning, ready to assist refugees fleeing south. It was in Bangladesh and in various parts of Africa. It was back in Vietnam from 1963 until the fall of Saigon, then stayed in the area, in nearby countries to assist those escaping from Indochina.

The world's largest cooperative resettlement effort, JVA/Thailand, was run under contract to IRC. And, like other relief agencies, it also ran medical and educational programs throughout Southeast Asia and extensive resettlement operations back in the States. More recently, the Committee has been involved in programs in Lebanon, Pakistan, the Sudan, and Jordan, while maintaining its activities in Asia and throughout the United States.

Until his recent retirement, Sternberg continued to hire people on the basis of his assessment of their ability to do a job, not in terms of specialized training. He remains one of a number of leaders who feel that good refugee workers are not made in the classroom. "We don't ask for degrees, but do want a willingness to work long hours, and a commitment to something that is more than a job."

The DP

"The Displaced Person" is an apt sobriquet for Ingrid Walter, the former head of the Lutheran Immigration and Refugee Service. Her early experience as an ethnic German Protestant, born and raised in Estonia, and her wanderings, having been buffeted back and forth by the winds of war in the 1940s, were clearly the basis for almost everything she was to do as an adult, including her career.

After spending some time in Austria, Walter's family moved to Germany. The end of the war found her in a DP camp where, despite very limited education, because of her language skills, she was recruited to serve as an interpreter with the American Christian Committee for Refugees, a predecessor to Church World Service, in Pasing. Finally her own number came up and she was able to emigrate to the United States in 1948. She was sponsored by a Congregational church in New Jersey.

"Before I came I had quite the title. I was one of the highest Class II persons in Germany, Senior Resettlement Officer. So, when I arrived and started to type with one finger, they all said 'Oh, oh. She doesn't even qualify as a secretary.' They put me in secretarial school immediately. . . . I made it through the year and graduated."

After short-term employment in several places, she heard of an opening at the Lutheran Immigration Service and applied for the job as a temporary stenographer. It proved to be more than temporary. She stayed at the agency the rest of her working life, moving slowly and steadily up the ladder: stenographer to secretary to administrative assistant. Then she started taking college courses, eventually getting a degree in Business Administration from NYU. After that she became assistant to the assistant director, then assistant director herself, then, in 1975, acting director. In 1977, the former DP and teenage-interpreter from Estonia became the director of one of the leading American refugee agencies.

Asked to say what her agency was like when she first went to work for it and to describe the changes she had seen over the years, Ingrid Walter shook her blondish head in an animated way, her eyes sparkled, then she began a lengthy monologue about how LIRS had gone through many ups and downs since it was founded in 1948, the year the Displaced Persons Act was passed.

The person who had been displaced herself explained that the Lutheran World Federations Assembly noted that "that year one out of every ten Lutherans in the world was a refugee and one of every three displaced persons in Europe was a Lutheran. . . . The Lutheran churches decided that, if there were Lutherans looking for new homes, why should they go to Baptist homes or the homes of others. Shouldn't we take care of our own?

That remained the prevailing sentiment until the 1960s. Then things changed and we began assisting various groups of people regardless of their religion."

The first major non-Lutheran group to be assisted was Asian, mostly Muslims who had been expelled from Uganda.

I asked the LIRS director if she thought the change in policy toward dealing with outsiders, that is, non-Lutherans, was the result of a resurgence of a kind of universalistic, Good Samaritan spirit. She smiled and said, "No. I think it was something different. We had developed the expertise to resettle people. . . . We had become professionals."

This was to become even more significant in the aftermath of the failed Czech uprising in 1968. As she explained, ". . . contrary to previous programs where people registered according to their religious affiliation— Jews with HIAS, Catholics with USCC, Lutherans with us, a new phenomenon occurred. The AFCR [the American Fund for Czechoslovak Refugees] became the center of registration. It was then on the basis of nationality rather than religion. This same practice continued when LIRS and the other 'religious' volags began to work together on the resettlement of refugees from Indochina. LIRS is still deeply involved in that activity."

When I last spoke to the Displaced Person from Estonia it was on the eve of her retirement. It was an appropriate time to ask what she thought was going to happen at LIRS and the other agencies whose long-time directors, such as John McCarthy at USCC and Carel Sternberg a counterpart at IRC, were themselves about to leave. Unlike the others interviewed, Ingrid Walter seemed rather reluctant to speculate either about her agency's future or that of the others. But she did express concern over increasing bureaucratization, the other side, as she saw it of the professionalization that made her agency—and others—better equipped to deal with their missions. In fact, she also worried a bit about the trend toward greater ever professionalization. She said that, in her day, people came into the field because of a special commitment, "an addiction," she called it. She worried that about the new trend toward greater specialized expertise might lead workers away from a more personal sense of involvement.

The End Checker

Wells Campbell Klein, the Director of the American Council of Nationalities Service, was the only person in the refugee field personally known to me at the beginning of my research on refugee workers. Although very close friends in graduate school days at Cornell in the mid-1950s, we had lost touch with one another sometime in the early 1960s and didn't meet again for nearly twenty years. We finally got back together sometime in 1981.

Though now nearly white-haired and a bit stockier, Wells Klein looked very much the way I remembered him: still dressed in a 1950s "ivy" style tweed jacket, gray trousers, heavy cordovan shoes. He sounded similar too; echoing words heard long before about the needs of refugees and the general disinterest in those who might be able to help them most.

Through a series of informal get-togethers, then more organized meetings over a tape-recorder, Wells Klein told me, once again, the story of how he first got involved in working with refugees, a field in which his father, Philip Klein, a well-known professor at the New York School of Social Work, had played a critical role during and after World War II. He related how, after he graduated from Sarah Lawrence, one of only thirty-five men who attended the previously all-women's college immediately after the war, he had held a series of temporary jobs "flitting," as he put it, "from one thing to another."

Then one day a friend called and said she heard of a job at CARE that Klein might be interested in. He was. Two days later he was in Yugoslavia, an "End Checker" (making sure things went where they were supposed to) for a big PL-40 food program.

After the job was finished, he returned to New York to work for CARE in the home office. His stay was brief for he was soon sent back to Yugoslavia as a Mission Chief. He remained with CARE for a number of years running a variety of programs.

One of the countries he worked in was Vietnam. It was just before the fall of Dien Bien Phu and Klein went there to set up a CARE program to deal with the flood of refugees from the north, some 950,000. His next stop was in Ithaca, New York.

"As you know better than anyone," he said, "I found that graduate school was not really the thing for me . . . After coming out of Vietnam and Laos and all the activity, the involvement, the stimulation, I found the shores of Lake Cayuga too bucolic. I was concentrating in anthropology with a minor in economics and a specialization on Southeast Asia. I had one Ford Fellowship to start my studies and then another to do fieldwork in Laos. I turned them back. You just don't turn back Ford Fellowships, but I did. I decided that, since I never planned to be an academician (though I had planned to get a doctorate), it would mean two, three, four more years. It just wasn't for me and I left."

"Are you sorry now?" I asked.

"No. In retrospect I think it was a very wise decision not to stay with it. I mean, I need action. I need to be involved. It just wouldn't have worked."

He returned to CARE in New York. But, after several years and a dispute over the management of a medical program in Algeria, he left the agency with which he had for so long been affiliated. Then, following what he described as some unproductive years as "a sort of superannuated hippie," he was asked to go back to Vietnam, this time by the Chairman of the Board of the International Rescue Committee. It was 1965.

Over the next several years he held a number of posts, including a stint as de facto Deputy Director of the U.S. Office of Refugee Coordination and as Director of the U.S. AID Vietnam Bureau on Refugees and Social Welfare.

Back in Washington he got to know "the Kennedy people."

"I would often go over to the Hill to talk to Dale DeHaan or somebody else on Kennedy's staff." During that same period, Wells Klein was offered a job as Director of the American branch of International Social Services, then headquartered in Geneva. While there he arranged a merger with ISS and Traveler's Aid. But "it was not a good move. I was sort of squeezed out."

After a few months he took over the directorship of the almost defunct American Council of Nationalities Service, ACNS, a consortium of thirty-two community-based local agencies, most of them known as "International Institutes," scattered around the country. ACNS which later merged with the U.S. Committee on Refugees based in Washington, is now one of the most vigorous of the volags involved not only in initial re-settlement activities but in job, language, and citizenship training programs through its constituent institutes. [In 1993 its name was changed to the Immigration and Refugee Service of America, IRSA.]

The Deputy

Dale DeHaan is an impeccable dresser with a bit of a flair for European style. He looks more like Hollywood's version of a foreign correspondent or the owner of a fine art gallery than the layman's image of one who works on behalf of refugees. But that is what he does and what he has been doing for most of his adult life.

DeHaan grew up in a Dutch Calvinist home in Michigan, went to a small midwestern university and then to the University of Amsterdam, where his main interest was in international politics. His involvement in refugee work, he reported, was quite accidental.

He had moved to Washington in the late 1950s, having worked on JFK's presidential campaign. "After his election," he reported, "Kennedy said 'Why don't you stick around?'" DeHaan did. For fifteen years.

He first worked in the office of Senator Philip Hart who was looking for someone, preferably from Michigan and with a foreign policy background. Hart was chairman of a committee on refugees in the Senate. DeHaan was immediately put to work in some refugee-related issues. "Once involved," he said, "I wanted to stay with it. It sort of grabs you."

The work was seen to be both challenging and frustrating.

"Too often," DeHaan, who soon became staff director of the refugee subcommittee, said, "refugee matters were seen as 'do-good' issues that, when push comes to shove, get short shrift—despite all the Statue of Liberty-type political rhetoric." But he met others who did seem to care.

In his position, he had increasing contact with those in the private sector who were advocates for and assisters to refugees. He noted that, "From the beginning of my work in the Senate, I learned that the voluntary agencies may not have had much political clout but they did have a good deal of knowledge. And, if we could stay in touch with the agencies, and their people, we could learn a lot, and so both Hart and Kennedy, but particularly Kennedy, made a point of bringing these people in and talking with them." That was how The Deputy came to know Jan Papanek, Gaynor Jacobson, John McCarthy, Carel Sternberg, and the others.

His contacts proved useful in preparing for debates over such legislation as the Refugee Assistance Act of 1962 and the Immigration Reform Act of 1965, and, later, in dealing with a series of international events including the exodus from Cuba, the flight to Hong Kong, the Czech uprising, the expulsion of Asians from Uganda, and, especially, the fall of Saigon.

Reminiscing, DeHaan said, "I always remember when, in 1975, we suddenly had the evacuation from South Vietnam to deal with. The State Department put a task force together that did not include a single representative of the volags. . . . They were totally ignored. Ted Kennedy moved to correct the situation. . . . John McCarthy of USCC was chairman of the ACVA [American Committee of Voluntary Agencies] Committee on Migration and Refugee Affairs. We brought him along with others. They were the experts. There was a stable full of them. One was Wells Klein. Wells had worked for CARE before and for ISS [International Social Services]. He and others supplied the committee with reports, especially about what was going on in the field."

The passage of the Refugee Act of 1980 was, for DeHaan, the culmination of years of effort. But, by then, he was far from Washington. In 1978 Dale DeHaan literally became The Deputy, the Deputy United Nations High Commissioner for Refugees.

"HCR," he said, "was very different from what I had done before. Instead of dealing with a lot of senators and people in the Executive Branch of one government, I had to deal with many governments."

Asked how the American efforts looked from his then-new vantage point, DeHaan said that " . . . compared to many others, the Americans as a group were really out front on issues of resettlement. . . . This was true of officials and members of NGOs."

In the case of the NGOs, DeHaan pointed to the differences in political cultures. "Not many understand or use the sort of lobbying or have the same kind of grass-roots volunteerism that is so familiar to Americans."

The third phase in a career in refugee work began in 1981 when DeHaan returned to the U.S. as Director of the Migration and Refugee Program of Church World Service (CWS), which functions, in the jargon of the organization, as "the ecumenical focal point for denominations or communities that are members of the National Council of Churches."

After moving to New York and settling into the headquarters of the National Council of Churches on Riverside Drive, DeHaan said he found CWS as byzantine an operation as anything he had seen in Washington or Geneva. He described the agency as an anomaly among the species called volags. It was hydra-headed, with a complex nervous system, and an over-riding credo that tended to play down if not denigrate professionalism in favor of pastoral commitment. This seemed an odd place to put a prag-matic, cosmopolitan, highly professional civil servant. Something, he con-fessed, of which he was quite aware. But it was also a challenge.

The Refugee Program at CWS was founded in 1948 but had been or-ganized from the start in a somewhat different way from its counterparts. This had to do with the core requirement of far more in-put in policy mak-ing and implementation by "lay persons" than most of the other volags, in-cluding those also church-related. Unlike the U.S. Catholic Conference's Migration and Refugee Service, it is not organized hierarchically. Unlike HIAS, it tended to favor the "congregational" rather than "case-manage-ment" method of resettlement. This meant that local congregations rather than agencies or individuals, were primary sponsors and caretakers, pro-viding more direct, hands-on support from the untrained true (though sometimes coopted) volunteers than is generally the case.

After nearly fifteen years of working at CWS, DeHaan commented that "in the agencies I have found that the staff members are, by and large, very hard workers. And they're not a bunch of wimpy do-gooders. There are some very hard-nosed people. . . . My one worry is that they be given enough air to breathe because they are so creative." He was interrupted by the question "Who are they? Ministers, former Peace Corps volunteers, social workers?"

"It's a mixture, the same as in the other agencies. But all of us are going to have to face the reality of the fact that a new generation will be taking over fairly soon. In many places it's already happening. There have been two key retirements from HIAS a few years ago. They were both fantastic people. John McCarthy of the Catholics has just retired; so has Carel Sternberg of IRC. Ingrid Walters is old now too. I haven't heard anything of Jan Papanek going into retirement but he is well over eighty. Wells Klein and I are the old-timers now!"

I asked DeHaan what he thought of those coming in to replace the older generation.

"Well, in a way, some of the newer people are more professional. I don't mean this in a negative way. It's just that they are less likely to be social worker types and more apt to be lawyers, managers. . . . "

He ended the last interview I had with him with the hope that the sense of "calling" (his word, not one proffered) that brought many into the field in the first place would not be lost in the push toward professionalization. He worried that certain very special people might be turned away. He ex-plained this in the following way: "Let me draw a parallel here with the

UN because I think this applies to the voluntary agencies as well. It's sort of what I look for in interviewing people. . . . "

"They used to say that UNHCR, of all the UN agencies, had one of the best reputations in terms of getting the job done. Of course, it varied from year to year . . . but, nevertheless, in general, I think it was true. People would say to me, 'Well, why do you think this is any better than UNDP or some other program?' My first answer was, and remains, we have more committed people here. I said, you know, you can't deal with these problems unless you've got some commitment. Even at the lower levels, I think you've got to have commitment. It's more important than how fast can you type or fill out a form.

"Of course, this is a judgment call. It also depends on the nature of your constituency. And it therefore varies from agency to agency.

"HIAS, for example, has always been more professional than most agencies. Over the years it has an outstanding record in terms of refugee resettlement. It uses NYANA and Jewish Family Service to run its monitoring system and each refugee family is part of a case with social workers assigned. But then, of course, it is more homogeneous. CWS, by contrast, is multiheaded and dependent on the view of many about what the mission is, a kind of Good Samaritan, religiously oriented ideology that even varies somewhat from one denomination to another."

"You see," he continued, "unlike most other voluntary agencies—religious and non-sectarian—we do not have a formal policy-making board. We have a committee, the Church World Service Committee. It meets three times a year and oversees the activities of the agency. The Committee is made up of the leaders of the member denominations. Most, but not all, are clergy. What complicates things further is that each of the constituent bodies has its own committee. . . . Our decentralization is both good and bad. Good because people get involved at the grass roots; bad because it is so hard to coordinate and to rank priorities."

The Professor

Le Xuan Khoa is currently Executive Director of the Indochinese Resource Action Center (IRAC) based in Washington, D.C. [Since 1995 it is called the Southeast Asia Resource Action Center.] He is from the northern part of Vietnam. Trained in Oriental Philosophy in Hanoi and Paris, he moved to Saigon from Hanoi in 1953, the year before the Geneva agreement that divided his country into two parts. A high school teacher for a time, Le Khoa had joined the philosophy faculty of the University of Saigon in 1960 and was affiliated with the University until the communist takeover in 1975 when he sought asylum in the United States. At the time of his departure he was Vice President of the University.

While he did serve for a brief time as Deputy Minister of Culture, he claims that he had little involvement in the politics of South Vietnam during the turbulent war years. He did, however, have many contacts with the Americans, and with those in the U.S. Embassy.

Knowing it was very difficult to send students overseas for graduate work, as he had done, Le Khoa said he proposed inviting visiting professors from abroad, especially from the United States to come to Vietnam. And some did come. In addition to conducting that exchange program, he helped to oversee the translation of some forty textbooks with the support of the Vietnamese American Association, a private organization. Assistance was also provided by the American Library and the USIS office to get the translations printed very cheaply. He thinks that many of the books are still being used in Vietnam.

"Two days before the fall of Saigon, April 1975, I got a message from a friend from the U.S. Information Service saying there was a bus to the airport if my family and I wanted to go. We had just one hour. And we—my wife and my kid and I—went. We flew to Guam and then from Guam to Pendleton [a marine base in California being used as a resettlement center]. We stayed there [in Pendleton] for one month, leaving there the first of June." Then they moved to Washington, resettled by Church World Service and sponsored by an American friend.

To find work, Le Khoa said he made out three kinds of resumes: one downplaying his academic credentials; one "with some of it"; and one "full of everything." He sent them to thirty to forty potential employers.

He first got a job as a cashier in a 7–11 store but was soon working for the Office of Refugee Resettlement which was planning to publish a newsletter for Vietnamese refugees, providing information about settlement in the United States. After a brief time, although invited to stay on at ORR, he went to work for a private agency—one which, it turned out, was under contract to ORR itself, conducting surveys of refugees.

After a brief stint in Philadelphia, where he trained Indochinese health professionals to work with their American counterparts, when the contract for the project was terminated, he returned to Washington where he became involved with an organization that had been started in 1979, IRAC, then called the Indochinese Refugee Action Center.

IRAC's founders were eager to assist the increasing numbers of Vietnamese, Loatians and Cambodians coming into the United States. It received its initial funding from both private—including foundations—and government (ORR) sources.

As IRAC grew, it became more institutionalized. Le Khoa applied for and was accepted as Deputy Director, working primarily on issues of training and technical assistance to help Indochinese newcomers move toward self-sufficiency and "to mainstream activities like any other ethnic minority." In this, IRAC, although it did not do primary resettlement, was beginning to take on many of the "settlement house" characteristics of the older volags. One of its principal tasks became working with and supporting a variety of ethnically specific (i.e., Vietnamese- , Laotian- , Cambodian- , Chinese-American) "mutual assistance associations" (known as MAAs) across the country.

Le Xuan Khoa was made Director of IRAC in 1982. Since then he has strengthened the organization in a variety of ways, while maintaining its main functions, especially in relation to the MAAs. To achieve its intercultural functions, the board was reorganized.

"At this point we have seventeen on the board; ten of them are Indochinese—three from each of the countries of origin and one ethnic Chinese. Of the remaining seven, three are representatives of the three major minorities, the Jewish community, the Black community, and Hispanic."

The Oriental Philosopher from Saigon, a most energetic and charismatic individual, is greatly admired by his fellow refugees from Southeast Asia and by his colleagues in the refugee field. Yet, unlike many of the volag leaders who are committed to a life of refugee work, Le Khoa does not see himself as a professional refugee worker. He claims that what he is doing is assisting his community and related communities to find their place in American society. Someday soon, he says, he will go back to teaching or, barring that, to writing.

"I have two projects in mind. The first is to write a book on the history of the Indochinese in America; the second is an autobiography."

The Vicars of the Volags

Those whose stories are briefly summarized revealed varied reasons for having come into the field of refugee resettlement work. Their personal and professional histories, and those of a number of the others already interviewed at length, along with the far briefer responses to questions posed in various trips to refugee sites and those asked in the mailed survey, tell of involvement motivated by values learned early in life, political convictions, personal and situational factors. Many, even in stressing one of these seemingly separable "variables" more than others, noted or implied linkage. There is clear evidence that growing up in environments that stressed universalistic values but that also emphasized the importance of protecting and aiding those threatened by persecution were important motivators of those who were to have careers in social work or international social service. Such seems to have been the case of John McCarthy, Gaynor Jacobson, Wells Klein, and Dale DeHaan. (Klein was the only head of a refugee agency and one of the few of the hundreds interviewed in the entire study whose mother or father had been a refugee worker.) The rest of those whose stories are briefly told in the preceding section, Jan Papanek, Carel Sternberg, Ingrid Walter, and Le Xuan Khoa, were, in one way or another, victims, individuals who had been forced to flee their homelands or, in the case of Papanek, to claim asylum, taking on the characteristic and paradoxical quality of long-time exiles, the sense of permanent instability. None of the "refugee group" had been trained for or intended to pursue careers in a "humanitarian regime"—though Jan Papanek was groomed to be, and became, a diplomat.

Whatever got the leaders of the volags started, like most others of those briefly talked to and observed in action, or heard from, or interviewed at length would be seen by others as professional altruists,[2] an expression discussed with each of them and which most found unsuitable. The reaction was not because it has a sort of self-contradictory ring to it (like the familiar oxymoron "paid volunteer") but because it sounds somehow exploitative.

There are good reasons for such sensitivity, and each of the volag leaders who were interviewed expressed it. They know, perhaps more than anyone, the arguments that are made about those who work with many relief and resettlement agencies, especially those that take any amount of public money or any from specific churches or political groups and the contention that they must be motivated far less by the spirit of selfless Samaritanism and more by the fact that they have been co-opted to do someone else's bidding or because they themselves want to further particular aims. They know that the critics say that religious supporters are giving only to impose their faith on others and win converts; that political supporters (private or governmental) are promulgating a particular ideology, be it anti-Fascist, anti-Communist, anti-Arab Fundamentalist, anti-Zionist. Even those who are said to claim that what they do is done solely for humanitarian reasons know they are seen as making calculated choices which suggest that the lives of certain persons are more valuable and deserve more attention than those of others. And they are aware that there are critics who say they are really driven by the marketplace. The leaders of the refugee agencies and, it turns out, many who work with them, are not only familiar with the stereotypes but recognize that some have more than kernels of truth.

Yet, on the basis of what is known about them and their own commitments, they doubtless argue that the issue is not so easily reduced to an either/or dichotomy, especially one that sounds like the popular expression that "If you're not part of the solution, you're part of the problem." This assumption is based on many offhand remarks made by the leaders and also by many of their staffers, too.

While there is little doubt that there are some, perhaps many, for whom refugee work offers opportunities to do well by "doing good," on the basis of a decade examining American programs and getting to know many who manage and run voluntary agencies as well as the members of their diverse staffs, when it comes to motivations there appears to be more altruism than self-interest, more concern about protecting others' beliefs than in proselytizing, and, paradoxically, often more idealism than pragmatism, a fact that often rankles those who worry about cost overruns and unrealistic case loads.

If there is a common idea that unites the American refugee resettlement workers whose disparate thoughts and activities are briefly reported, it is still the concept of caregiving. While most describe work that requires them to play many parts, some clearly political, even the heads of the agencies, sophisticated cosmopolites with years of experience in the field still seem to define themselves as mainly being advocates for the dispossessed, purveyors of aid and comfort, and agents of their integration into what they would define as safer havens than the ones where so many refugees are first encountered. Those in whom many refugees are asked to place their trust and faith do appear to take very seriously their responsibility to assist. They would say that theirs is not a *business* of caring but a business of *caring*.

REVIEWS

The Intellectual Migration
Revisited

I

REREADING Stuart Hughes's *The Sea Change* in conjunction with some research on the sociology of exile, I noted an acknowledgment "to those who sustained my spirits and contributed to my thoughts in ways of which I suspect they were mostly unaware." Hughes then mentions several people. One of those named is Lewis A. Coser.

Hughes's book is one of several significant works on the migration of social thought from Europe to America in the 1930s and 1940s, on the contributions of those Laura Fermi called the "illustrious immigrants." Many such immigrants—members of the Bauhaus, the Frankfurt School, the Vienna Circle, as well as unaffiliated academicians, artists, and writers—already had made their marks prior to their transAtlantic passage. Others received their graduate training in the United States and then gained prominence in their respective fields. What the older and younger generations had in common was the fact that they lived and worked as marginal men and women who, even as they became a part of the new society, remained apart from it in crucial ways.

Georg Simmel called such persons "strangers." He suggested that, unlike the visitor or the wanderer, the stranger "comes today and stays tomorrow." His position is "determined, essentially, by the fact that he has not belonged to the group from the beginning, that he imports qualities into it, which do not and cannot stem from the group itself." In new environs he is both "near and far at the same time." Neither Hughes nor Fermi nor other writers whose books are often cited as standard works on the movement of refugee intellectuals set their texts in such an explicitly Simmelian framework. Given the nature of the subject, it was quite likely that, sooner or later, someone would return to the master concept of "the stranger" and its explication—someone like sociologist Lewis Coser whose comments and suggestions to Stuart Hughes more than a decade ago might well have been along just such lines.

*Review of *Refugee Scholars in America: Their Impact and Their Experiences*, by Lewis A. Coser. Originally published in *Society*, May/June 1986, pp. 88–90.

Coser, himself author of numerous essays and books on social theory and social issues, contributor to a number of critical debates on a broad panoply of sociological concerns, had done little by way of addressing his own situation and that of the others in that quasi-ethnic category "refugee scholar." Several summers ago, I had a long conversation with him about this. It began when Coser asked me about my study of refugee workers, then turned to my broader interest in the study of alienation in its literal sense. The latter, I remember saying, was an area in which he himself had much to contribute.

That twilight meeting on Cape Cod proved to have a latent function as Coser acknowledges in the preface to his latest book, *Refugee Scholars in America: Their Impact and Their Experiences.*

Having been a catalyst, I did not become a consultant. While knowing that the seed planted in Wellfleet was germinating in Stony Brook, Palo Alto, and Paris, I never saw any of its fruits until I received a copy of the book several months ago. Like the marginal people who concern us both, I approached the task of reviewing *Refugee Scholars in America* with a sense of detached involvement.

II

As I read it, I kept thinking, "this is another *Men of Ideas*, only this time, properly, the tail wags the dog." The importance of the volume is not merely or mainly the many word portraits of the several dozen social scientists and humanists he writes about, but the cement that binds it all together and the Coserian asides that add so much to an understanding of the lives of those he discusses and their contributions to their fields and to this society.

In a preface which sets the boundaries of his study, Coser explains that he restricted himself to certain disciplines, eschewing the temptation to tell the whole story. The result is that he does not deal with those in the natural sciences or the arts. Moreover, he writes, "Since my topic is the transmission of knowledge and cultural elements across the Atlantic, it stands to reason that I have had to exclude young refugees who [like himself] pursued a significant part of their higher education in this country." Included in this neglected cohort are the historian Peter Gay and the sociologist Reinhard Bendix, both of whom have written autobiographically on the subject themselves.

Coser further admits to limiting himself to those who seem to have been successful and whose success is measured by their scholarly impact. He notes that there are many refugee intellectuals, most especially "those who choose, or were forced, to teach in small Southern colleges both black and white . . . [who] were often the first ambassadors of European scholarship and cosmopolitan culture in these settings." They are rightly referred to as the unsung heroes of American higher education. (Perhaps first among the many was the last Ernst Borinski of Tougaloo.)

To discuss any of these people in proper sociological fashion it is essential to define the refugee scholar. Coser does this in his first chapter, an essay on loss and the generation of prestige. He distinguishes between immigrants, those who are drawn to a new society by the hope of advancement; exiles, those who seek temporary asylum to wait out the storms at home; and refugees. To Coser, refugees have some of the qualities of both immigrants and exiles. Like the latter, they often leave because of categorical persecutions, having been pushed out rather than pulled away; like the former, their departure is generally an irrevocable one. One may quibble with these distinctions, but they do seem appropriate as operational definitions for Coser's purposes. Most of whom he writes are not immigrants or exiles but refugees. Most are Jews who, having experienced or witnessed racial and religious persecution by the Nazis, made the painful decision to leave to seek new lives in new environs, in many cases going away with great trepidation and almost no prospect of returning home.

These refugees whose lives and works are assessed in several subsequent chapters are different in at least one other significant respect. Unlike most immigrants and many exiles, these German and Austrian scholars "usually came from positions fairly high on the status ladder where they had lived in relative comfort and were accustomed to receiving a certain deference and respect." For many, emigration meant more than being uprooted, it meant losing status or having difficult times in retaining it in milieus in which the rules of the academic game are played differently.

Those with the most transferable skills and the best contacts had the easiest time adjusting. Coser briefly contrasts the experiences of hard scientists and those of others who faced the prospects of readjustment in the midst of a depression-wracked economy, resulting in all sorts of unanticipated consequences. He noted that "it is part of the wonderful irony that attended to much of the early reception of refugee scholars in America that most of them were hired at first by colleges or minor universities where teaching rather than research was at a premium." It was a humbling, sometimes humiliating experience. Many had little patience with the demands of daily classroom routines and worried that such chores were not really useful in advancing stalled careers or increasing visibility. While some learned to live within the more narrowly restricted worlds of the provincial campus and made important contributions as conveyors of outside ideas in the academic hinterlands, most still longed for environs more conducive to a self-image as *Herr Professor Doktor*.

Those who seemed most satisfied with their situations and most appreciated by new colleagues were often those who managed to obtain appointments in the large universities of the Middle West or California rather than in the ivied East where they had originally hoped to find placement.

There were exceptions but, by and large, only private academic bastions were less receptive to the newcomers and their ideas than the more free-wheeling public multiversities.

The social psychologist Kurt Lewin was one who was buffeted about until he obtained a tenured slot at the University of Iowa. Well known before his emigration, Lewin had to overcome many difficulties in reestablishing himself in the United States. He was luckier than many other refugee psychologists. According to Coser, "The psychologists as a group were only minimally successful, both in their personal careers and in the reception of their teachings: the psychoanalysts were phenomenally successful in both respects." Although Lewin did restart his interrupted career, made many important contributions to field theory, and influenced a generation of students who came to be known as Lewinians, even he never really penetrated the inner sanctum of the psychological establishment. Lewin is the first of several who are profiled in a chapter on psychology and psychoanalysis.

Coser also reports on the productive careers of "the Gestalt triumvirate": Wolfgang Köhler, Kurt Koffka, and Max Wertheimer: and on the unhappy fate of Karl and Charlotte Buehler, who never managed to find their place in America.

The psychoanalysts were on a rather different track. They moved in and up with considerable alacrity. Coser provides summaries of the creative innovativeness of Erik Erikson and Wilhelm Reich, the neo-Freudianism and social criticism of Erich Fromm, and the culture-personality orientation of Karen Horney. Readers are also offered some hard statistics to bolster the view that, in the aggregate, these analysts and their colleagues made quite a difference. Their impact was ubiquitous.

> On the average, refugees published four times as many books and more than one-and-a-half times as many papers in psychoanalytic journals as did their American-born colleagues. Refugee psychoanalysts have produced on the average 79 percent, 82 percent, 63 percent, and 52 percent, respectively, of books, [and] articles in psychoanalytic journals . . . psychological journals and . . . popular journals.

In few other fields could newcomers make such impressive claims. Indeed, in contrast to the widespread influence of the psychoanalysts, and, to a lesser though still significant extent, economists and political scientists (dealt with in later chapters), only a small number of refugee sociologists had such a major effect on their discipline in the United States. Coser attributes this, at least in part, to their left-leaning political proclivities which, along with their Jewish identities, were anathema to the Nazis—and not always welcome in this country.

The field of sociology, a once important rallying point for critical social thought, was largely obliterated by its brown-shirted opponents. Those who could escape, did, and most came to the United States. Once here, instead of starting American branches of their old intellectual schools or staking out new intellectual turf, Coser claims that most tended to "serve as transmission belts for sociological theory, but without adding to that knowledge in more than marginal ways." In fact, it was more than marginal. In the same section Coser contradicts himself a bit indicating that what they transmitted was to have a significant impact of its own. He quotes Edward Shils's statement:

> The refugee in the social sciences brought the awareness of the possibility of decay in the social order, of the possibilities of disruption of what once seemed stable. They brought the exhilaration of intellectual melodrama—they brought Freud and Marx and a respect for the name of Max Weber.

The sociologists brought a comparative and historical and sometimes radical perspective to the atheoretical character of much of American sociological thinking. Among the most prominent of the conveyors of ideas and writings largely unknown or ignored on this side of the Atlantic were Hans Gerth, Kurt H. Wolff, Hans Zeisel, Max Rheinstein, Joachim Wach, and Rudolf Heberle. All are briefly mentioned by Coser.

Then there was the New School for Social Research, the "University in Exile," founded by Alvin Johnson. Along with Black Mountain College in North Carolina, Roosevelt University in Chicago, and the Institute for Advanced Study at Princeton, the New School was established to provide anchorages for scholars fleeing the tempests of Europe as well as forums for exchanging ideas. According to Coser, for some it became "a kind of gilded ghetto for those refugee scientists who called a protective bulwark against native grown academic influences"; for others it was a bridge to American colleagues while still allowing the refugees to feel that they "were teaching *in paribus infidelium.*" In what he calls a collective portrait, Coser summarizes the history of the New School and the selection of its twelve charter scholars, including sociologists Albert Salomon and Hans Speier. They were soon joined by many others, some of whom formed the core of a graduate faculty, an organization whose culture was much like the character of its members: half-European, half-American, not quite a part of either world, but in a real sense an amalgam of both. As Coser rightly states:

> The success of the Graduate Faculty can partly be measured by the quality of its graduate students. In all fields taught by the faculty, a significant number of students later achieved considerable eminence on the American science. In sociology, for example, Peter Berger, Maurice Natanson, Bernard Rosenberg, Ephraim Fischoff, Helmut Wagner, and Thomas Luckmann received their Ph.D. degrees in the early years of the Faculty.

Many affiliated with the New School also found employment in government service, a career choice "that came easier to them than to the Marxists of the Frankfurt School." The latter group was quite different in orientation. Far less eclectic, as critics of the social order, they were internal exiles in their native Germany, a status they seemed to continue to hold once in this country. Coser highlights the attitudes and actions of the long-time leader of the school, Max Horkheimer, as well as those of Herbert Marcuse, Leo Lowenthal, Friedrich Pollock, and Theodor Adorno.

Special and separate attention is given to three other scholars each of whom, in his own way, had a profound effect on American sociology. First and foremost of this unlikely triumvirate is Paul F. Lazarsfeld, who is aptly labeled as the "Founding Father of American Social Research"; second, the phenomenologist Alfred Schutz; and third, the controversial author of *Oriental Despotism*, Karl Wittfogel.

Among the refugee scholars considered in a chapter on economists and economic historians are Ludwig von Mises, Oskar Morgenstern, Fritz Machlup, and Gottfried von Haberle—all influential Austrian classicists; econometrician Jacob Marschak; Alexander Gerschenkron and Albert A. Hirschman—"two students of economic backwardness and development"; Karl Polanyi and Paul Baran, described as "mavericks" for their unorthodox views of economic history and economics, respectively; and three students of economic behavior: George Katona, Peter Drucker, and Fritz Redlich.

Within any psychology, psychoanalysis, sociology, and economics, those grouped in any one sector of a social science typology are often in reality very strange cellmates. This is also true in political science. Schools of thought abound as do methodologies and debates over the very functions of the discipline. Such differences are clearly apparent in any examination of the refugee scholars who studied government or politics; behaviorists like Karl Deutsch and those, such as Hannah Arendt, Leo Strauss, and Eric Voegelin, who bridled at the very notion of such detached positivism. Coser writes about all those mentioned plus "that advocate and critic of power politics," Hans Morgenthau. Vignettes about each give the reader insight into their particular political and intellectual bents—and to Coser's own assessments of the individuals and their contributions.

The poignancy of estrangement is particularly evident in the all-too-brief chapter on European writers. It begins with portraits of Alfred Doeblin and Leonard Frank, graphically described by Coser as whales stranded on the California coast (where they worked in Hollywood's dream factory); and Herman Broch and others who "deliberately insulated themselves from American cultural influences and pursued their writing careers untouched by anything that happened in America; they might as well have lived in Tahiti." Reactions such as that of Broch were not universal. There were writers like the great Thomas Mann who used their acquired double vision to react to challenging new environments while keeping council with fellow émigrés. There were those like Vladimir Nabokov who drank deeply of America's cup of life and wrote about it, becoming, if not American writers, then "American men[and women] of letters." Coser gives Nabokov and those like him a special sobriquet, "reluctant insider."

Nabokov, like many of those who shared the same chapter, could have also been placed in other parts of Coser's book—perhaps in the very next one on the humanists. That chapter is in many ways the most broadly based for it encompasses a range of scholars who brought to America new ideas and effected far-reaching changes in a variety of unrelated fields: Roman linguistics; Erin and other art historians; Reich, Leo Spitzer, and Rene Wellek in comparative literature; Werner Jaeger and other classicists; and a quartet of eminent historians, Hajo Holborn, Felix Gilbert, Hans Rosenberg, and Paul Oskar Kristeller.

The introduction to the final chapter on philosophy and theology is a fitting end piece. In it the author discusses the favorable reception of Rudolf Carnap and the logical positivists of the Vienna Circle, the negative reaction to Aron Gurwitsch and others whose Husserlian phenomenology was quite unpalatable in the mainstream of philosophical thinking until nearly two decades after the end of the war, and the shifting views of the philosopher-theologian Paul Tillich. Here the reader is reminded that, while refugee scholars do share certain things in common which distinguish them from other refugees and from other scholars, there are important distinctions to be made among them, differences based on field and fate and fortune. Some were to find they had something appealing to offer and that their hosts were ready to receive it. Others learned through bitter experience that, whatever they had done before—or wanted to do in America—there were still others who, by calculation of conversion, modified their earlier convictions to become refugees *à la mode Americaine*, a label Coser assigns the man who was to become the progressive leader of liberal theology in this country: Paul Tillich. Says Coser of Tillich: "The erstwhile firebrand from Germany became an American institution, a revered and highly respected voice that, far from being critical of things American, provided soothing relief from the anxieties and the spiritual unease of the times."

II

Refugee Scholars in America is a compendium of information and opinion about a select (and selected) group of social scientists and humanists whose loss to the intellectual soil of Europe, because of their victimization, was, paradoxically, a gain to the intellectual life of this country. While Coser's quick sketches are sometimes uneven and occasionally disjointed, and the introductory essays often too short for those, like me, who find his assessments of the interplay of personalities and politics most intriguing, these are minor annoyances. The more serious one is, perhaps, unfair. As the author himself acknowledges, not all dispossessed scholars who sought refuge in America made it here, and not all who made it here had an impact—or even a satisfying life. I would like to know more about them, but that is obviously beyond the scope of this study.

In all, Lewis Coser is to be commended for reminding American readers of the enormous importance of the contributions of refugee scholars to our lives, our thoughts, and our culture. He sums it up in a statement with which he ends the first chapter:

> American culture by and large prizes and values objective and analytical thought. It therefore welcomed the contributions of the refugee intellectuals, even if it was also a little distrustful of their cold intelligence, unregardful, as is often seemed, of received verities and pieties.

Returning to the theme of alienation, Coser adds some additional thoughts: the European scholars found that, while Americans were willing to listen to their voices, they were often heard at a distance. When all is said and done, they were still outsiders. Those who wished to make their home in America may have been acculturated quickly, but there was still a barrier to their full acceptance and to the redefinition of themselves as Americans, regardless of what it said on their new passports: "Strangers may learn to speak the language of their new community with considerable fluency, but they are unlikely to speak it without at least a slight accent, which remains the stigma of otherness."

"Their children," Coser notes, "speak without accents."

Pellegrini

Dami centue lire
e mi ni vaiu a lamerica
Maladitu lamerica
e chi la spirminta

Give me a hundred lire
And I'm off to America
Goddamn America
And the man who thought it up.

S O SANG little boys in the streets of towns and villages in Sicily (and, with some dialectical variations, in those of the *Mezzogiorno* of Italy) around the turn of the century when millions left such places hoping for a better chance in that far-off land "discovered" by one putative *paisano* and named for another. The song, also sung here, is a fitting prologue to Jerre Mangione and Ben Morreale's *La Storia: Five Centuries of the Italian American Experience.*

Mangione, professor emeritus of English at the University of Pennsylvania, is the author of the classic autobiographical novel *Mt. Allegro,* about the Sicilian community in Rochester, New York, where he grew up, and many other books on Italian American and other themes. He is widely recognized by students of acculturation as a sensitive chronicler of the problems of negotiating the difficult passages between two cultures and the insights of those who write about the marginality of refugees, immigrants, and minorities in general. His coauthor, Ben Morreale, shares many common identities and abilities. Professor of literature and history at the State University of New York at Plattsburgh, Morreale is also a novelist who writes about Italian Americans and others. His recent work of fiction is a novel, *A Few Virtuous Men.* Their collaborative effort, which has already been warmly received by a cross section of commentators, is an engaging, lyrical, and loving tribute to the authors' pasts and a paean to

*Originally published in *International Migration Review* 27, Winter, 1993.

countless countrymen. It is intended to be both a font of information and a corrective to what they feel are the distorted lenses through which many have long viewed Americans of Italian ancestry and their communities.

La Storia, meaning "history" in Italian, is, in fact, closer to what it sounds like to English-hearing ears. The book is an epic story written for a wide public by the two storytellers who rely on a combination of sources to relate the grand scope and minutiae of the Italian American life. Despite the extensive referencing, the book remains highly personal. Throughout one senses that this is the Mangione-Morreale "take" on history. It has a particular spin to it.

Not surprisingly, *La Storia* begins with the voyages and landings of the now-controversial Genoese "Admiral of the Ocean Seas," Christopher Columbus. (I would guess that neither of the authors anticipated the negative flak he would receive when they planned publication for 1992, the year of the Columbus Quincentennial.)

Neither Mangione nor Morreale is a professional historian, and there are a number of places in their volume where this will become apparent to those who are. For example, readers of the *International Migration Review* acquainted with its longtime editor and author of the important study *Piety and Power*, Silvano Tomasi, will do a mental double take when they read in a footnote on pages 332–333 that he is identified as "a highly respected Italian American historian" and "a member of the Jesuit order." Silvano Tomasi is many things, including a damn fine historian; but he is not a Jesuit.

There are other errors of fact and various places where specialists steeped in the nuances of specific aspects of the subject will be wont to disagree with Mangione and Morreale and their interpretations, but, to me, while not to be dismissed—for these are not trivial matters—they do little to detract from the overall impact of this richly detailed and illustrated (in photographs as well as words) lengthy and generally balanced testimonial to the struggles and tribulations and triumphs of a significant cohort of Americans.

The story is told in twenty-seven chapters. After the Prologue, referred to above, the book begins with a discussion of the Italians in the colonial period and a thumbnail portrait of the land they left. Then it turns to the fever to emigrate, the time before and after *Risorgimento*, and the America to which the vast majority came in the period of the Great Migration, 1880–1924. This was a period when many, especially peasants from Sicily and Italy, initially saw themselves as temporary sojourners. Like the Chinese "coolies" of an earlier period, they often came, frequently having been recruited by labor contractors, with the intention of making money and returning home. Many of those others were to refer to as "birds of passage" were to make several trips before deciding to stay in *lamerica*. Most settled in the northeast but some went far afield.

In a section that addresses what is, perhaps, least well known to American general readers, the authors discuss life for Italians in the southern and western United States, with a special focus on New Orleans. They also write about more familiar if hardly well understood topics, too: character, identity and assimilation; stereotypes; work and the padrone system; politics and political parties; neighborhoods like New York's Mulberry Street and Boston's North End; crime and punishment; and social mobility.

Most interesting are the latter parts of the book, where the authors really come into their own. Two that are particularly noteworthy, especially to those who are fascinated by such literary ethnographies as Pietro di Donato's *Christ in Concrete*, Mangione's *Mt. Allegro*, and Mario Puzo's *The Fortunate Pilgrim*, are chapters 21 and 26, which both deal with Italian American writers, the first about those in the period from 1890 to 1960, and the second, 1960 to the present. These chapters are complimented by a very useful listing of the titles of over 800 novels, short stories, plays, and poems at the end of the book, one of the most comprehensive bibliographies on the subject available.

Like other books of its genre, those written about the experiences of other American ethnic groups—the Jews, the Irish, and African Americans—*La Storia* highlights the activities, troubles, and, especially, the accomplishments of Americans from Italy and names them, by the hundreds! Many of those cited are little known to most Americans.

To the pantheon of prominent Italian Americans one more name should be added: Jerre Mangione. Long before Gay Talese told other Americans about what it meant to be *pellegrini* (pilgrims) in a new land, Mangione was doing it. He still is.

On the Slopes of Mount Allegro

S EVERAL YEARS ago the editor of *Contemporary Sociology* asked me to review the reissued version of Jerre Mangione's classic memoir *Mount
Allegro*. I did so with pleasure for it had long been one of my favorite works
of "literary ethnography," a wonderful portrait of Italian American life. It
is something else, too, as I noted in my review:

> . . . *Mount Allegro* has additional meaning for me, for my mother and her
> brothers grew up in the very same Italian and Jewish (formerly German and
> Irish) section of Rochester that Mangione describes. Many of his accounts of
> Papa, Uncle Nino, Compare Caligero, Mr. Michaelangelo, Mr. Bernstein,
> Mr. Solomon, and *gli Americani* have a special ring of verisimilitude for I had
> heard the stories—or some like them—long before I first read Mangione's
> book nearly forty years ago.

The stories I remember best are about the Carbonas, Quadrozzis, To-
meis, Regners, Levys, and Felds. But mostly they are about the Felds, my
Polish-born maternal grandparents, and the Carbonas, their next-door
neighbors from Southern Italy. Here are a few of them.

Both families had come to America in the early years of the century.

After several years of struggling in New York and Albany, my grandparents moved to Rochester, drawn by the opportunity to find work as custom
tailors in the city that was rapidly becoming the center of the men's clothing industry. Wolf Feld (who became known as William) took a job at
Hickey-Freeman's. His wife, Celia, did piece work at home.

The Carbonas, John, a shoemaker, and his wife, Jenny, came to Rochester a few years later. Within a short time the two families became next-
door neighbors. Each family had mortgaged itself for life, purchasing
nearly identical houses on a street that would be known a half-century later
as the border of the "riot area."

*Originally published in *Congress Monthly*, November/December 1986.

The two men, both quiet and thoughtful, rarely engaged in lengthy discussions. But they were good friends. Their wives, two poorly educated street philosophers with different worldviews and religious orientations—one was a devout Catholic; the other, like her husband, an active member of the Workmen's Circle and secular Jew—were close companions and fellow confidants. In accents that were nearly perfect echoes of those heard in *Abie's Irish Rose* and on *Life with Luigi*, they shared their hopes and their fears. They gossiped. And they argued about everything.

Together they watched the world around them change. They watched their families grow up. The Carbona children, Roma, Jimmy, and Leah, stayed quite close to the nest, remained in the immediate neighborhood, and raised their own families there. The Felds went farther afield. My Uncle Harry, a violinist, took a teaching job in South Carolina and eventually moved to New York; his younger brother, Sam, joined the Indian Service and spent his entire career in the Dakotas. Both of them, and my mother, Lillian, who moved to Syracuse, then to the northern Adirondacks, then to Tucson, did keep in touch with the old neighbors. For years they exchanged letters and holiday greetings.

The older women remained close. They attended parties in one another's homes. My grandmother dressed up for Carbona christenings and confirmations and weddings as if they were for members of her own family. On Easter Sunday a troop of Carbona children and nieces and nephews marched through our parlor showing off their finery. On Christmas delicious pastries were delivered to our house by those same children. And quid pro quo, almost every week plates of gefilte fish and paprika-speckled chicken and pots of soup with homemade noodles were taken next door to be enjoyed by the Carbonas.

The families shared hard times as well. One of my most vivid memories was my grandfather's funeral, when the rabbi called the names of those most carefully chosen to bear his pall. He read from the list my father had prepared: Rose, Berman, Astrachan, Greenstone, Pelton, and Quadrozzi. Mario Quadrozzi was Leah Carbona's husband.

Funerals inevitably involve reminiscing—and cosmic thoughts. Shortly after my grandfather died, my grandmother and Jenny Carbona, by then both in their late seventies, were sitting on the sun porch of our house, slowly swinging back and forth on an old-fashioned glider. My wife and I were inside. The window was open and we eavesdropped on a fascinating discussion about life and death and religion. Finally, trying to give some closure to an obviously irreconcilable difference of opinion, we hear my grandmother say: "You know, Mrs. Carbona" (she was always *Mrs. Carbona*), "I figure it this way. We got the father. You got the son. So what?"

Mrs. Carbona thought for a moment then said to Mrs. Feld (she was always *Mrs. Feld*), "You right."

Neighborhoods change and, as Jerre Mangione relates in an afterword to

the new "Morningside Edition" of *Mount Allegro*, his did, too. Young
people leave. Old people die. New people move in. The rhythms of life are
affected. The sounds and smells are different. The faces often are different
too.

Sometime in the late 1950s, the people next door to our house moved
out and sold their home to a black family. Mrs. Carbona was very upset; so
were many others on the street. My grandmother, perhaps more liberal
because of the attitudes of her commitment to socialism or because of the
attitudes of her college-educated children and politically active grandchildren—or perhaps because her second son had married a Cherokee woman
from Oklahoma in the early 1930s—was deeply disturbed at the attitudes
of her neighbors. On the same old glider she admonished Mrs. Carbona,
reminding her what it was like forty years earlier when the local residents
opposed the intrusion, as they saw it, of Italians and Jews.

"They're different," I heard Jenny Carbona say. "*Ma sono negri.*"

My grandmother argued and argued, but to little avail. Mrs. Carbona
was not going to be budged. Nor were the others. They were worried
about their neighborhood; worried about their property values.

Still, the black family moved in. Mother, father, and five little kids.
Most of the people on the street seemed to ignore them; to treat them as if
they were invisible. But my grandmother saw them and welcomed them.

Soon the children were in and out of our house, ever eager to enjoy
some pint-sized loaves of twisted bread, *challa*, that "Mimi" made for them.

Not long after they had become part of the local scene, I happened to be
in Rochester. I asked my grandmother how things were going. She told me
that Mrs. Carbona was still somewhat upset and that, in part, she had a
point. I was not surprised that Mrs. Carbona had not yet come around, but
was troubled by my grandmother's seeming change of heart. I pressed her
a bit for an explanation.

"Well," she said, "they are young people and we are old. We like peace
and quiet. They're very noisy. Maybe we've forgotten what it is to have
many children running around."

"But," she added with a characteristic shrug, "it will work out."

Two years later, she became very ill and had several lengthy bouts in the
hospital. My mother and I made the painful decision that since she could
no longer manage alone, we would have to sell the house. We put it in the
hands of a local realtor. We said there were to be no restrictions of race,
creed, or color. He found us a buyer almost immediately, a young man
who, it turned our, was a recent arrival from the *Mezzogiorno* who had
come to work at Hickney's. In an age of accelerating change, it seemed that
history was repeating itself. The Carbonas were delighted.

Another year passed and I was back in Rochester to see my grandmother, now living permanently in the Jewish Home. Not having a place
of our own, I stayed with the Carbonas. Late one night I returned from the

Home to find Mrs. Carbona, then eighty-five, still awake, waiting to serve me some of her jet black coffee and specially prepared *meringhe*.

We talked for a while and, still curious about "race relations" in that little corner of the world, I asked her how she felt about the neighbors.

She replied with animated vehemence. Wringing her hands, she exclaimed, "They're terrible. They don't seem to like us. They don't behave nice."

"The Negroes?" I asked her.

"No," she said, "they're O.K. It's those *ee-mee-grants*."

Unsentimental Journey

The teachers were mostly WASP, but nevertheless they knew their immigrant children. Some were kind to us and helped, others were rough. In the fifth grade I had a teacher, a Miss Prescott, who was forever telling us that her great-great-grandfather was the General Prescott of the battle of Bunker Hill. She would always talk to us in a very precise way; she always made us talk precisely too.

AARON KATZ

Aaron Katz and many other elderly Jewish immigrants, and Neil and Ruth Cowan who quote them and tell of their Americanization, offer us a richly documented evocation of a recreated milieu: the world of many of our parents and grandparents. While the Cowans' book is grounded in the frequently cited researches of many specialists on immigration and Jewish history who have analyzed the odyssey from émigré to hyphenated American, an understanding of that experience is enriched and deepened by their recorded reminiscences—the "oral histories"—of many aging friends and relatives.

Oral history, a fancy term for the verbatim recording of personal memoirs long used by ethnographers studying non-literate societies, has become a popular method employed by journalists, sociologists, and historians of immigration. As the late Barbara Meyerhoff so aptly demonstrated in her award-winning volume, _Number Our Days_, the technique is especially useful in getting information from those who represent "the last of a generation," those who are, quite literally, a dying breed. But, as Myerhoff was ever wont to point out, to be successful, oral history must be practiced not as a passive exercise on the part of the interviewer but as an interactive process between the questioner and the storyteller, the former stimulating nuanced recollection to try to minimize the pitfalls of selective memory and the understandable desire to tell "good" stories.

*Review of _Our Parents' Lives: The Americanization of Eastern European Jews_, by Neil M. Cowan and Ruth Schwartz Cowan. Originally published in _Congress Monthly_, vol. 57, no. 1, January 1990.

Authors Neil Cowan and Ruth Schwartz, respectively a public-affairs consultant in New York and a professor of history at the State University of New York, Stony Brook, are to be commended for their adroit employment of the technique. Using what they learned as both primary data and illustrative material, the Cowans take their readers on a refreshingly unsentimental journey back in time, back to the encapsulated world from which their fathers and mothers came, then forward to and into the New World where, with millions of others, the greenhorns became Jewish-Americans, a special variant on the uniquely American social construction, "the *American* ethnic group."

"The immigrant Jews—our parents and grandparents, the men and women we interviewed," the Cowans write, "were different [from other 'ethnics'] precisely because they were Jews. They assimilated to a culture whose everyday structure was overwhelmingly Christian, a paradoxical situation that did not exist for Irish, Italian, Greek, German, or Swedish immigrants."

Each of the Cowans' eight chapters is an essay on some aspect of the phenomenon of being Jewish in a secular-Christian *and* open society; each a commentary on acculturation powerfully enriched by excerpts from interviews with "Aaron Katz," "Irving Farber," "Jennie Grossman," "Charlie Moses," and many others who, assured their real names would never be revealed, were encouraged to tell as much as they could about their everyday lives in the old days (meaning the turn of the century, for all of those interviewed had come to America between 1895 and 1915). Beginning with the question, "Tell me the earliest memory you have of your childhood," the old folks were then asked matter-of-fact queries about such mundane aspects of living as the physical layout of homes and neighborhoods, the sorts of facilities and amenities they had, the numbers of persons sharing their space. They were also asked about more personal matters—health, sex, attitudes toward education, experiences in the workplace; and about social relationships within their communities and with those who were both nemeses *and* mentors: the *goyim*.

The approach worked well. The Cowans got people to unburden themselves, sometimes in unanticipated ways. They discovered, and conveyed, many interesting "findings." For example, they found that contrary to the stereotypes of loving, supportive, and happy Jewish families devoid of the serious problems that beset others, many had had domestic difficulties, sometimes quite serious ones; that not all were puritans, ever faithful, ever sober; that instead of belonging to communities of highly charged political activities, distinguishable only by the radical banners under which they marched, most were apolitical and many were hardly what would today be called "intellectuals." The Cowans show that while pride in the achievement of children was real, generational conflict was rampant and communications between parents and their offspring were frequently fraught with misunderstanding. They give ample evidence to explain what it meant to be truly marginal, living in but not yet of America. They, and their storytellers, offer important insights into what it took, then what it meant, to make it in this country.

Despite all the tumult, the conflict, the anxiety, the fears, and the dreams which were endemic to the estate of those they studied, the authors write that "never before in the history had Jews found themselves assimilating to a culture quite like America in the early days of the twentieth century: expansive, expanding, growing more secular with every passing year. Unable to turn to their parents—even could they have heard the questions—had no answers, they created a culture, a Jewish culture, all their own." In a fitting denouement, they quote one of their interviewees, "Sam Smilowitz," who told them:

> "It is the most fantastic thing in the world to be an American. It is unbelievable! Pie in the sky! Streets are paved with gold! We have fallen into the most wonderful world conceivable. I am always astonished by it. I can't imagine how lucky can I get, could I have been, to have been born at this time, to have been spared my ancestors' hardship in Europe."

Going to the Mountains

I F RIP VAN WINKLE had slept a while longer, say, two hundred years instead of twenty, he would have *really* been amazed to see the dramatic change that had taken place around him. Sleepy hamlets would have turned into bustling towns; farming would have been mechanized; unbelievable horseless carriages would be sputtering over hill and dale, and all sorts of newcomers would be coming into the area—including a cluster of Yiddish-speaking city folk seeking respite from crowded tenements and musty factories. Needing to "take the air," the Jewish sojourners would spend a few days or a week or, perhaps, a fortnight in old farmsteads turned into boarding houses or in places they called *kuchaleyns*, a "Yinglish" term for a room or set of rooms where you cooked for yourself.

The Jews who went to Rip's mountains in the early days of this century were, in reality, a third wave—and a vanguard. According to Stefan Kanfer, those called "Hebrews" had been to the area well before the American Revolution and some, mainly from Germany, had not only peddled their wares throughout the region during the first half of the nineteenth century but also tried to settle in, to become farmers themselves. A handful of utopians had even tried to establish their own little peaceable kingdoms, including one appropriately named *Sholem.* They found the mountains to be a pretty inhospitable place where a combination of social and economic—to say nothing of cultural and religious barriers—repeatedly thwarted their good intentions. In time, most of the Jews who went into the region intending to stay grew disillusioned and returned to the city. A few who remained were later to offer lodging to those so puzzling to our imaginary Rip and his descendants.

Within a decade after the onset of the great migration of East European Jews began to alter the character of urban America, Rip's turf would begin to undergo its own metamorphosis. With accelerating speed it was trans-

*Review of *A Summer World: The Attempt to Build a Jewish Eden in the Catskills*, by Stefan Kanfer (New York, 1990). Originally published in *American Jewish History: An American Jewish Historical Society Quarterly Publication*, vol. 79, no. 4, Summer 1990.

formed from a modest refuge for hard-working men and women seeking temporary asylum and a chance to clear their lungs into a glitzy retreat for the nouveaux riches. Soon grand hotels began to dominate the landscape. Eden was rapidly becoming "The Borscht Belt."

Within the confines of the area, hoteliers provided their clientele with something that was familiar even as it was different. The paradox is explained by the clever idea of offering Jewish food, Jewish entertainment, even Jewish traditions (like religious services, especially on the High Holidays) in a pseudo-Gentile resort atmosphere replete with indoor games and dancing lessons and outdoor sports—swimming, boating, horseshoes, golf, skating—and other kinds of special activities geared to families, couples, and, especially, to "singles."

Owners, managers, and social directors relied heavily on the growing desires of those who, though hardly steeped in a tradition of rural romanticism, increasingly saw themselves as taking playtime in the country. They were quite willing to shell out hard-earned dollars for the amenities proffered by those who catered to their whims and their status-anxieties. Describing the growth and development of the Jewish resort industry, Kanfer suggests that the great commentator on Jewish life in America, Abraham Cahan, got it right in his wonderful novel, *The Rise of David Levinsky*. There Cahan described an early Catskill resort, "Rigi Kulm." (If *David Levinsky* offered a portent, the recent film *Dirty Dancing* and the word-pictures painted by Jackie Mason in his one-man show on Broadway a few years ago provided us with an equally half-real, half-caricatured retrospective of the whole scene, just before it was to change forever.)

In time the Rigi Kulms of the "Jewish Alps"—Grossingers, The White Roe, The Concord, The Lakeside, the Nevele Hotel and Country Club, and many others—became not only places to spend a holiday but places to be seen and to be discovered. As the ever-escalating competition between them increased, so, too, did the need for innovative shows and more and more entertainers. The hotel circuit became the testing ground for talented singers, vaudevillians, and stand-up comics, many of whom were to go on to become headliners and stars. Their ranks included Eddie Cantor, Jan Peerce, Robert Merrill, Danny Kaye, Milton Berle, Sid Caesar, Jerry Lewis, Red Buttons, Gene Barry, Joey Bishop, Henny Youngman, Alan King, Buddy Hackett, Jackie Mason, Eddie Fisher, and Joan Rivers. Later, best-selling authors, popular psychologists, and with-it rabbis would also begin appearing on stage—and in seminars—offering a new brand of "enlightened" entertainment.

As readers of advertisements in newspapers as different as *The Jewish Daily Forward* and *The Sunday New York Times* would know, the Jewish celebrities and their ("honorary Jewish") Italian, Irish, and Black counterparts became chief attractions in the heyday of the Borscht Belt. And what a day it was! But it is over, or nearly so. The Catskills have not returned to their pristine character à la Washington Irving to be sure; but neither are they the raucous realm of Jewish acculturation that made them a special place to two generations of new Americans. In those resorts that are struggling to survive, every effort is made to adapt to the changing social scene. A recent example is illustrative: In February 1990, one of the most venerable of the old hotels was promoting weekends not for the traditional target population of "singles" but for *"single parents."*

Kanfer's lively anecdotal history fills in the blanks for readers who have only a vague notion of what "the mountains" meant to Jewish New Yorkers and what its hotels' *tummlers* meant to American popular culture. While it includes discussions of the activities of others besides the hotel operators, entertainers, and guests—Jewish communists, bootleggers, mobsters, and Hasids, *A Summer World* is mainly the story of the growth of an industry geared to the insecurities of newcomers enroute to becoming fully participating Americans and of its general decline at a time when the *arrivistes* finally made it.

A sequel to *A Summer World* would likely show that, rapidly distancing themselves from the world of the ersatz Rigi Kulms, the grandchildren of those who went to the "Jewish Alps" now seem to prefer the real thing.

Maven's Delight

I

ALTHOUGH not a language maven like Edwin Newman or William Safire, I too, have long been fascinated by manners of speaking English. I collect oxymorons. For example: "same difference," "genuine fake," "ordered chaos," "cruel kindness," and "obligatory options" (a reference to built-in-heaters on cars sold in Florida for which the customer must pay). I am intrigued by metaphors: "America as a melting pot . . . a seething cauldron . . . a salad bowl"; euphemisms: "revenue enhancement" (for unwanted taxes) and "visa falcon" (for security clearance); slang expressions such as "awful" meaning wonderful and "gross" meaning terrible; and acronyms of all sorts: NATO, AIPAC, NOW, CORE, and FAIR (the last standing for the rather restrictionist Federation of Americans for Immigration Reform, sometimes called by its opponents, unFAIR).

I am also interested in those "foreign" (meaning non-English) words that have become so common in everyday use they no longer require italicization. Many are French in origin: accolade, aide, bloc, camouflage, chalet, chef, chic, commune, crèche, critique, cul-de-sac, debris, detour, divorce, elan, gauche, laissez-faire, liaison, macabre, nuance, panache, pari-mutuel, penchant, sabotage, sauce, savant, tour, and thousands more. Some are Spanish: Casanova, guerrilla, patio, peon, poncho, posse, and veranda. Some are German: gesundheit, kindergarten, realpolitik, rucksack, wanderlust. Some are Italian: brio, cognoscenti, concerto, novella, pasta, tempo. A few are Hindi: guru, pundit, pyjama, yoga. We use Japanese words without thinking about where they come from, words like futon and tycoon; and Chinese words like kowtow and typhoon; even Anglo-Indian ones: calico, dandy.

Then of course, there are the many German- and Hebrew-rooted Yiddish terms and expressions that have also become a part of the continuously evolving American language, a very special part. Such words and sayings, and the manners of speaking which add so much pungency to the

*Review of *The Joys of Yinglish*, by Leo Rosten (New York, 1990). Originally published in *Congress Monthly*, vol. 57, no. 5, July/August 1990.

popular culture, are worthy of serious research. They have already been the subject of learned discourses by ivory-tower linguists. They are also—actually, mainly—the source of continuous and equally intense debate among those who know it best, the cornerstone kibbitzers now resident in the Jewish Home(s) for the Aged from Manhattan to Miami.

Those who have examined the process note that some words are taken over directly from what might well be the ultimate oxymoron, *pure Yiddish*. Some are metaphrases, literal translations put into English. Some, indeed, many, are examples of verbal acculturation (i.e., "literary mishmash"). Finally, there are English constructs with Yiddish- or East European-Jewish syntax and/or inflection. All are parts of those *American* figures of speech the well-known novelist, raconteur, and lexicographer Leo Rosten calls "Yinglish."

Rosten's latest volume gives plenty of examples of each. In the first category are commonplace terms heard throughout the country, spoken these days not only by Jews but by those who have no more idea of their origin than they do about detour, pyjamas, wanderlust, typhoon, and dandy. A sampler must include all those "k" words like kibbitz, klutz, kosher, and kvetch, as well as chutzpah, glitch, mensh, nebbish, nosh, shlep, yenta, and zaftig. (Rosten claims that at least 400 individual words from Yiddish are now a part of colloquial English.)

In the second case, there are expressions like "bite your tongue" (*bays dir ditsung*); "a hole in the head" (*lokh in kop*); "Big deal!" (*a grosyer Kunst*); "knows from" (*vos vays ikh fun . . .*); "likewise" (*mir oykh*); "talk to the wall" (*red tsu der vant*), as in, "Talking to you is like talking to the wall!"; and "Enough!" (*Genug!*).

Under the third rubric are all those wonderful new American-Yiddish or "Yinglish" words like boychick, cockamamy, f'r instance, gunsel, moxie, nudge, nudnik, shamus, shlock, shmo, shnook, shtik, tush; and statements like "Oedipus, shmoedipus!" and "Art-shmart, I call it garbage!"

Finally, there are the Anglo-Yiddishisms. Many are sparkling words like "regular"—as in "He's a regular guy, a real person if you know what I mean," refulgent phrasings like "So sue me!" and "All right already!," and what Rosten calls stratagems of mockery, irony, or contempt: "Look who's talking"; "Smart, she isn't." Usually terse and to the point, sometimes these linguistic artifices are enhanced by a bit of storytelling. To get the full effect, they require a build-up before the put down. F'r instance:

It is told that when John Austin, the Oxford philosopher some time ago, said that in every language he knew a double negative came out affirmative but he knows of no language where a double affirmative came out a negative. From the audience, philosophy professor Sidney Morgenbesser is reported to have said (in classic Yinglish): "Yeh, yeh."

Interesting, *n'est ce pas?* . . . er, *nu?* But what does it all mean?

II

Consider a well-known advertising poster widely displayed in New York some fifteen to twenty years ago. Godfrey Cambridge, or a young Asian-looking man, or an American Indian, each is portrayed holding a sandwich above the caption: "You don't have to be Jewish to like Levy's rye bread." Can the same be said about Yinglish?

While increasing numbers of white bread–loving Americans are larding (poor choice of word I admit) their language with "Jewish" terms, expressions, and intonations without realizing where they come from, there is little question but that Jews know and seem to get special pleasure in *their* contribution to the ever-changing American language.

"What are you," you might be asking in a tone properly edged with sarcasm, "a sociologist?" In fact, I am. Trust me.

The fact is that Yiddish and Yinglish cognoscenti (mavens?) are readily ranked along both ethnoreligious and geopolitical axes. Put in plainer English, the most attuned to the nuances are Jews living in the heartland of Jewish settlement—New York, New York—or in any of the other incubators of Yinglish like the Windy City, Miami, and L.A. They know it best. Next are Jews living in the suburbs of Long Island and New Jersey along with many adult members of New York's other ethnic communities and Big Apple politicians of all stripes and their California counterparts. Then there are the Woody Allen buffs, even Gentiles living in Minnesota, who *think* they get it. Finally there are those, maybe millions, who watched *Chicken Soup* on TV in the fall of 1989 and found Jackie Mason weird and wonderful instead of an embarrassment to those who *knew* what he was talking about and many of the allusions.

III

To many, television is a principal font of Yinglish for those in the hinterlands. But, according to Rosten, it is far from the only source. In a recent article, "From Yiddish to Yinglish," in *Encounter*, Rosten offers a somewhat more detailed explanation of how it happens that the words and phrases of a particular minority have become so much a part of the lingua franca. While most often heard on television today, Yiddish English has been infiltrating the popular culture for years. It has come in via the cryptic comments of comic strip characters drawn by Harry Hirshfeld and Bud Fisher and Al Capp; the quips of vaudevillians like Jack Benny, George Burns, Milton Berle, and the Marx Brothers; the songs of Tin Pan Alley and Broadway; on the radio (*The Fred Allen Show, The Goldbergs*); the commentaries of syndicated columnists such as Walter Winchell and Leonard Lyons; the fiction of Irwin Shaw, Norman Mailer, Herman Wouk, Philip Roth, Jerome Weidman, Saul Bellow, Joseph Heller, Bernard Malamud,

Stanley Elkin; the movies; even through the stories and columns of such non-Jews as Damon Runyon, O. C. McIntyre, Jimmy Cannon, and Jimmy Breslin, writers who caught the fever and spread it.

Rosten's newest book elaborates on these themes with rich examples and humorous asides. In many ways, it is very much an extension of his other "dictionaries" of Jewish Americana. So what else is new?

Not an awful lot. The alphabetical A–Z format with the interspersing of definitions with anecdotes is familiar to anyone who has read Leo Rosten's earlier lexicographies. Yet, even if some of the text is a bit too familiar to those who know his other books, *The Joys of Yinglish* is fun for all to browse through, non-Jews and Jews alike, as they all try to play those intergenerational parlor games called "I bet you don't know what this means?" and "Tell me where this word (phrase, expression) comes from?"

Read it, you'll like it.

JASPs

"JASPS," I once wrote rather facetiously, "are *Jewish* Anglo-Saxon Protestants." It was a throwaway line but it did provide a new sociological acronym to refer to certain upper-class Jews who, while not religious converts to Christianity, seem more comfortable with the manners and mores of Episcopalians and Congregationalists (the descendants of the Puritans) than with those of their putative *landsleit.*

My label referred to those who want to eschew their "Jewish" traits in order to assimilate, to be seen as *Americans* first, rather than as Jews. It is not easy to accomplish. Even the most assiduous in their pursuit of acceptance seem ever conscious of their background and ever aware that others know it too. Such people have often been described as those who can't live with their ascriptive identities and aren't permitted to live without them.

Henry Morgenthau III, a Deerfield- and Princeton-educated writer who is the son of a United States Secretary of the Treasury and the grandson of an American Ambassador to Turkey, is author of a family history that offers many examples to support such a view. He describes growing up in an atmosphere in which being Jewish—despite numerous attempts to mask it or, at least to underplay it through all sorts of patterns of avoidance of Old World traits and adoptions of WASPish ones (like celebrating Christmas and holding Easter egg–hunts)—was seen as "a kind of birth defect that could not be eradicated."

In Morgenthau's bulky book, such self-conscious concerns about status and acceptance—his own and those of the others he describes—are leitmotifs running thorough some thirty chapters. In the introduction he says, in respect to those whose story he is about to tell, there is "one constant— that elusive, amorphous something called 'being Jewish,' generating love, hate, pride, and fear, it remains inescapably present." Still, for all the concerns about being Jewish and trying to be, so pointedly detailed in the

---

*Review of *Mostly Morgenthaus: A Family History,* by Henry Morgenthau III (New York, 1992). Originally published as "A Singular Clan" in *Congress Monthly,* vol. 59, no.3, March/ April 1992.

book, it would be a mistake to characterize *Mostly Morgenthaus* as simply or even mainly a 500-page study in assimilationist angst. It is, for author and reader, something more: a richly detailed and loving tribute to a remarkable and socially conscious—as well as socially striving—family. It is also an interesting series of "takes" on some of the main events and key political figures of the twentieth century seen from an angle of vision quite different from that of professional historians or social scientists.

While bolstered by a wide array of the same sorts of source material the specialists might use—diaries, memoirs, memoranda, studies of the period, conversations with scholars and with kith and kin—this book was never meant to be an analytical assessment. It is, rather, a personal accounting, something between a triple biography and a family scrapbook, replete with two sets of photographs of many of those introduced to the reader in the text.

Part I, "Lazarus: Up and Out," is about the author's ambitious, inventive, aggressive, and highly erratic great-grandfather; the Germany in which he grew up and made and lost his first fortune; and the new world in which he tried to reestablish himself and his family. The second part, "Henry's Self-Improvement," is a detailed examination of his grandfather's rather calculated movement from the margins of ordinary society to the margins of High Society; from a practice of law dealing in real estate to involvement in Democratic politics; from the role of "token Jew" to his ambassadorship and critical involvement in debates over the future of Europe at the end of World War I.

Despite his financial and diplomatic success (most notably in protecting Christian interests in the Ottoman Empire and trying to reduce the suffering of Armenians), the first Henry Morgenthau never got what he wanted most: a cabinet position in the administration of the singular figure to whom he had hitched his wagon, Woodrow Wilson.

In "Henry Jr., the 100 percent American," the most interesting part of the book, Henry III explains how his father, a far more retiring individual than either the flamboyant Lazarus or the hard-driving Henry Sr., who started his adult life as a gentleman farmer and was, for a time, publisher of the *American Agriculturist*, was to become one of the most important figures in New York State and then in the federal administrations of his Dutchess County neighbor, Franklin Delano Roosevelt. Henry Jr. devoted his life to public service and he was amply rewarded.

The author describes his father's service on the Taconic Parkway Commission and Agricultural Advisory Commission, then, in FDR's second term as governor, as Conservation Commissioner where, teaming up with such notables as Harry Hopkins, plans for what would become the Civil Conservation Corps and the National Youth Administration were first formulated. He tells of the important roles Henry Jr. played in the run-up to Roosevelt's first presidential election and in each of his four administrations, where he was both Treasury Secretary and adviser on matters that ranged beyond the traditional limits of his department's purview, including foreign affairs. He notes the significance of the fact that, despite his father's initial resistance to being seen as a special pleader for Jewish causes, after 1943 he became an outspoken and unabashed advocate. Henry Jr. worked diligently to aid the victims of Nazism and establish the War Refugee Board. Later, he became an active supporter of the new state of Israel.

The book, while centered on the lives of the three key figures, also includes colorful portraits of the members of their crowd—their business partners, political cronies, close social acquaintances (WASP, JASP, and other), interspersed with anecdotes about their distant and close relatives, especially wives and children. The first part is much more than political biography. It includes the author's remembrances of childhood and adolescence—happy times in the New York, Dutchess County, and Washington homes of prominent, well-connected, and powerful parents as well as bitter encounters with the stigma they wanted so much to eradicate. While the focus is on Henry Jr., we learn a good deal about his wife Elinor, confidante and friend of Eleanor Roosevelt, and their other children, brother Robert (the most politically active of his generation), formerly U.S. Attorney for the Southern District in New York State and currently the four-time elected District Attorney of Manhattan, and sister Joan, a physician. (Joan will be remembered by readers more for her coming-out party held at the White House in 1940 than for her many other activities and accomplishments, including her years on the staff of Mt. Sinai Hospital and, more recently, her directorship of the Health Services at Smith College.)

While not central to his attempt to recapture the past, Henry III also introduces his readers to the next generation, most notable "Henry the Fourth," actually named Henry ben Henry in an only partially successful compromise to satisfy Morgenthau tradition and Orthodox in-laws.

What the future holds for young "Ben" (his nickname) and brother Kramer is hard to say. Readers of their father's book will wonder whether what he has likened to a relay race—"with each succeeding generation [of Morgenthaus] getting off to a running start, [then] snatching the baton for the next lap"—will continue on the same course or turn off in a new direction.

I think it is safe to predict that if they follow the path "born-again" Henry III has decided to take—he is the first of the clan to enthusiastically embrace the religious Orthodoxy of his great-great-grandparents—*their* Jewishness at least will be less problematic. And few will ever think of the next generation of Morgenthaus as "JASPs."

Down East Jews

THIRTY-FIVE years ago, fascinated by the concept of "marginality," I set out to learn something about the lives of "isolated members of minority groups," focusing on small-town Jews and their neighbors. I quickly discovered that save for anecdotal material, there was a paucity of information on the subject.

Much of 1957 and 1958 was spent interviewing and corresponding with people who lived in villages having fewer than 10,000 residents (and most of them in far smaller ones) in non-metropolitan counties of New York State, western areas of Vermont, and northwestern Pennsylvania. All were communities where there were fewer than ten Jewish families.

Much of what was discovered from both Jews and Christians at the time, and in a follow-up survey of the memories and experiences of the original Jewish participants and their by-then grown-up children conducted eighteen years later, has been corroborated in the studies conducted by others in various parts of America, all far removed from the centers of Jewish concentration. To a person, each researcher has reported how different life was (and is) for the countrified but still essentially urban folk they met in comparison to those left behind in the ethnic enclaves of Boston, New York, Philadelphia, Chicago, and other big cities.

Although many investigators say that motivation for moving into remote areas was found to be far more economic than romantic, and all describe the difficult struggles the Jews had in overcoming entrenched attitudes about them (and about other strangers) and finding niches, they also tell of the satisfaction expressed by those who felt they could and did find "the best of two worlds." Their subjects, like mine, frequently spoke of the enjoyable pace of small-town living while saying they still managed to retain some sense of their roots, of their Jewish identity. They also indicate how the presence of the Jews often seems to have led Christian neigh-

*Review of *Crossing Lines: Histories of Jews and Gentiles in Three Communities*, by Judith S. Goldstein (New York, 1993). Originally published in *Congress Monthly*, vol. 60, no. 2, February 1993.

bors to recast generalized attitudes toward those with whom the Jews were invariably identified.

While having a somewhat different goal and examining places slightly to considerably bigger than what I defined as "small towns," in *Crossing Lines* historian Judith S. Goldstein provides further evidence of the pains, pleasures, and paradoxes of being marginal men and women, often having to assume the mantle of "Ambassador to the Gentiles."

Goldstein's book is about three communities in Maine: the city of Bangor, a center of the once-powerful timber industry; the exclusive resort area of Mount Desert Island; and the border town of Calais. Her social history of the three places and the people—natives (meaning Yankees not Indians) and newcomers, year-round residents and summer folk who lived in each of them in the century between the Gilded Age and the Reagan Era—is a welcome addition to the continuing examination of an important segment of American Jewry and to the broader study of the "exemption mechanism" (or "but-some-of-my-best-friends-are . . ." syndrome) in which clearly prejudiced people make exceptions to their proclivities to discriminate.

Crossing Lines is divided into three uneven parts, each focused on one of Goldstein's target communities. The amount of space given to each corresponds to both the size of the locale under consideration and to the relative size of the Jewish entity in each. Bangor, the largest of the three, is typical of many small cities in New England and the Mid-Atlantic states. It is a place to which many immigrants went in the late-nineteenth century, seeking opportunities for employment and new lives. While Jews had been in the area since the 1840s and a permanent congregation was organized in the 1880s, the largest migration took place in the period between 1890 and 1910. By 1889, Goldstein reports that there were 1,800 in Maine. (At the same time there were 66,000 Jews in Massachusetts, 110,000 in Pennsylvania, and close to 700,000 in New York.)

Unlike other parts of New England, there were few if any Sephardim in the censuses of Maine's Jewry. The earlier settlers—and some of those few, seemingly select Jews who were to summer near Bar Harbor (including the likes of Jacob Schiff and Henry Morgenthau, Sr.)—were German or of German origins, but most came from Eastern Europe after having spent a period of time in large cities along the eastern seaboard. The majority were poor, poorly educated, and, at best, semiskilled. They had little money and few possessions other than fierce ambition and a desire to realize their personal visions of the American Dream. As found to be the case in the hinterlands of New York, Vermont, and Pennsylvania—and in various states of the South, as well as in Colorado, Utah, and northern California—Goldstein also indicated that most who headed "down east" to Maine from Boston and New York were peddlers of dry goods and clothing. In time these "dealers" established small shops and department stores that were to become as commonplace as the Civil War monuments and band gazebos on the village greens. (They still are, as observant visitors to the places studied by Judith Goldstein and a hundred other Maine locales can see for themselves.)

For much of Maine's history suspicion of outsiders in general and Jews in particular was hardly uncommon. Finding acceptance was difficult. Sometimes it proved impossible, and the unwelcome newcomers would move on. Such, for example, was the case of some of the Jews who first settled in the towns of Eastport and Lubec and then moved to far more hospitable Calais, where they were to become an integral part of the wider community as well as the core group for other Jews scattered in even tinier places in Washington, Aroostock, and Hancock counties. Still, as those like the Cutlers of Bangor and the Unobskeys of Calais established themselves, provided needed services (mainly as retailers, but also as cattle dealers and, later, as doctors and lawyers), and became involved in community activities, the process of exemption seemed to take hold. "Our Jews," as some of the Gentiles were wont to refer to local acquaintances, were perceived as being somehow different—even when it was clear that some of them clearly fulfilled some of the old stereotypes, especially those relating to "intelligence," "shrewdness," and "financial prowess."

One of the paradoxes of life both for the minority group members and those in the dominant one in the sorts of places Goldstein writes about is that owing to their relatively small sizes, intergroup interaction, including informal meeting at a personal level, is far more commonplace than in big cities. Jews and Gentiles have daily opportunities to get to know one another at first hand. For the Jews, particularly those in the smallest towns, to have any social life at all such associations are crucial. Concomitantly, for such persons, acculturation to the ways of the "Yankees" is generally more rapid than for those who live in the highly ghettoized enclaves in one or another of the major urban centers.

Because there was a sufficient critical mass to have a congregation, and eventually several of them, the Jews of Bangor were never as isolated as those in the other two places Goldstein studied or the ones I visited years ago. Yet, many "Down East Jews," including those from Bangor, tried to eschew so-called "Jewish" traits and played down what might be construed as citified habits to become more like the locals. Goldstein remarks that "the Bangor Jews were proud that they were not like New York Jews. The Bangor style of being Jewish was to act and look like a Gentile."

Away from metropolitan areas, sociologists have found that the intensity of interfaith interaction generally varies according to relative separation from others of one's group (in this instance, in terms of how many Jews are nearby) and with the conspicuousness of the minority as an entity. The rule of thumb is that the fewer the number of Jews in a particular place, the greater the likelihood of personal socializing with Gentiles.

Acculturation involves more than adapting manners of behavior. It involved challenges to beliefs. In the case of Maine's Jews, the desire to become more WASPish had more to do with style, status, and acceptance than with apostasy. And it had, in the minds of most Jews, nothing to do with conversion. In fact, while parents encouraged their offspring to model behavior on those around them (to which the kids eagerly responded), one proscription was clearly expressed: no intermarriage. It happened of course, especially in the early days, and it is happening again, but for most of the period from the 1880s to the 1980s that is the time-frame of Goldstein's book, the wishes of most parents were realized. Endogomy was the rule, exogamy the exception to it. (On the latter point, she offers a glimpse into the estrangement of Maine's U.S. Senator William Cohen from his father's faith, caused, the author contends, by the local synagogue's refusal to permit him to become *bar mitzvah*, despite his preparation for it, because his mother was not Jewish.)

In my own research I found that despite the same concern about intermarriage and rejection of it by more, one-third of the Jews interviewed in the 1950s identified non-Jewish individuals as their closest friends. This high a percentage would have been a very unlikely finding in a survey of the attitudes and behavior of urban-dwelling Jews conducted at the same time and would probably still be rather unusual today. However, as Judith Goldstein shows, in what, to me, is the most important part of her book, relative separation and the size of the community are not the only variables that effect intergroup relations. Another important one is the social climate of the place itself. The workaday towns of Bangor and Calais had very different cultures than the resort region of Mount Desert Island, a place built on the idea of isolation and exclusivity, where super-rich "rusticators" from Boston and Newport, New York and Philadelphia rather than locals set the tone and determined the status hierarchies.

In each of the places she writes about, Judith Goldstein found that caste-lines of privilege that had denied even the most successful Jews full access to all the institutions of the communities in the past have given way to a true equality of opportunity. Her conclusion suggests that one can no longer assert with certitude what the historian John Higham wrote many years ago: "[While] assimilation improved their status, the Jews reaped more and more dislike as they bettered themselves."

"But They Don't Look American"

S EVERAL years ago a student of mine, with a name like Vickie Kim, gave me a personal example of why she felt it was difficult for Americans of Asian background, even those outwardly successful, to feel fully accepted in this society.

Early in the semester, she recounted, a new resident in her dormitory (whose name, which she told me, was distinctly Italian) looked her over very carefully, smiled, and asked her where she was from.

"Montclair, New Jersey," Vickie answered.

The questioner looked puzzled and so Vickie said, "Oh, you want to know where my parents are from?" [Long pause] "I told her, 'Monterey, California.'" As an afterthought, Vickie commented that "I never thought to ask her what country she was from. I mean," she said, "I just assumed she was American."

Obviously, her new housemate hadn't made a similar assumption. The problem was that Vickie didn't "look American."

Hawaii-born Ronald Takaki, professor of ethnic studies at the University of Hawaii, also a third generation American, relates a number of similar experiences in a new book, *Strangers from a Different Shore*. He tells his own story in an introduction aptly titled "Their History Bursts with Telling," relating how, as an undergraduate student at a midwestern university, he found himself constantly being invited to attend foreign-student activities, being asked questions about how long he'd been in the country, and repeatedly being complimented on his amazing proficiency in English. The American was assumed to be a foreigner, even by real foreigners and by those who are often described as "hyphenated Americans" themselves.

Given how commonplace such experiences are, particularly in areas where there are rather few contacts with large numbers of Asian Americans, it would be surprising if those with surnames like Chang, Nyuyen,

*This selection is based on a review of *Strangers from a Different Shore: A History of Asian Americans* by Ronald Takaki (Boston, 1989), originally published in *Newsday*, August 20, 1989, p. 15; and of *The New Chinatown*, by Peter Kwong (New York, 1988), originally published in *The Christian Science Monitor*, April 21, 1988, p. 17.

Singh, Kim, and Takaki did not have an overwhelming feeling of alienation, of being outsiders in their own land. Some do and it is debilitating.
Others find ways of adapting, sometimes using the classic practice of developing increasing pride in who they are and where they came from, through
selective interaction with others who share their labels and their identity,
through political mobilization. In such terms they are not very different
from the members of much larger if not always older immigrant groups,
especially those from southern and eastern Europe, who didn't seem to
"look American" either.

II

Despite a history of immigration that is as old as that of most of those now
labeled "white ethnics," dating back to the middle of the nineteenth century, many second-, third-, and even fourth-generation Asian Americans
are still considered as persons who are apart from rather than a part of the
main body of American society. To be sure, gross stereotypes have undergone a profound change in recent year. As I noted several years ago [see
Chapter One], no longer were those whose ancestors came from Asia
being seen as mysterious orientals, kowtowing inferiors, scabbing laborers,
or, as was the case for Japanese Americans early in World War II, dis-
loyal intruders. Such negative portraits were being replaced by far more
favorable ones. Beginning in the 1970s, "Asians" (usually meaning Asian
Americans) began to be described in the aggregate as calm, diligent, community-minded super achievers.

Recently a number of voices have been raised in protest against the
tendency of outsiders to define the reality of the experiences of the twenty-
odd "nationality" groups that fall under the broad Census Bureau rubric
"Asians and Pacific Islanders." They have called for ways of addressing the
general lack of knowledge about those sojourners, immigrants, and refugees who crossed the Pacific and stayed to become Americans.

Responding to the challenge, many have attempted to close the information gap, to help the general public realize that widely touted American
pluralism is not limited to whites and blacks and Latinos. In a surge of new
writing about the Asian in the West, many have focused on specific places
such as San Francisco's Chinatown or on specific issues such as the continuing debates over reparations for Japanese American internees. Takaki's
book is different.

Touching many bases, it is at once a comprehensive history of Americans not only from China and Japan but also from Korea, the Philippines,
India, and Vietnam; a fine sociological examination of their common and,
more often than not, different backgrounds, fates and experiences; and an
interesting commentary on the growing desire of young adults from all
sectors to "break the silence" and to be recognized as full partners and participants in their own terms.

Takaki's book, a careful blend of research, reportage, personal insight and critical analysis, is divided into four major sections. These are constructed both chronologically and communally. For example, in the third section, dealing mainly with the period from the early part of the twentieth century to World War II, Takaki discusses the settling of the Japanese and the rise of the second generation, the *Nisei;* the emergence of Chinese ghettos; the struggle of Koreans; the arrival of Asian-Indians—once called the "Hindoo Question," and the often-forgotten Pilipinos. His penultimate chapter describes the post-1965 period when, as a result of changes in our immigration laws, over half of all legal entrants to the United States came from Asia, including nearly one million Indochinese refugees.

Takaki's book concludes with a variation on what historians of American immigration have long called "Hansen's Law" (the expression refers to something Marcus Lee Hansen wrote in reference to Swedish Americans he was studying: "What the son wishes to forget, the grandson wishes to remember"). It is about Asian roots and the meaning of memory.

Beyond its rich ethnographic content, *Strangers from a Different Shore* is also a powerful essay about the character of ethnicity in contemporary American society; it fills a voice in public knowledge about Asian Americans and clarifies many misconceptions about their cultures, subcultures, hopes, dreams and demands.

III

The New Chinatown is another "insider's" book on Asian Americans. It has many common themes with others of its genre, not least a commentary on the label "model minority." To Peter Kwong, it is a misleading and somewhat patronizing stereotype often used by journalists and social scientists to characterize—and praise—those who, in the aggregate, seem to be especially capable of turning adversity to advantage, overcoming the odds, and "making it" in America. This, he says, is hardly a true reflection of a complex reality. Then, having offered the disclaimer, he goes on to do what he says the outsiders do, recounting how well many Asians have done in a society where many were convinced they were unassimilable, commending them for being such excellent exemplars (models?) of what can be done with drive, determination, and solid support from many families willing to sacrifice everything to see their children succeed! In fairness, he does also offer an important caveat: many is not all, perhaps, not even most.

Statistics on the achievements of Asian Americans do indicate that they are leading or close to the top in many measures of socioeconomic status. But such general findings tend to obscure important differences among the nearly twenty Asian and Pacific Island cohorts (the largest being Chinese-, Japanese-, Pilipinos-, Korean-, Indian-, and Vietnamese-American) and *within them.* The latter distinction is often overlooked or underplayed, contributing to what are legitimate concerns of those who worry about the effects of generalizing. There are numerous examples of success in many of the trans-Pacific migrant communities, but they are most often to be found in the ranks of those who are best prepared—socially, economically and, in many ways, psychologically—to function in the New World. Others, especially among the immigrant population, are limited in a variety of ways. They have a very hard time.

According to Kwong, most of New York's Chinese Americans, the main focus of his study, tend to belong to one of two such subgroups. There are the American-born "Uptown Chinese," who come close to fulfilling all the attributes of the model minority characterization. The others, the "Downtown Chinese," collectively represent a type of ghetto-dwellers familiar to students of an earlier period of New York's history: people who live in ethnic enclaves where they face discrimination from outsiders because of their background or color or inability to speak English, and where they endure exploitation from kith and countrymen who capitalize on their need to survive and the desire they often share with those uptown to give their children every opportunity to spring the trap that ensnares them.

In *The New Chinatown*, Kwong shows that Chinese-owned and operated restaurants and garment factories are the principal employers of thousands. While both businesses are highly competitive, there seems no shortage of jobs for those willing, as were their putative forebears, to work for "coolie" wages. Today's unskilled laborers, many of them illegal aliens, wait tables or wash dishes in places where local people gather and others go to "eat Chinese"; or they do piecework under appalling conditions reminiscent of those exposed by muckraking journalists a century ago. Even though many garment workers are organized, union leaders have difficulty forcing compliance of their unions' regulations in the closed and, in many ways, still-secret society.

Peter Kwong, a Chinese-born, American-educated political economist particularly concerned with the segmented American labor market, provides considerable evidence to show both the similarity of Chinatown to other urban ghettos and its unique features, not least its near-feudal structure, which is undergoing significant changes, and its social problems, which continue to plague the oldtimers and the new immigrants, too.

While Kwong does discuss the major social organizations and other elements of Chinatown's stratification system and its complicated polity, he fails to convey any sense of the vibrance of a community he claims is "dynamic." There is a sterile, reportlike quality in his writing. The result is that the reader learns quite a bit about the author's view of Chinatown but puts the book down thinking there is something missing. There is.

One never really gets to "hear" or "feel" or "see" the new Chinatown. Or the older one, for that matter. For that, one has to turn to writers like Ronald Takaki.

Some Americans From Asia

I N A RECENT issue of *Reviews in American History*, Sucheng Chan briefly
summarized the changing character of the historiography of the Asian
American experience. Chan noted that early writings tended to be tracts
attacking or defending trans-Pacific immigration in terms of the costs and
benefits to those *in this society* or equally ethnocentric assessments of the
difficulties of assimilating such "alien" people who did manage to come.
Later on the emphasis was to shift somewhat. There were some excellent
community studies conducted by members of the groups themselves; there
were critical assessments of public policies and governmental actions,
especially relating to the wartime relocation of Japanese Americans and its
meaning both for the victims and the society by sympathetic outsiders;
then came several books and a spate of magazine and newspaper articles
that seemed to turn those once viewed as pariahs into paragons, "model
minorities." William Petersen's *New York Times Magazine* article, "Success
Story: Japanese Style," January 9, 1966, in which that now controversial
sobriquet was first used, was, in many ways, a watershed. Since then, scholarship on the subject has taken off in a variety of directions, generating a
number of thoughtful studies which offer new insights into old debates
about the origins, motivations, and patterns of adaptation and acculturation of Americans from Asia and their relationships with others in this society.

Paralleling the new trend of research and writing is the redefinition of
the United States as a country of *racial* cohorts—White, Black, Hispanic,
Native American, Asian—rather than a "melting pot" or a "nation of nations." Such a characterization stems, at least in part, from policies devised
to redress the effects of past discriminations and to enhance inclusion of
those in the latter four categories, each an administratively designated
"minority." The term "Asian American," for example, which in the 1960s

*Review of *Asian Americans: Chinese and Japanese in the United States Since 1850*, by Roger
Daniels (Seattle, 1988). Originally published in *Reviews in American History*, 18, 1990, pp.
430–435.

became a positive—or at least neutral—substitute for the disfavored "Oriental," has become an even more generic rubric for those from some twenty different countries stretching from the "Near East" to the Pacific and including more than half the world's population. Those known by census takers, affirmative action officers, and many others as "Asian" (or "Asian American") today are not only from East and Southeast Asia— China, Japan, Korea, and the countries of Indochina—but may come from the Philippines and other Pacific Islands or from the Indian subcontinent. While recognizing its utility for certain political purposes, a number of specialists have voiced their concerns about the unintended consequences of arbitrarily putting all peoples from one geographic area—or those who seem to look alike—into one basket, blurring critical distinctions of culture and character. Their own responses are either to continue to limit the perimeters of inclusion when they use the term "Asian American," or to use it in its broader, currently fashionable sense—and then qualify it!—while favoring more traditional nationality-based or ethically specific labels.

Among scholars particularly sensitive to this problem is historian Roger Daniels who, despite his own title, *Asian Americans*, clearly sees the necessity of disaggregating the cohort. His new book is a history of two of the largest subgroups, Chinese and Japanese. (Daniels is also the author of a long interpretive essay, *History of Indian Immigration to the United States*, recently published by the Asia Society, in which he discusses yet another group which he sometimes defines as "Asian," too.)

Twenty years ago, Daniels alerted fellow historians to the fact that most of those who wrote about immigration history tended to focus on the "excludes" and on the patterns of exploitation and discrimination. He urged them to avoid the trap of writing only "negative history," which he described as "history that recounted what was done to these immigrant people rather than what they did themselves" (p. ix). His own early works, especially the two volumes, *The Politics of Prejudice: The Anti-Japanese Movement in California and the Struggle for Exclusion* (1962; 1978) and *Concentration Camps in North America: Japanese in the United States and Canada during World War II* (1972), themselves suffered somewhat from the syndrome he (and Chan) identified. But, based primarily on the archival record, they provided important baseline information and striking portraits— not just of action but of reaction—on which much subsequent scholarship has been based.

Asian Americans is something more. Here, while still relying on such critical documents, he clearly extends the scope and method of inquiry. He details the migration, reception, settlement, and development of the two American subcultural "provinces"—"Chinese America" and "Japanese America"—in a wider geopolitical setting, comparing their respective members to each other, to other "Asians," and to other immigrant populations. In the last instance, he contends that those whose histories he has closely examined are, in many important ways, similar to that of those who came from Europe. For example, the Chinese "coolies" were not unlike other contract laborers who came to America as temporary sojourners, intent on making money and returning home to enjoy a better life than those who stayed behind.

Like the Irish who preceded them and the Italians who were to follow, the Chinese, exploited by their bosses and resented by other laborers, were said to "work cheap and smell bad." They were relegated to the margins of society where they established enclaves with others who shared their fate and their culture and within which infrastructures were created based on old-country ties and indigenous organizations that both assisted them and, in many cases, controlled their actions. Like other immigrant groups, the Chinese—and, later, the Japanese—carved out occupational niches in the wider society as well. And, like many other groups, they suffered from the problems resulting from an imbalanced sex ratio. (As late as 1920, less than 10 percent of Chinese Americans were female.)

While they were similar to the European immigrants in certain ways, they were different as well; not just in their lifeways but in the way they were treated. Daniels quotes the observant Senator Oliver P. Morton of Indiana, chairman of a special joint committee of Congress of "The Chinese Question," who stated, in 1877, "If the Chinese in California were white people, being in all respects what they are, I do not believe that the complaints and warfare made against them would have existed to any considerable extent. Their differences in color, dress, manner, and religion were, in my judgment, more to do with the hostility than their alleged vices or any actual injury to the white people of California" (pp. 53–54). Twenty years later, some time after the passage of the Chinese Exclusion Act of 1882, the first piece of national origins–based restrictive legislation, another senator, George Frisbee Hoar of Massachusetts, claimed that "Chinese exclusion represented nothing less than the legislation of racial discrimination" (p. 54).

The Anti-Chinese Movement (and the subsequent Anti-Japanese Movement that took hold around the turn of the century) was more than a campaign to stop immigration. It was an effort to rid the country, especially in California and the Pacific Northwest, of "undesirables." The campaigns for restriction and exclusion were replete with racist rhetoric that was both protective of labor and jingoistic, a portent for what was to come in subsequent decades.

The first several chapters of *Asian Americans* deal with the coming of the Chinese, the efforts to keep them out, and the establishment of the community itself. The fourth and fifth are about the migration of the Japanese, who began coming to the territory of Hawaii and to the mainland of the United States in significant numbers around the time of the Chinese exclusion. Daniels notes that the country the Japanese left behind in the late nineteenth century was very different from the chaotic, poverty-ridden homeland of the Chinese. Japan was trying to modernize overnight, to move from feudalism into the industrial era. Emulating Great Britain, it saw itself as a world power, a place to be reckoned with. It was claimed that the Japanese authorities cared deeply about their émigrés, not so much out of humanitarian concern (though there is evidence that Japanese officials did try to monitor the treatment of their nationals overseas) but mainly that they should behave well so as not to bring disgrace upon the national honor and invoke the wrath of their hosts—lest they be viewed and treated as Chinese!

Daniels discusses many other ways in which the two groups differed. For example, "[while] there were clear similarities between immigrant experiences of Chinese America and Japanese America, there were even more important differences. Geographic distribution and patterns of employment were decidedly divergent, and the demographic history of the two groups was markedly distinct" (p. 155). For example, the Japanese group arrived later but its women—wives and "picture brides"—came sooner and in far greater numbers than did women from China. For the Japanese in the United States, the family was the core of the communal existence. Moreover, while *Nihonmachi* (Japanese enclaves of Japantowns) existed in many western cities where many were employed in wholesale and retail trades or in personal services, by 1940 more than half of the Japanese in the United States lived outside of such centers, working in agriculture, forestry, and fishing.

In contrast, the second generation of Chinese immigrants, the *Nisei*, were far more apt to take on many cultural aspects of the host society, even to the extent of confirming "Hansen's Law" by rejecting the ways of their fathers. The *Nisei* wanted to be American. Their incarceration, along with their parents, was not only a legal outrage but a blow to their self-images as good Americans.

"About the war's impact on Asian Americans," Daniels writes, "there can be no debate: it marked a crucial turning point in the history of each {Chinese and Japanese] community."

As an expert of the *Nikkei* (persons of Japanese ancestry) and, especially, their experiences during and after "relocation," it is not surprising that Daniels devotes most of chapter 6, "Asian Americans and World War II," to the plight of Japanese Americans, but he also mentions what is far less widely discussed, the war's impact on Chinese Americans. Moreover, as he correctly observes, despite very different wartime experiences (the fortunes of Chinese Americans rising somewhat as those of Japanese Americans plummeted precipitously), "the long-term changes for each community, however, were similar; in each instance, the center of gravity changed decisively from the Old World to the New."

Daniels describes the reintegration of the *Nikkei* and the changing attitudes of most Americans toward them and their homeland in the period from 1945 to 1960. He also discusses what was going on within "Chinese America" and the domestic spillover of postwar sentiments that linked images of Chinese people—here and abroad—to the shifting policies of the U.S. government toward China, a country alternatively viewed as a loyal ally whose brave soldiers helped to rid Asia of the Japanese Yoke, a Maoist's prison, and the source of years of debate about "Who lost China?"; then the place of "Ping-Pong Diplomacy"; and then, after the Nixon-Kissinger trip and the "Opening," as an ally in opposition to the mutually shared view of the menacing Soviet Bear. Most important here is Daniels's contention that, in sharp contrast to earlier times, the major dynamic in the Cold War era attitudes toward the Chinese was ideological rather than racial. It was not the "Yellow Peril" that aroused anxiety but the "Red Menace." Thus, depending on the time and the prevailing policy, there were "good" Chinese and "bad" Chinese. (There were—and are—also "uptown" and "downtown" Chinese, the rich and successful and the poor and encumbered, a subject discussed at length by Peter Kwong in *The New Chinatown* [1987], but only briefly considered by Daniels here.)

The last part of Daniels's book is about the recent past, when the trickle of renewed immigration that began in the 1950s became a steady stream owing to the sweeping changes of the Immigration Reform Act of 1965 which removed old restrictions, including the quotas of the 1920s, and gave equal access to petitioners from all over the world. The Refugee Act of 1980 provided even more opportunities for Asians, in particular those from Indochina (many of whom were "ethnic" Chinese). By 1985, more than 95 percent of all legal immigration to the United States was non-European, nearly half of it from lands across the Pacific (the rest from across the Rio Grande).

In what is perhaps the most interesting part of the book, the epilogue, Daniels offers his thoughts about what is happening today within the Japanese and Chinese American communities. Their members may be seen in a far more favorable light now than in earlier periods, but they continue to be subjected to stereotyping, scapegoating (the Vincent Chan case being the most notable but hardly only example), and both blatant and subtle forms of discrimination; they continue to wrestle with their own multiple identities and with their external referents; and their patterns of socialization, interaction, and exogamy belie the claim that the cohort is more significant than that of the group.

While lacking the verve of some recent highly polemical volumes and the visceral impact of the newest autobiographical ethnographies, Daniels's solid scholarship, clearly presented evidence, and closely reasoned arguments make *Asian Americans* a most useful text for understanding the history and reception and, to a limited extent, the social institutions of Chinese and Japanese Americans. It is also an important addition to the more general study of American immigration.

Writing About a Culture
of Racism

*In my view, racism, although the child of slavery,
not only outlived its parent but grew stronger and more
independent after slavery's demise.*

T HAT SENTENCE is, in many ways, the principal theme of this most welcome collection of essays by George M. Fredrickson, author of the
prize-winning books *White Supremacy* (1981) and *The Black Image in the
White Mind* (1987). Throughout its seventeen chapters, all but two of
which have been published previously (four as review/essays in *The New
York Review of Books*), Fredrickson argues for recognition of what he calls
"the autonomy of cultural racism" and for greater efforts by both historians and sociologists to show how this particular ideological construct,
deeply rooted in the fabric of society, affected (and continues to affect) patterns of power and dominance in this country. Contending that economic
and political factors are necessary for explaining racial exploitation in
America—and particularly southern—history, Fredrickson claims that
they are insufficient to account for the growth and persistence of what
might well be called America's second "peculiar institution," racism itself.
"America," the author hypothesizes, "was not born racist; it became so
gradually."

Since the papers included here were originally prepared for different
purposes, Fredrickson's "case" is not presented in a conventional fashion.
Yet, the theme is pervasive. It appears time and again as the author examines and, in many instances, reexamines the work of many historians of
slavery, racism, and social inequality in America.

The book is divided into three parts: assessments of debates about slavery and race in the Civil War period, the historiography of the nineteenth
century, and the character of race relations' policies and practices in the
United States and several other multiracial societies, including South Af-

*A review of *The Arrogance of Race: Historical Perspectives on Slavery, Racism and Social In-
equality*, by George M. Fredrickson (Middletown, Conn., 1988). Originally published in *Reviews in American History*, 18, 1990, pp. 256–261.

rica. In the last set of papers Fredrickson urges the broadening of the database for historians who "for the most part have refused to interest themselves in the theoretical grounds of their discipline and have avoided the kind of transitional or comparative approaches that might shed light on the origins and destiny of the modern world."

The first section, a series of enlightening and hardly controversial descriptions of important participants in the struggle to defend or abolish slavery, includes five papers addressing pro-slavery thinking and the roots of racism; the antislavery but clearly racist attitudes of the southern abolitionist Hinton Rowan Helper, author of *The Impending Crisis of the South* (1857); the ambivalent attitudes of Abraham Lincoln toward those he was responsible for freeing; a trilogy of commentaries on William Lloyd Garrison, Frederick Douglass, and Lydia Maria Child; and "The Travail of a Radical Republic: Albion W. Tourgée and Reconstruction."

I found the essay on Helper most interesting. Originally written as an introduction to a new edition of *The Impending Crisis of the South*, which Fredrickson claims is one of the most important single books published in the United States in terms of political impact, the essay focuses on the extent to which racial paranoia is deeply embedded in and arises from class consciousness and status anxiety. Here Fredrickson makes an important distinction between the pro-slavery racists and such anti-slavery racists like Helper himself. Helper, and many others—including some northern abolitionists—saw slavery as economically repressive not morally reprehensible. They wanted to be able to expand opportunities for free *white* labor hindered by the plantation system. They supported the movement to free the slaves without believing that they were either equal to white people or capable of adapting and competing in an open society. In a phrase, they believed them to be racially inferior.

The sketches of Garrison, Douglass, and Child, although originally written and published at different times, are combined to give a composite picture of three middle-class radical reformers committed to the ideals of a liberal capitalist society in which social distinctions based on meritocratic principles rather than inherited or ascriptive criteria ought to be the bases of social status and social mobility. Despite the abolitionist goals they shared, their backgrounds, experiences, religious orientations, and political proclivities led them to take different paths to achieve their goals. Fredrickson points to Garrison's anti-colonialist "perfectionist Christianity" and to Douglass's acceptance and elevation of the ideals and rhetoric of the American Revolution, in spite of his oft-stated outrage over the hypocrisy of a Declaration of Independence that had proclaimed the principles of justice and freedom as being for white men only. In Child's case, the issue is one of linkage, the emancipation of slaves being seen as a correlate to the struggles of white women like herself who were beginning to fight for gender equality.

Garrison and Douglass and, to a lesser extent, Child are familiar names

to general readers of American history; the same may not be said of Albion
W. Tourgée, author of the novel *A Fool's Errand*. While ostensibly fiction,
Tourgée's book described the rise of the Ku Klux Klan as a political organization established by prominent whites—not "rabble"—to limit the
powers of the federal government and prevent the enfranchisement of
freed slaves. As Frederickson shows, Tourgée also provided a critical assessment of what he saw as the failure of Radical Reconstruction to adequately prepare freedmen for citizenship or to offer what today would be
called "development assistance."

The second section is a seven-part critique of southern historiography
dealing with many aspects of slavery, Reconstruction and segregation, and
their effects on black and white Americans. In many ways, the first essay is
a reprise of the widely known controversy relating to Stanley Elkins's landmark book, *Slavery: A Problem in American Institutional and Intellectual Life*
(1959), in which, among other things, the view is posited that the "total institution" of slavery had a devastating effect on the psyche of blacks, leaving them with little sense of their own self-worth and few structural
supports. Many critics of Elkins recognized the problems of internalizing
disgrace but saw the relationship between the slave experience, black culture, and personality traits as far more complex. Some, like the late Herbert Gutman, pointed to the real strength of the unrecognized internal
organization of black slaves and to the importance of kin-relationships to
them. Gutman contended that the slave holders were not only generally
indifferent to the complex kinship arrangements prevailing in the quarters
but hardly aware of their existence. Fredrickson implies that many historians were equally blind to these facts of everyday life on the plantations,
which may have led to assumptions about slaves being devoid of norms and
values—or even a culture or subculture—of their own.

"The Challenge of Marxism" is a thoughtful and critical review of Eugene Genovese and Elizabeth Fox-Genovese's book, *The Fruits of Modern
Capitalism* (1983), in which the authors further develop (and modify somewhat) Genovese's general thesis that American slavery was a paternalistic
form of class hegemony, a position Frederickson argues is too narrow and
restrictive to fully explain the character of the institution and its effects on
both society and the members of the two principal and clearly interdependent racial cohorts, black and white.

The next chapter offers a series of perspectives on how historians of the
nineteenth-century South have dealt with the continuities and discontinu-
ities between antebellum and postbellum experiences and, more particularly, how they perceived the essential character of the (white)
South—whether basically democratic or aristocratic. Historians have long
been divided on the issue. A few, such as W. J. Cash and David Potter,
have claimed that in many senses, it was both. Theirs is not a fence-sitting
position. What is important is the angle of vision. Does one look at society

from the top down or from the bottom upward? (This "dual perspective" is discussed in considerable detail in R. A. Schermerhorn's seminal work, *Comparative Ethnic Relations* [1970], a volume somehow overlooked in Fredrickson's surveys.) In this instance, planters might well have viewed the world far differently than farmers—and certainly from slaves. It is in this context that Fredrickson introduces the concept of a "herrenvolk democracy," a label favored by sociologist Pierre van den Berghe, author of *Race and Racism* (1967) and many other books on the dynamics of intergroup relations. In such a society, certain groups, the *herrenvolk* (similar to the "Aryans" in Nazi Germany), are free to enjoy the rights and privileges of inclusion while others are beyond the pale, restricted by racial group membership imagined or real.

No writer on the historiography of slavery and the South can overlook the significance of C. Vann Woodward, whose work is the subject of one of the chapters. Acknowledging his own indebtedness to this mentor of many, Fredrickson boldly states that Woodward's *Origins of the New South* (1951) is "the finest single piece of scholarship and writing in the field of American history that has appeared in the past half-century or more" (p. 144). While many may disagree with such a definitive statement, few would dispute the importance of Woodward, whose best known book, *The Strange Career of Jim Crow* (1955), is reported to have been seen by Martin Luther King, Jr. as "the historical bible of the civil rights movement." In a critical essay on the book, its legacy, and its critics, Fredrickson suggests that the work set the agenda for historians of the late nineteenth and early twentieth centuries, then examines the work of some of Woodward's legatees and critics.

First there is Eric Foner's *Nothing but Freedom* (1983) and then Steven Hahn's *The Roots of Southern Populism* (1983) which, in rather different ways, both offer examinations of the curtailed hopes of "peasants" in the political economy of emerging capitalism. A third volume, Charles Flynn's *White Land, Black Labor* (1983), challenges Hahn's Marxist hypothesis that white racism can be best characterized as a form of class consciousness. Flynn, like many others, says Fredrickson, views the South of the period as having two overlapping social systems, one based on caste, the other on class. (This is a common theme in many early sociological studies of the post-emancipation South, particularly those by black scholars such as Allison Davis, Bertram W. Doyle, Charles S. Johnson, and Hylan Lewis.)

In a review of Joel Williamson's prize-winning *The Crucible of Race* (1984), Fredrickson praises, especially, its "biracial view" of southern history. But Fredrickson, the consistent critic of pure economic determinism, is also reluctant to buy into Williamson's overpsychologizing of "states of minds" removed from social, structural, or political considerations. Fredrickson's criticism here is based not so much on Williamson's psychocultural interpretation of the rise and fall of racial extremism but his tendency to overlook or underplay other factors. Still, Williamson's typology of liberal, radical, and conservative "mentalities" seems to me a most useful paradigm, especially for understanding differences between the racism of the 1880s (which he sees as conservative) and of the 1890s (which is viewed as radical).

"Slavery and White Supremacy: Comparative Explorations," part three, contains five chapter/essays. Each considers one or more studies of the social conditions under which racial attitudes emerge in bi- or multiracial societies. As in other parts of the book, Fredrickson's own research provides substantive bases for the assessments of others' work, yet here it is far more obvious than elsewhere, especially where he presents *his* views on "The Social Origins of American Racism," stressing the particular character of an ideology that emerges from a way of life and develops into a system of thought and continuing social practices, and in "White Images of Blacks in the Old South." In the latter, Fredrickson, turns his earlier interest in the black image in the minds of whites (the subject of one of his major books) inside out. He begins, once again, with Elkins's "Sambo" and such critics of the thesis as John Blassingame and Ronald Takaki (whose *Strangers from a Different Shore* [1983] addresses another example of American racism, that directed against those from Asia), and others.

In another essay, Fredrickson, especially in his comparison of American and South African racial policies (the subject of his book *White Supremacy*), builds an argument based, at least in part, on the writings of such sociologists as Pierre van den Berghe, Michael Banton, Sami Zubaida, and John Rex. What is particularly interesting is that mid-course in his essay, Fredrickson consciously shifts from a structuralist to a Weberian mode of analysis. Quite explicitly he calls for a rapprochement between historians and sociologists by proposing a framework for the comparative study of race relations in societies of colonial origins.

The last essay concentrates on segregation in the United States and apartheid in South Africa, extending and, to some extent, reformulating points made earlier in *White Supremacy*, in light of Fredrickson's own recent research and that of John Cell, author of *The Highest State of White Supremacy* (1982), Stanley Greenberg, author of *Race and State in Capitalist Development* (1980), and others. He shows how the comparative approach offers ways of seeing common themes and sharp differences, not least those relating to the presence or absence of judiciary systems capable of liberating blacks (and others) from political and legal oppression.

Reviewing a book that is, at bottom, a book of reviews is a challenge. Each essay provides the critical reading of an experienced scholar with very strong and well-grounded opinions about those whose work he knows well and with whom, in many cases, he has debated directly or in print over interpretations of the slave experience, the roots of racism, and the character and meaning of social inequality in the United States (and in other lands as well). I—and certainly those whose works Fredrickson critiques—could pick many nits over interpretations and emphases (in my own case regarding some of the sociological perspectives he favors and those he ignores), yet, on balance, I find this an amazingly consistent book—not only in the clarity of the arguments and the felicity of the writing but the persistent murmur of the leitmotif, sometimes "heard" more loudly than others but always there: American racism began first as a way of life in the Old South, then became a system of thought, an ideology that now pervades the entire social system.

Down Home and Up North

O NE OF the best-known Negro spirituals tells how "When Israel was in Egypt's land . . . oppressed so hard they could not stand" they left the country of their slavemasters for a "Promised Land." It was a fitting anthem for black Americans who hoped to escape the land of *their* former enslavement and continuing segregation. They longed to move "north to freedom."

Early in the twentieth century their own Exodus began. Demographers called it an internal migration, for they crossed no borders. But, for those who made the trip, it was like going to another country.

Escape from the racist policies of the Old South was not the only reason people wanted to head north. There were powerful "pull" factors as well, not least the promise of steady work and better wages in Chicago (their *Guldene Medina*) and other cities around the Great Lakes and the upper eastern seaboard. For forty years the flow flooded and ebbed, paralleling the rise and fall of the economy "down home" and up North. Still, as recently as 1940, nearly 80 percent of America's black population continued to live below the Mason-Dixon line, half of them in rural areas where the vast majority were sharecroppers.

The invention of the cotton gin in the late eighteenth century had revolutionized the cotton industry, served as the principal catalyst for the plantation system, and was one of the greatest stimuli to a vastly expanded traffic in human chattel. A century-and-a-half later the mechanization of cotton picking wrought a second major change in the Southern economy. According to Nicholas Lemann, in the days before mechanization, a good field hand could pick 20 pounds of cotton in one hour. The mechanical picker could now pick as much as 1,000 pounds an hour, each machine doing the work of fifty men. This was good for the planters but devastating for the sharecroppers. It was then that with few other means of making a

*Review of *The Promised Land: The Great Black Migration and How It Changed America*, by Nicholas Lemann (New York, 1991). Originally published in *Congress Monthly*, September/October 1991.

livelihood, vast numbers of rural blacks individually or in family- or communally-based groups, set out for the Promised Land.

For those who made the trek northward, much of the appeal would prove to be quite illusory. To be sure, some began with routine, menial jobs and then managed to pull themselves up, joining the slowly growing black bourgeoisie, and moving up and out of the ghetto before it became their permanent jail. But the others, the majority, would be left behind in "a world unto itself completely cut off from the institutions and mores of the wider society," an environment of despair where anomie prevails and disorder is worse than poverty.

Writing of the migration in the preface of his great novel *Invisible Man*, Ralph Ellison captured the promise and the pathos of the odyssey:

> In relation to their Southern background, the cultural history of the Negroes in the North reads like the legend of some tragic people out of mythology, a people which aspired to escape from its own unhappy homeland to the apparent peace of a distant mountain; but which in migrating, made some fatal error of judgment and fell into a great chasm of maze-like passages that promise ever to lead to the mountain but end ever against the wall.

While, as noted, such was a close to the reality of what hundreds of thousands of blacks did come to face in the Northern ghettoes that became their new homes, it does not speak to a powerful corollary to their migration: the impact of the great shifts in population were to have on those in the wider society, on white Americans outside the Black Belt for whom the Negro, for most intents and purposes, had been, as Ellison aptly put it, "invisible."

One of the principal theses of Nicholas Lemann's book is that the entire society, not just its black members, was to be profoundly affected by what happened in the mid-1940s, something only a few prescient observers had anticipated. Explaining that turn of events, directly attributable to the migration, is, to me, the most original and important aspect of Lemann's carefully crafted tale of three cities: Clarksdale, a small town in the Mississippi Delta ("the locus of our own century's peculiar institution": sharecropping); Chicago (whose South Side is "the acknowledged capital of Black America"); and Washington, D.C., which, though Lemann doesn't say it in so many words, is the policy-making capital of *white* America.

The Promised Land is a brilliantly conceived and imaginatively written multilayered sociological analysis of contemporary history. It tells the story of Ruby Lee Daniels Haynes and her family's and friends' and lovers' and rivals' experiences over fifty years after moving from the Delta to Chicago, a city whose black population grew almost exponentially from under 50,000 in the first decade of the century, to 109,000 by 1920, to 813,000 by 1960. It is also a commentary on this country's confrontation with the implications of that prototypical family's movement; an examination of the politics of race (detailed in a lengthy middle section on "Washington");

and an assessment of what has happened, due to the fabric of a society increasingly rent by racial confrontations and near-institutionalized polarization between the mostly white "haves" and the mostly black members of what some have come to call "the urban underclass" made up of those, like Ruby and the others, who left the Mississippi Delta and other similar places for a better place and a better life. Throughout the body of the book one feels the tension as the author builds toward a singularly depressing conclusion: neither Ruby nor the wider society have been able to deal with what race has done to both.

The Promised Land is, in many ways, in the rich tradition of the Chicago School of Sociology whose principal figure, Robert E. Park, was like Lemann an investigative journalist too. Like Park and his students (many of whom he quotes), Lemann does not limit his sociology to armchair speculation. He introduces those he had come to know thorough his exhaustive research; poor migrants like Ruby Daniels, caught in the vortex of a social maelstrom; local officials in the South and in the North; civil-rights leaders; Washington bureaucrats; key political figures in each of the post-war administrations, most particularly those prominent in the heyday of reform when a conservative Kennedy was forced to act and a pragmatic Johnson (signer of the Civil Rights Acts of 1964 and 1965 and shaper of the "War on Poverty") tried to make improving race relations the cornerstone of his domestic agenda; and the idea-men, too.

Lemann writes about Paul Ylvisaker, Nathan Glazer, James Farmer, Lloyd Ohlin, Richard Cloward, Michael Harrington, Saul Alinsky, Daniel Patrick Moynihan, and many others who were directly or indirectly involved in fashioning various campaigns to achieve the dual goals of abolishing racial injustice and reducing economic deprivation. He goes further, examining and trying to explain the struggles that went on between sometimes overlapping but often quite separable political *and* ideological factions over approaches to meeting these goals. In the former, for example, there were the conflicts between Kennedy's legatees, not least brother Bobby, and the Johnson people; in the latter, there were such disagreements as those over strategies between those in LBJ's administration who advocated Head Start- and Job Corps-type programs that Pat Moynihan, then in the Nixon White House as Domestic Adviser, was to label "Maximum Feasible Misunderstanding."

In an "Afterword"—one that tends to lean toward many of Moynihan's concerns—Lemann seems to reverse course, at least a little. He says that "thinking about the history of American race relations can easily give rise to bitterness and fatalism, but it is encouraging to remember how often in the past a hopeless situation, which appeared to be completely impervious to change, finally did change for the better." As evidence he offers the general progress of many blacks toward achieving middle-class status largely as a result of changes wrought by the civil-rights struggles. Fair enough. But then, like others frustrated by what they know of those who haven't made it and are falling farther and farther into the abyss of isolation, despair, and dependency but with few practical ideas of how to deal with the situation, the hard-hitting Lemann turns to the rhetoric of liberal compassion. He says, for example, "[The] real impediment in the short run is not lack of political support—which in racial matters always comes after the fact, if it comes at all—but the weakness of spirit."

That's what Ruby Daniels's pastor might have said, too, but, as Lemann knows and shows, "Over Jordan" imagery is not enough.

The Real McCoy?

―――――

I

The *Bonfire of the Vanities* is Tom Wolfe's Dickensian chronicle of Jimmy Breslin's beat. It is an epic tale of life and politics in New York. Sociological fiction (or fictional sociology, take your pick), it was written by an observer with a very sharp eye and a pretty good ear for urban types, New York–style. A technicolored tale of blacks and whites, Gentiles and Jews, Wolfe's book is filled with wrath and rage and well-drawn principals who are at once believable and also tintypes. This blending of character and caricature, together with a rather straightforward if melodramatic plot, succeeds in striking many responsive and chilling chords.

Bonfire is already a runaway bestseller and the topic of many talk-show debates where most of the discussion tends to focus on two issues: how accurate this story of class warfare and ethnic conflict *really* is, and if it is a reflection of reality, what effect will it have on race relations in New York and elsewhere across the country?

Whatever the answers, Wolfe, in whose opening pages a Koch-like mayor is being harassed by black demonstrators calling him "Goldberg," "Hymie," and other polarizing epithets, would doubtless say that the questions are irrelevant to *his* objectives. He is, after all, a founding member of the New Journalism and though a novel (Wolfe's first), *Bonfire* is in many fundamental ways another piece of his finely honed and evocative "tell-it-like-it-is" (or "how-I-think-it-is") reporting style.

While there are similarities, *The Bonfire of the Vanities* is quite different from his other works, and, especially, from the latest blockbuster, *The Right Stuff*, a lengthy exercise in narrative non-fiction that reads like a novel. *The Right Stuff* was full of heroes; *Bonfire* is almost completely devoid of them. *The Right Stuff* was a comic book writ large; *Bonfire* is fare for the tabloids—where, in fact, much of its drama is "reported."

*Review of *The Bonfire of the Vanities*, by Tom Wolfe (New York, 1988). Originally published in *Congress Monthly*, vol. 55, no. 4, May/June 1988.

The new book is a story about Sherman McCoy, a thirty-year-old WASP bonds trader who went to Buckley, St. Paul's, and Yale, and works at the venerable firm of Pierce and Pierce. He lives with his wife Judy and daughter Campbell on Park Avenue during the week and in Southampton on the weekends. Until his undoing, he knows little of the vast majority of his fellow New Yorkers and could care less about them. His comeuppance begins when he starts cheating on his wife with Maria Ruskin, a foxy young gold digger with a beautiful body, a Southern drawl, a penchant for excitement, and an aging husband, Arthur Ruskin, a Jew who runs an air-charter service flying Arabs to Mecca.

II

Driving back to Manhattan from JFK where he has gone to pick up Maria in his $48,000 Mercedes sports car, McCoy makes a wrong turn and ends up in the South Bronx. While trying to find his way out of that alien world, Sherman and Maria are confronted by a wheel in the roadway. He gets out to move it and two young black men appear. McCoy is confused and frightened. He panics, throwing the wheel at one of them. A brief altercation ensues, and, while he is out of the car, Maria slips into the driver's seat. He jumps into the passenger seat. She throws the car into reverse, hears a thud, puts the car into forward gear, and speeds off. Did they hit the smaller youth? they ask each other, each thinking that indeed they did. Despite Sherman's concern that they ought to report the incident, Maria talks him out of it. And they don't.

They had hit and knocked down Henry Lamb, breaking his wrist and causing a head injury so severe that he soon lapses into an irreversible coma. Before he slips away, Henry reports that he was run down by a two-door Mercedes with a license plate whose number begins with "R . . . " He says nothing about Roland Auburn, the other youth (who turns out to have a considerable police record), nor does he say who was driving the car—only that there were two people in it: a white man and a white woman.

The hit-and-run incident becomes the cause célèbre many have been hoping for, not least Reverend Reginald Bacon, a charismatic black minister, ward heeler, and clever manipulator of various dissidents ever searching for an issue to vent their ire at the establishment. He mounts a campaign to avenge the attack on Henry Lamb, whom he portrays as a squeaky-clean honors student from the Edgar Allan Poe Project.

Responding to the groundswell of support for those who want McCoy drawn and quartered, the fictional assistant to the mayor of New York puts the whole scenario into a single sentence: "The guy who hit the wrong kid in the wrong part of town driving the wrong type of car with the wrong woman and, not his wife, next to him."

Abe ("Captain Ahab") Weiss, the Bronx D.A., whose office spends most of its time prosecuting "minorities" and who is up for reelection in a county that is 70 percent black and Puerto Rican, sees great value in McCoy's undoing. The Park Avenue swell becomes Weiss's perfect foil for countering the arguments of Reverend Bacon and his minions and others who charge that there is only justice for white people in New York.

Among the other principal stokers of Wolfe's bonfire are Albert Vogel, a liberal lawyer who chases causes; Ed Fiske III, a representative of St. Timothy's Episcopal Church (a place that seems strikingly like St. Bartholomew's on Park Avenue); Peter Fallow, a down-and-out British journalist who writes for a tabloid, *The City Light;* Tommy Killian, McCoy's Irish lawyer; two detectives from the Bronx, Martin, another "harp," and Goldberg, who is said to be so tough "he acts Irish"; Annie Lamb, the mother of Henry, the victim; McCoy's Jewish boss, Eugene Lopwitz; his father, the Lion of Dunning Sponget & Leach; and a whole hive of fellow WASPs.

III

I said there are almost no heroes in *Bonfire.* One of the few is a tough little hawk-nosed, sharp-eyed judge, Myron (Mike) Kovitsky, who is the first to attempt to deal directly with the mobs who gather to seek vengeance and publicity once the culprit is identified and brought to dock.

McCoy, unsuccessful in covering up the act committed by Maria is found out and taken to "a prodigious limestone parthenon done in the early thirties in civic moderne style," the Bronx County Building on 161st Avenue. There he is treated like a common criminal and publicly humiliated by court officers, the press, and the people of the neighborhood. An innocent in the rough-and-tumble netherworld in which he finds himself, McCoy is totally unprepared for what he must face when he is officially charged with reckless endangerment, vehicular homicide, and leaving the scene of an accident—and accused of the additional crimes of indiscretion, haughtiness, and having been born on the right side of the tracks, of being a rich cavalier who cares nothing for the poor, fatherless youngster who never had his advantages.

McCoy's fall is precipitous. He, who first sees himself as Master of the Universe and is so regarded by his coworkers, cannot cope with his new estate. The ordeal of arrest and arraignment weakens him, turning him into a self-pitying cipher who nearly gives in to his thoughts of blowing his brains out with a blast from his shotgun. But he doesn't. Instead he is somehow reborn as a tough guy ready to take on the mobs that so unhinged him.

Reading about his sudden and dramatic transformation, I kept thinking what Wolfe's own characters would say about it: "Whatdayya, whatdayya? This don't ring true."

It doesn't. In fact, in the last part of this book of nearly 700 pages, the sense of versimilitude slips away as Wolfe, an American Tory, tries to make his fellow Yalie, McCoy, into something it is unlikely he would become. I could not but feel that the character Wolfe created would remain the old (and real?) McCoy, a con artist and survivor, though now admittedly older, wiser, craftier—like his adversaries, like Chuck Colson and John Dean.

The criticism looms large but should not overshadow the sheer power of *The Bonfire of the Vanities*, a book which is difficult to pick up (it weighs five pounds) and very hard to put down; a book filled with colorful, Wolferian word-images—anorexic ladies called "social X-rays" and tootsies on the arms of much older men called "lemon tarts"; attempts to keep the seething racial caldron from bubbling over called "steam control."

Despite my quarrel with the uncertain conversion of Sherman McCoy, I think Wolfe is accurate in suggesting that liberals are often conservatives who have been arrested—an inversion of an even more popular view that conservatives are liberals who have been mugged.

In a long essay on Tom Wolfe in *The Christian Science Monitor*, Hilary DeVries called him "the police reporter at the garden party," a chronicler of cultural revolutions. To his critics Wolfe says, "If you don't think this is a correct picture of New York today, then do your own reporting. I say you'll come back with what I did." They probably would, especially when they noted how much *Bonfire* reflects the lives of thirty-year-old Wall Streeters making a million bucks a year (at least until October 19, 1987), and the likes of Boesky, Goetz, Howard Beach, Hizzoner, and the separate slices of the Big Apple, some rotting faster than others.

Race and the American City

O N A gray winter morning not too long ago, Jim Sleeper, a middle-class Jewish, liberal-left journalist, got in line to buy a paper at a Forest Hills newsstand. A well-dressed black woman seemed to cut in front of him. He was annoyed. She was too, thinking, apparently, that it was he who was the queue-jumper. She jostled him and Sleeper blurted out, "I didn't do it to ya lady." She snapped back, "Well, it was your kind."

This brief anecdote, told in the beginning of a chapter aptly titled "The Liberal Nightmare," provides us with a capsule commentary on American urban race relations in our time. It is a theme that appears time and again in *The Closest of Strangers*, a depressing study in the sociology and politics of resentment, New York–style.

The Closest of Strangers is, in many ways, a complement to Tom Wolfe's controversial novel about New York, *The Bonfire of the Vanities*. It even has many familiar characters. But Sleeper's story ain't fiction. This time, the names are as real as are the paroxysms of a city, once the quintessential pluralistic society, that is being torn apart by polarization into hostile racial camps.

To explain how it came to such a state, Sleeper, then an editor at *New York Newsday*, reviews the history of racial and ethnic politics in New York from colonial times to the present. He focuses on two centuries of discrimination against blacks and describes the waves of immigrants who came to settle in the Golden Land with whom they had to compete in what, owing to persistent prejudice and restrictive practices, was never a fair race. Included are those from Germany and Ireland who arrived in the 1840s and 1850s and those who came later, Jews and others, mostly Catholics from Eastern and Southern Europe, sometimes collectively designated as "white ethnics." Sleeper examines the ascendancy of the postwar liberal agenda in which Jews played an especially prominent role, and attempts, some quite

*Review of *The Closest of Strangers*, by Jim Sleeper (New York, 1991), and *Devil's Night and Other True Tales of Detroit*, by Ze'ev Chafets (New York, 1991). Originally published in *Congress Monthly*, vol. 58, no. 2, February 1991.

successful, to build coalitions to end racial discrimination and promote integration. He discusses what he calls "the confluence of diverse radical currents that submerged that liberation tradition and tried but failed to replace it with a larger social vision," and he reflects on the plight of those in the working class (of all races) who often become scapegoats for those he feels most responsible for the current troubles: militant blacks and apologetic whites.

According to Sleeper, one significant result of the changes that have been taking place since the mid-1960s is that New York, almost from its beginning a living mosaic of cultural and religious as well as racial diversity held together by the tenuous glues of political and economic interdependence, is rapidly becoming an agglomeration of formally recognized *racial* cohorts: the "victims"—blacks, Hispanics, and Asians (each an officially designated "minority")—and the "oppressors"—whites (a residual rubric under which everybody else, the Jews and WASPs, the Irish and Italians, the rich and the poor, etc., are grouped). The newly institutionalized alignments are a logical if unpredicted extension of policies developed in response to those who demand and then were given group rights.

In making his case, Sleeper contends that somewhere along the line civil rights activists, contravening their own traditional ideology, changed their strategy, shifting from "demanding equality of individual opportunity, which entails color-blind respect for a person's merits and rights beneath the skin, to demanding equality of condition, which submerged individual dignity beneath a color-based emphasis on the putative rights of historically deprived racial or ethnic groups." In twenty-five years," he says, "[the federal] government moved from ensuring that people were not formally categorized on the basis of race to ensuring that they are so categorized today, whether they want to be or not." More often than not, Sleeper suggests, "liberal legalisms" embodied in such practices have led to the ossification of what Martin Luther King wanted to change when he said that he looked forward to the time when his children would be judged not by the color of their skin but by the content of their character.

Clearly opposed to the excesses of affirmative-action policies, Sleeper has been labeled by some as a "neoconservative," railing against the bleeding hearts and the black protesters with whom, his critics say, he would once have been clearly identified. Those who make such claims miss his basic point: race-specific favoritism and emphasis on victimization (and the rhetoric of "my suffering is greater than your suffering"), however well intended, has tended to aggravate polarization rather than enhance the entry of blacks and other minorities into the mainstream. Such practices have led to greater alienation of those who otherwise might be encouraged to form alliances to attack problems of mutual concern, at least those relating to poverty and crime and drugs.

A careful reading of Sleeper's text illustrated his awareness not only of the complexities of the situation, but of the tendency of too many to let the few strident voices of unreasonable separatism (and those who support them with cries of *mea culpa*) speak without challenge. Even so, there *are* places in the analysis where, I feel, Sleeper is too limiting in his assessment of the parties responsible for what is now happening in the racially tense city (there are other key stirrer-uppers besides the "black militants" and the "liberal apologists") and too quick to cast blanket condemnations over all of those in each of his targeted camps. Moreover, I worry that some of his generalizations about the current state of affairs and his criticism of much of the city's black leadership, taken out of context, might be used as justifications for those quite ready to pull their wagons in a circle, despairing of any other possibility of avoiding racial warfare.

New York is often seen as the prototype of urban America, past, present, and future. It is—and it isn't, as comparisons between Jim Sleeper's *The Closest of Strangers* and Ze'ev Chafets's new book, *Devil's Night and Other True Tales of Detroit*, indicate.

Sleeper makes it clear that New York is a multiracial city under siege. Chafets makes it clear that Detroit used to be one, too, but that for all intents and purposes, it lost the battle. It is no longer functionally multiracial. As Chafets rightly points out, Detroit is "the first major American city to cope with going from white to black." Moreover, while most of New York's bonfires are figurative conflicts, Detroit's are literal conflagrations. They flare up on "Devil's Night" Halloween Eve, when local people now carry an old tradition of hell-raising to an illogical extreme: they set fire to their own communities and, with others—many of whom come from surrounding towns—watch it burn.

Chafets, a Pontiac-born Israeli writer, grew up in Detroit. When he left in the 1960s, it was still the auto capital of the world, a rich industrial giant; a place where hard-working blacks and hard-working whites labored side by side on the assembly lines of the auto factories. It was a boom town; a city undergoing a great architectural and cultural renascence; a metropolis on the move. It was also "Motown," the home of rhythm and blues, a music that pulsed through the various neighborhoods and racial ghettoes— Southern and Northern, white ethnic, Jewish, Arab, and WASP, too. It was not, however, a unified society. Even more than New York, Detroit was riven with intergroup and, especially, interclass rivalries and deep-rooted social tensions.

When he left home, Chafets was well aware of the promise of his city. He also knew its dark side. He had been personally touched by both. His best friend was a working-class African American; his grandfather, a shopkeeper who served everyone, was mugged, robbed, and beaten to death by two black youths. Chafets returned to Detroit in the late 1980s. Even his early days in the city did not prepare him for what he found.

His report, like Sleeper's commentary on New York, is set in a historical context. But Chafets's history is far shorter, limited by his own memory and that of those interviewed as he engaged in a kind of ethnographic search for the true character of Detroit today.

Devil's Night is partly about the decline and fall of a city that was struggling to make it but suffered a series of serious setbacks, not least the terrible race riots in 1967 that accelerated the steadily increasing white flight to the suburbs, leaving it mostly black; that saw its economic base further erode as Japanese cars gained the favor of a fickle public; that saw its social fabric torn asunder, dramatically characterized by its new sobriquet, "Murder Capital, U.S.A." It is also about what Chafets describes as a poverty-ridden black metropolis.

If there is a single word that reverberated through Sleeper's assessment of New York, it is *antagonism*. Although Chafets and those to whom he spoke never use it, the word I would choose to sum up *his* portrait of Detroit is *anomie*. There is a pervading sense of breakdown, of normlessness in almost every tale he tells.

Not surprisingly, the white people Chafets spoke to in the suburbs and in the city described Detroit in very different terms from those used by the poor, working-class, and professional blacks he met and got to know. To most of the former, Motown today is simply one big, dangerous, urban nightmare. Many blacks share this vision, some openly expressing the sentiment that "the trouble with us is us." But, to at least some black Detroiters, including certain politicians, preachers, policemen, and publicists struggling to pull things together, Detroit is an island of self-determination and promise in a sea of white racism and hostility.

Chafets himself likens the city to the Jewish state: "Israel, like Detroit, is a place where people with a history of persecution and dependence finally gave up on the dream of assimilation, and chose to try for the first time, to rule themselves." It is an interesting but rather far-fetched analogy, as Chafets's own "data"—what he saw and heard and experienced as he roamed the city—make clear. (The closer parallel might be Detroit's blacks as Michigan's symbolic equivalent not to the Jews of Israel but to Israel's Palestinians!)

Both Sleeper and Chafets offset their generally depressing portraits with some hope that things will change. They so do in rather different ways. For Sleeper, the "only way to address racism, to break the spell, is to stop casting events as purely or primarily racist in character." In other words, he sees efficacy in a return to the *status quo ante*, when viable integration was seen as an achievable goal. He cites organizations such as Saul Alinsky's interracial Industrial Areas Foundation as the sorts of models needed to provide the means to reach them.

For Chafets, integration in his old hometown is no longer a realistic option. Instead, for Detroit's predominantly black population to reverse the course on which they seem to be heading, Chafets implies that they must move toward greater independence (again, the Israeli analogy). Detroit's black leadership would probably agree. They know that only through a bootstrap type of economic, political, social, and moral rearmament can they rebuild their lives and their shattered communities. But few residents there have the wherewithal to manage the first—the economic problem— without considerable outside help. Since there is no equivalent black constituency like the real Israel's Jewish donors ready, willing, and able to provide the millions and millions needed to shore up the collapsing edifice, without a massive infusion of "white" assistance or government aid, the future of Detroit looks very glum indeed and, despite its own very real racial issues, far worse than New York's.

The House We Live In

What is America to me?
A name, a map, the flag I see.
A certain word "Democracy"...

FIFTY YEARS ago a skinny young crooner named Frank Sinatra popularized the words of Lewis Allan and Earl Robinson's patriotic ballad. I can still hear him singing, "The house I live in. My neighbors, white and black. The people who just came here, or from generations back. The town hall and the soapbox. The torch of Liberty. A home for all God's children—that's America to me."

The words evoked a special feeling of inclusion, especially for many of us who were the children and grandchildren of immigrants. The colorful star-spangled paean spoke to *our* idealized America.

It is still the America of Lawrence H. Fuchs, a stubborn believer in the possibility of achieving "the more perfect union" in a society whose principles are rooted in the spirit of liberty, justice, and reform and supported by a political structure that, he argues, has repeatedly if often grudgingly met the challenges brought by exploited and disenfranchised groups and sympathetic confederates. Their protests, legal and extralegal, have forced the country to honor its own vaunted ideals by recognizing increasing diversity, encouraging ever-greater participation, enhancing achievement, and perhaps most important of all, providing ever-better mechanisms for righting historic wrongs.

For years Fuchs has claimed that those successes are directly attributable to something de Tocqueville identified long ago "when he discovered that which distinguished the national spirit, character, and identity [of the United States] was not sectarian religion or ancestry but a culture of politics. The Americans were not a Protestant nation in the same sense that the French were a Catholic nation, or the Germans a folk. The unifying

*Review of *The American Kaleidoscope: Race, Ethnicity and the Civic Culture*, by Lawrence H. Fuchs (Hanover and London, 1990). Originally published as "A Man and a Metaphor: Characterizing a Nation" in *Sociological Forum*, vol. 6, no. 4, 1991, pp. 731–738.

culture of the United States was not religious or racial but political." And by virtue of this basic fact of American life, those in the American polity, Fuchs has often added, can make a difference, for it is *their* society.

A Harvard-trained political scientist who holds the Meyer and Walter Jaffe Professor of American Civilization and Politics at Brandeis, Fuchs has devoted his own career as much to participation as observation. He was the first Peace Corps field director, appointed by President Kennedy in the early 1960s. More recently he was executive director of the Select Commission on Immigration and Refugee Policy during the days of the Carter administration. Many of his articles, reports, and books clearly reflect the hands-on approach of a social scientist some have described as "a citizen-scholar *par excellence.*" Particularly noteworthy are such early works as *The Political Behavior of American Jews* (1955), *American Ethnic Politics* (1968), *Those Peculiar Americans: The Peace Corps and American National Character* (1968), *Black in White America* (1974), *The American Experiment* (1981), and the staff report of the Select Commission (also published in 1981), which he edited.

His latest book, *The American Kaleidoscope*, a weighty tome in many different ways (including its sheer size), is a compellingly written, comprehensive distillation of years of study and years of involvement. It has an unmistakable Fuchsian orientation, reflecting the author's own political proclivities and those of many much-admired social philosophers, social scientists, and liberal politicians who were his models and mentors.

Especially influential in the shaping of Fuchs's thinking were other citizen-scholars who had rejected the rhetoric of draconian Americanization as well as the myth of the melting pot, who promoted instead the idea that a viable pluralism in which hyphens connect an array of racial and ethnic groups to a common core was the best course for an increasingly heterogeneous polity. It was a goal advocated by Jane Addams, Randolph Bourne, John Dewey, and Horace Kallen; a goal deemed reachable by both Robert MacIver and Gunnar Myrdal. MacIver's contention that for a variety of historical and sociological reasons, racial and immigrant—ethnic group harmony was possible to achieve in the United States in ways quite unimaginable in most other societies, and Myrdal's "optimistic conclusion" that if Americans applied their creed consistently they would overcome racism, had a special impact on Fuchs's thinking, reinforcing his own assumptions about the true strength of American democracy. The increasing successes of the civil rights movement, the enactment of new laws to protect minorities, and the passage of the Immigration Act of 1965 that abolished the highly restrictive quotas imposed in the 1920s seemed to give empirical credence to both MacIver's and Myrdal's views.

Fuchs's own brand of pragmatic liberalism, a sentiment—and faith—shared by many like-minded Americans, was severely shaken in the second half of the 1960s. It was not only the events of those turbulent times—urban riots, the breakdown of old civil rights coalitions, the shifting allegiances, and the increasing emphasis on the "one" rather than the "many"—that disturbed him, but also many of the initial responses to them. The writings of several respected friends and colleagues added to the disquietude about some of the methods being used to redress legitimate grievances and remove categorical impediments to access.

One of the books was Harold Isaacs's *The Idols of the Tribe*, a hardhitting attack in which Isaacs warned against replacing the idea of strength in diversity with a kind of chauvinistic balkanization or, as he put it, "retribalization." Another was Nathan Glazer's *Affirmative Discrimination*, which saw certain well-intended policies which legitimized group rights and special consideration for administratively determined "minorities" as both unconstitutional and counterproductive as a means of resolving the legacies of slavery and discrimination. John Higham's *Send These to Me: Immigrants in Urban America*, also gave Fuchs pause. And it inspired him. In Higham's volume, the distinguished historian and authority on nativism forcefully argued that Americans had a serious problem "in rediscovering what values can bind together a more and more kaleidoscopic culture."

In the preface to his own attempt to portray that culture, Fuchs says he decided to examine the premises of Isaacs and Glazer and the problem posed by Higham. It turned out to be a fifteen-year quest, during a period marked by a rollercoaster of successes in certain areas, such as immigration reform; continuing disagreements in others, not least the continuing conflicts over group rights and entitlements; and setbacks, too, especially in terms of the sharp reduction in government support for civil rights causes. In the end, despite some serious misgivings, Fuchs retained his belief that the United States still had the means to meet the new challenges and would be able to continue to reform itself within the bounds of liberal democracy, within the kaleidoscope.

His (actually Higham's) America-as-a-kaleidoscope metaphor is an interesting one. It is another to add to the growing list that includes "melting pot," "salad bowl," and "orchestration of mankind." But like each of the others, it has certain clear limitations.

A real kaleidoscope is a closed system in the form of a tube one holds up to the light, looks through, and turns to watch the varying pieces of multicolored glass make ever-changing but always symmetrical patterns. The imagery is vivid and "functional" (in more ways than one!) but it may be a somewhat misleading referent.

The United States is multicolored and ever-changing like the shards in the turnable instrument, but the relationship between the real parts (read: *social groups, classes, institutions*, etc.) in our society are far from being randomly scrambled. Each "turn" of the real world results in alterations to be sure, but barring a serious jarring of the entire framework, these are generally limited to modified patterns easily traced to their most recent past. Societal change is socially and politically, not haphazardly, determined.

Of course, when society is viewed synchronically (that is, holding the social kaleidoscope—to stick with the allusion—still), it is evident that some parts are bigger than others and therefore closer to the center of the system, *but the character of their arrangements and the nature of their symbiosis remain illusory*. More "data" are needed to understand both hierarchy and interdependence.

Larry Fuchs knows this. Indeed, much of his book illustrates these very complexities; the sources of inequity; the different ways old minorities and new immigrants have been treated, interacted, grown, and changed—adopting some ideas, adapting others, and sometimes successfully challenging some of the traditional ways of "making it" based on well-ingrained ideas about color-blindness and meritocratic norms that are part of the civic culture.

Without calling it such, Fuchs offers an almost classic structural-functional analysis of the American political and social system centered on the concept of a "civic culture," an idea first labeled as such by Gabriel Almond and Sidney Verba in 1965. That culture, Fuchs says, evolved on the basis of three premises: first, that ordinary men and women can be trusted to govern themselves through their elected representatives; second, that all who live in the American political community (once limited to property-holding white males, then to all white males, then to all male citizens, then to all citizens, male and female) are eligible to participate in public life as equals; and third, that individuals who comport themselves as good citizens are free to differ from each other in religion and in other aspects of their private lives. The last idea was the basis of the notion of "voluntary pluralism," an idea that found its earliest expression in the colony of Pennsylvania but was eventually to be enjoyed throughout the emerging nation at least by those of European background and their progeny.

"The new American invention," Fuchs writes, " . . . in which individuals were free to express their ancestral affections and sensibilities, to choose to be ethnic [a term that, of course, did not enter the vernacular until many years after the "founding" of the nation] however and whenever they wished or not at all by moving across group boundaries easily, was sanctioned and protected by [the] unifying civic culture based on the American founding myth, its institutions, heroes, rules, and rhetoric. . . ." The most important of those rules—and the accompanying rhetoric—were found in such texts as the Declaration of Independence ("We hold these truths to be self-evident . . .") and the Bill of Rights, the latter becoming the Sinaidic tablets of America's "civic religion." Fuchs puts the argument succinctly in saying that "the American experience in representative self-government was blessed, but the congregation—the members of the polity—were covenanted as partners of God in fulfilling the promise of the blessing."

Fuchs's new book addresses some two dozen themes, presented in as many interlocking chapter-essays, some dealing with those who generally set the trends, some with those on the outside seeking admission. It is a volume filled with stories of migration, anticipation, struggle, compromise, debate, and tension. It is peopled with well-known figures, including Jefferson, Franklin, Lincoln, Tom Watson, Madison Grant, Israel Zangwill, Henry Ford, Senator Bilbo, FDR, Bayard Rustin, JFK, LBJ, Ron Karenga, Daniel Inouye, and David Dinkins; with ordinary, anonymous Americans who had come, or whose ancestors had come, from somewhere else; and with journalists, historians, and social scientists who recorded, described, analyzed, and sometimes reconstructed the social as well as the intellectual and political history of the country. Readers of *Sociological Forum* will be especially interested to note that while the works of many sociologists are cited—including those of Helen and Robert Lynd, Robert Bellah, Elliott Rudwick, Harry Kitano, Benjamin Ringer, Stanley Lieberson, and William Julius Wilson—the relevant theses of such landmark studies as Seymour Martin Lipset's *The First New Nation*, Robin M. Williams, Jr.'s *American Society,* and especially Milton Gordon's *Assimilation in American Life,* in which he makes a critical distinction between structural and cultural pluralism, all seem to have been overlooked or underplayed.

Fuchs first reviews the early days of nationhood and the notions of what it meant to be—and to become—an American. He then focuses on the immigration history of those from Ireland, Jews from Eastern Europe, and Poles, Slavs, Italians, Greeks, and others who were later to be collectively known as "white ethnics;" native Americans (who, Fuchs says, suffered from "predatory pluralism"); African victims of slavery, Jim Crow laws, and de facto segregation that defined them in caste-like terms; Asians and Mexicans, who, like many Italians, came as sojourners and stayed. Here he also addresses some of the tensions that now exist between the "new immigrants" and the old minorities as between Koreans and Blacks in New York, Cubans and Blacks in Miami—and the sources of the conflict. Data are provided for comparing opportunities for African-, Asian-, and Mexican-Americans.

Part Three is about the struggles for inclusion, especially by those who, today, are officially designated as "minorities": Blacks, Native Americans, Asians, and Hispanics. Fuchs briefly but effectively retells the story of the civil rights struggles in the streets and in the courts, the Voting Rights Act of 1965, the Black Power Movement, the challenge to old ways of addressing patterns of discrimination, the surge toward separatism and its consequences not only for African-Americans but for others, too. For example, he examines various aspects of "tribal pluralism" between those called Indians and the rest of the country and among the various tribes themselves. He writes about the special experience of Japanese-Americans during World War II, and the struggles of various Asian groups to break down the barriers and to find a satisfactory way, paraphrasing Louis Adamic, to find the right mix in the "chemistry of hyphenation."

The fourth part of the book is about the ethnic landscape as altered by both domestic struggles and changes in immigration laws in recent decades, both of which have led, in the main, to a quickening pace of ethnic interaction in a variety of settings—churches, schools the armed services, the workplace—and what he sees as a rising "multiethnic conscience." Fuchs celebrates the ever-widening diversity and notes the speed with which several of the newest groups, such as Cuban and Vietnamese refugees, have become new ethnics and new Americans. More significantly, he points to the often neglected fact that there are newcomers who are more advantaged than others in terms of professional or technical skills, language abilities, and cultural orientations that make it easier for them to cope with resettlement and to find ready acceptance in their new country. ("Mareilitos" and Haitians have had a much harder time than first-wave Cubans; Koreans and Indians with bachelor's degrees are much better able to deal with the inevitable problems of relocation than the Cambodians or the Hmong, Hmein, and Laotung tribes people from Laos.)

The presence of so many refugees and immigrants, including those more employable than some members of old American "minority" groups, has led to conflicts reminiscent of those of an earlier period. In addition, the more recent group-consciousness movement has strained old alliances (as, for example, between Blacks and Jews) nearly to a breaking point. This new "particularism," in contrast to old style "pluralism" as Diane Ravitch has recently noted, has meant that in many cases, instead of mutual respect and empathy being enhanced by an appreciation for a common if diverse humanity, ethnocentrism itself has been reinforced.

"Pluralism, Public Policy, and the Civic Culture, 1970–1989" is Fuchs's final subject. It is a kind of retrospect and prospect. In addition to a lengthy chapter on the civil rights compact, which includes a critique of the Reagan administration's civil rights policies, there are reminders of days not so long past when the thrust of many discussions relating to race relations focused on *integrating* housing and education, and *enhancing* political access and economic opportunity for those left out, arguments now couched in terms of disagreements over the idea of "counting by race."

Indicating how much the population has been affected by the Immigration Acts of 1965 and 1966, and by the Refugee Act of 1980, *all of which Larry Fuchs had a hand in shaping*, with over 90 percent of post-1960 legal immigration coming from Latin American and the Caribbean, and Asia, Fuchs discusses various aspects of the politics of immigration, the subject about which he has written so much elsewhere.

In his last chapter Fuchs returns to the distinction between insiders and outsiders, the increasing anxiety of those eager but unable to find work, and the even more alarming estrangement of those who have little prospect of gaining a meaningful place in the society. He emphasizes the fact that those who suffer most today as in the past are the "ethno-underclass" (a sobriquet as sure to evoke criticism as did William Julius Wilson's use of "underclass" alone). However, unlike the communities of the urban poor of an earlier time, when ghettos were often way stations on the path to mobility, hope has given way to thoughts of sheer survival, anomie is pervasive, and the entire fabric of the civic culture is under threat.

Fuchs only scratches the surface of the monumental race/class problem. Solving it is pivotal to the question of whether we will enter the twenty-first century as a society in which full participation is an achievable reality or whether the currently widening gap between those who are making it and those who remain on margins will lead to greater and greater polarization and the undermining of the law of life Fuchs genuinely believed all should be able to enjoy. By its very nature any attempt to address the issue requires the implementation of an imaginative dual (race/class) agenda and a massive two-front (participation *and* equality) campaign that, sadly, few of our current leaders or members of Congress seem prepared to carry out.

The prospect of a failure to meet the challenge of those who live lives of desperation, those who have not found a place even in Larry Fuchs's expansive house of many rooms, is far more frightening than any of the scenarios imagined by those concerned about the issues raised by Harold Isaacs, Nathan Glazer, and John Higham.

New Immigrants, Old Issues

A ccording to Ellis Cose, what the Irish faced 150 years ago, what East European Jews and Catholics from Central and Southern Europe faced a century ago, refugees and immigrants from Asia and Latin America have been facing in recent years. Indeed, the same sorts of questions asked about the earlier groups—and about the "absorptive capacity" of this society—are still being asked.

What should be the criteria for admission? How ought people be selected? How many should be permitted to enter? How should those who do come in be received? What are the consequences of the entry of newcomers for native-born, including other "minorities"?

Taken at face value, each of these is a fair question. Yet, often as not, they have been asked with the answers fixed in the minds of those who pose them.

Sometimes the fears expressed, especially about undercutting the labor market and replacing American workers with foreigners ready, able, and willing to work for considerably lower wages than most Americans, have been reasonable. More often they have been used as xenophobic rationalizations "to keep the country from losing its special character"—meaning the status quo ante.

Such nativistic attitudes may properly be construed as morally reprehensible and politically incorrect but, sociologically, they are readily explicable. Resistance to new immigrants, even by those (in some instances *especially by those*) but a few years "off the boat" themselves, offers one of the clearest examples of what William Graham Sumner was taking about when he coined the word "ethnocentrism" nearly a century ago.

People, he said, tend to like what is familiar and distrust what is different. Furthermore, they often rank others on a scale of social distance, with particular cultural criteria being used as measures of acceptability. The

*Review of *A Nation of Strangers: Prejudice, Politics and the Populating of America*, by Ellis Cose (New York, 1992). Originally published as "New Immigrants" in *Congress Monthly*, vol. 59, no. 7, November/December 1992.

"distance" often has to do with how close those who seek to emigrate are in "looks and outlooks" to those in the dominant group. Ascribed traits such as racial designation or religious affiliation are generally judged most harshly; but other characteristics, such as political beliefs and affiliations, are considered as well. So is the social-economic status of the would-be immigrant.

Of course, social class—and occupational-skill level—can cut two ways. While it is generally assumed that potential host societies favor only the well trained and highly skilled, the need for large numbers of laborers at various times and in various places has repeatedly provided exceptions to such conventional wisdom. Priorities have often been determined by the market. The case of guest workers in Europe is a classic example. But there are others, nearer at hand: consider the Chinese "coolies" brought here in the nineteenth century; the Mexican *braceros* brought here in the twentieth.

While not stated in exactly the same way, these are some of the matters addressed in Ellis Cose's new book about *A Nation of Strangers.* The title provides a clue to his thesis. It is a familiar title and a familiar thesis. Many scholars of race, ethnicity, and the immigrant experience—including such historians as John Higham, David Reimers, Ronald Takaki, and Roger Daniels, and social scientists such as Vincent Parrillo, Alejandro Portes, Ruben Rumbaut, and Lawrence Fuchs—have written extensively on the interplay of prejudice, politics, and the populating of America.

Cose, editorial-page editor of the *New York Daily News,* goes over much of the same ground. What he writes about is generally well known to specialists and students but not to many others. Those others are his primary target audience.

His fast-paced, jargon-free book begins with an overview of America's enigmatic character. Cose describes a nation that despite its early emphasis on the Rights of Man ("We hold these truths to be self-evident, that all men are created equal") is also, in his apt words, a society whose culture is "rooted in intolerance."

The original colonies were overwhelmingly Protestant and hoped to stay that way. They were also predominately white. Those who were "colored" were held apart by a caste-line privilege. In some cases, as in the treatment of native populations and slaves, limits on participation and opportunity were embodied in law.

In others, such as practices relating to associating with members of religious minorities, de facto patterns of discrimination operated that served to maintain the overall hegemony of the Protestant establishment. (Sometime later these were to be called "Gentlemen's Agreements.") But while there was frequent agitation for it, especially during the time of the exodus from poverty-ridden Ireland, there were no formal restrictions against immigration until the Chinese Exclusion Act was passed in 1882.

Cose notes that in the late part of the nineteenth century, "[while] Congress was choking off immigration from China, many American intellectuals were exploring political radicalism and scientific racism." The fear of foreign agitators combined with deeply rooted sentiments against certain groups led to the formation of the Immigration Restriction League founded in 1894. According to Cose, "[it] became an effective lobby for that idea, as well as for the general proposition that such ethnic groups represented inferior and unassimilable races."

It is important to note Cose's accurate use of the phrase "unassimilable races," for that is how others were seen by those white Protestants who pressed hardest for containing and then curtailing the immigration of many who were considered unsuited for life in the Land of the Free through draconic Quota Laws of 1921 and 1924, statutes that were not significantly amended until the Immigration Act of 1964. The more recent act, called by Cose a "reluctant reform," was promoted to especially redress the grievances of those now-called "white ethnics." It had important unintended consequences. The most significant was that the vast majority of those who were to take advantage of the policies (which permitted an annual immigration of some 20,000 persons from each country regardless of race or creed or color) were to come not from Europe but from Asia and Latin America. Their ranks were to be augmented by hundreds of thousands of refugees from Cuba, the Soviet Union, and the countries of Indochina.

Some commentators, such as Andrew Hacker, writing in *Two Nations*, suggest that as increasing numbers of Asians and Latinos, who are still looked upon by some as intruders, find it easier to move into the mainstream of society, recapitulating the experiences of the Irish, then the Jews, and other "white ethnics," only Americans from Africa, whose ancestors have been in this country as long as those of the Pilgrim Fathers, will remain the "odd men out." Some blacks are beginning to express their own brand of nativism in allegations that America (meaning white America) continues to take in new peoples (including other "people of color") when it can't even solve the problems of those long here. Their declamations are clear echoes of what certain white American Firsters have been saying for years.

Cose, himself an African American, is particularly sensitive to this reality and to the latest twist in the politics of immigration indicated in the recently passed Immigration Act of 1990, which includes three visa categories: for family, for employment, and for "diversity," the last being a very elastic one but hardly designed to enhance "multiculturalism." (In the initial plan, 40,000 visas were allocated for that third category, with 16,000 set aside for Irish petitioners!)

Many commentators on immigration argue that while far from perfect, there is little evidence that the new bill fosters restriction or cuts down on the numbers allowed in under the 1965 reform (or the Refugee Act of 1980). Cose says that "once lawmakers started down the road of letting certain groups in, other groups naturally followed; for Congress always finds adding easier than subtracting." But he is not altogether sanguine about this tendency as evidenced by this further statement: "By the most parochial of politics, Congress had ended up with a most expansive result—one ensuring that an already steady stream of strange people knocking on America's door would swell into a torrent, heightening not only the potential for ethnic enrichment *but also for ethnic turmoil.*"

I italicize the last five words of Cose's last sentence in his final chapter for they highlight one of his greatest concerns: finding a way to reconcile growing ethnic diversity (containing "the largest influx of nonwhites than any time since the height of the slave trade") with the potential for group-based competition and greater polarization between those who get left behind. The recent tensions between Korean immigrants and African Americans in Los Angeles and other cities are pointed indicators of the sorts of conflicts Cose fears.

We may have come a long way toward making this country more of a true nation of nations than the world has ever known but, as Cose rightly states, "Optimistic forecasts notwithstanding, racial animosity has proven to be both an enduring American Phenomenon and an invaluable political tool . . . It more resembles a virus that at times lies dormant but can suddenly erupt with vengeance—particularly during periods of stress."

The Limits of Tolerance

I

Despite a raft of recent articles and books and numerous panel discussions on the subject of multiculturalism, few have captured the character and significance—or the pathos *and* comedic elements—of America's recent "cultural wars" better than Robert Hughes, an Australian-born, ex-Catholic, anti-Marxist, free-thinking art critic and historian. Hughes is the author of prize-winning books on Australia and Catalonia. His latest, *Culture of Complaint: The Fraying of America*, is based on a series of lectures he delivered at the New York Public Library. Their evocative titles were: "Culture and the Broken Polity"; "Multi-Culti and Its Discontents", and "Moral in Itself: Art and the Therapeutic Fallacy." Taken as a whole the lectures show the author to be a quintessential outsider-within, using his marginality to great advantage. He knows us well.

Speaking of the sources of strain that underlie many of the concerns already expressed here, Hughes says, "What this culture likes is the twin fetishes of victimhood and redemption." He further notes that "there has always been a friction between the remains of the Puritan ideology of a hierarchy of the virtuous under the immutable eye of God, and the later, revolutionary, nineteenth-century American conception of continuous secular development toward equality of rights which were inherent in men and not merely granted by government."

Yet, like many foreign observers of our manners and mores who, since de Tocqueville's day, have tried to capture the essence of the culture, Hughes is impressed by "the fact that America is a collective work of the imagination whose making never ends," a society with "a genius for consensus, for getting along by making up practical compromises to meet real social needs." He clearly aligns himself with today's liberal-conservatives. He, too, wishes to see us preserve the best of the social richness of our multiethnic character as well as our rather unique capacity for cohesion,

*Review of *Culture of Complaint: The Fraying of America*, by Robert Hughes (New York, 1993). Originally published in *Congress Monthly*, vol. 60, no. 7, November/December 1993.

"for some spirit of common agreement." (Like the pragmatist and plural-istic John Dewey, Robert Hughes implies that in America, the hyphens ought to connect instead of separate.) Thus Hughes decries the extremes that threaten to break down the social compacts and rend the fragile fabric of society and the demagoguery on both sides, that represented by the likes of Pat Buchanan who, he says, "gave a speech so harsh and divisive [at the Republican Convention in 1992] that it might not have been out of place in the Reichstag in 1933"—*and* by Leonard Jeffries, Louis Farrakhan, and many of their defenders.

Saying that "paleo-conservatives and free-speech therapists are both on the same wagon, the only difference being *what* they want to ban," Hughes further notes the inconsistencies of their own positions. For example, those who call for free speech usually want it only for themselves; those who have a tender regard for fetal rights often support the death penalty for adults; those who demand racial equality favor race-norming and other preferential and/or categorical devices for redressing grievances.

II

Hughes is especially effective in pointing to Orwellian distortions of thought and language on all sides. Here he mentions those who referred to the stock market crash of 1987 as "equity retreat," the firing of large numbers of workers as "corporate rightsizing," and bombing the hell out of Baghdad as "servicing a target." (The last example is a reminder of Viet-nam-era officials who spoke of "protective reaction strikes" against Hanoi.)

Hughes comments on euphemisms devised by college administrators under pressure to lighten stigmatization—"differently abled" as a replace-ment for handicapped; "other-visioned" for the blind; "vertically-chal-lenged" for the short, etc. And he offers a particularly pointed example of such language-sanitizing in extremis: the attempt by the administration of The University of California at Santa Cruz to ban such expressions as "a nip in the air" and "chink in one's armor" as racist. The author facetiously suggests that they might also want to ban "fruit-tree" as being too homo-phobic! (This is a fitting example of what William Safire has recently la-beled "retro-slurs.")

Hughes not only explores that other much more complex and danger-ous form of literary policing, relating to the control of what is to be read and studied, he also expresses opinions that cut to the core of the debates. "The idea that the ex-colonial must reject the art of the ex-colonist in the interest of political change is absurdly limiting . . . its absurdity remains true no matter what form of 'colonization' is mean—economic, sexual, ra-cial. You can learn from Picasso without being called a phallocrat, from Rubens without becoming a Hapsburg courtier, from Kipling without turning into an imperialist."

What happens when the multiculturalists combine forces with the politically correct crowd? According to Hughes, "What ought to be a generous recognition of a cultural diversity degenerates into a worthless symbolic program, clogged with lumpen-radical jargon. Its offshoot is the rhetoric of cultural separatism." He cites his own discipline, history, using, among others, the example of how the great cultural hero, Christopher Columbus, who having undergone a near apotheosis at the time of the 400th anniversary of his "discovery," was excoriated as a dastardly exploiter on the occasion of the quincentenary of his "encounter." It is not the reassessment that bothers Hughes so much as the re-romanticization of the story. Now, it seems, the Europeans were all bad—rapists, torturers, materialists, sexists, etc.—while the indigenous people were noble innocents, free and fair and devoid of any of the usual sins.

III

Some will accuse Hughes of a kind of overkill, of using worst-case examples to present a thesis about the dangers of current trends. But a close reading of *Culture of Complaint* will show that he is quite careful to indicate that he is hardly averse to critical scholarship and the revisiting of old "stories" and being enlightened by seeing them from a new perspective. Four of the many cases in point Hughes mentions are the works of the English writer E. P. Thompson and his famous study *The Making of the English Working Class;* those by the black Caribbean historian C. L. R. James and his interpretations of what more imperial writers had said; the late Herbert Gutman's powerful reassessment of conventional ideas in *The Black Family in Slavery and Freedom, 1750–1925;* and Nicholas Lemann's *The Promised Land,* a recently published portrait of the northward movement of Southern blacks. (His own book, *The Fatal Shore,* about the founding of Australia, is a first-rate example of such careful, thoughtful, and evocative scholarship.)

It is clear that Hughes has little use for monocultural or class-based history; what he objects to is the substitution of one form of bias for another—in the name of liberation. Like Arthur Schlesinger, his prime target is the recent writing of the "Afrocentrists" and what Eric Hobsbawn has called "the invention of tradition," especially in consideration of the origins of slavery or in descriptions of black-Jewish relations and such canards as the central role of Jews in the slave trade.

Hughes is far from insensitive to the social, political, and psychological bases of many of the actions and expressions of those who denounce liberal, reformist ideas. He recognizes the hurts that pervade the psyches and affect the communities of those who have been denied access in a thousand different ways; those who demand recognition and crave self-esteem. But, he also argues that, no matter how great the injustice, "the desire for self-esteem does not justify every lie and exaggeration and the therapeutic slanting of evidence that can be claimed to alleviate it."

Pulling no punches, Hughes's book on the limits of tolerance is an important contribution to a continuing dialogue about the future of pluralism in America.

Notes

From Pariahs to Paragons

1. A Gallup poll conducted for *Newsweek* during the time of the debates over the Simpson-Mazzoli-immigration-reform-bill asked a random sample of adults the question, "Do you think the number of immigrants now entering the the the United States from each of the following areas is too many, too few, or just right?" Fifty-three percent thought there were too many coming from Latin America while 49 percent said the same about Asia. Far fewer felt that way about Africans (31 percent) or Europeans (26 percent). See *Newsweek*, June 25, 1984, p. 21.

2. *The Journal and Miscellaneous Notebooks of Ralph Waldo Emerson*, ed. William H. Gilman (Cambridge, Mass., 1961), p. 244.

3. See, for example, Calvin F. Schmid and Charles E. Noble, "Socio-economic Differentials among Non-White Races," *American Sociological Review* 30 (1965): 909–922; Stanley Lieberson, *A Piece of the Pie* (Berkeley, 1981); and Thomas Sowell, ed., *Essays and Data on American Ethnic Groups* (Washington, D.C., 1978).

4. The term "model minority" for Asian Americans was popularized by William Petersen in "Success Story: Japanese American Style," *New York Times Magazine*, ed. George DeVos (Berkeley and Los Angeles, 1973).

5. William Petersen, "Chinese Americans and Japanese Americans," in *American Ethnic Groups*, ed. Sowell, pp. 65–66.

6. Robert Lindsey, "The New Asian Immigrants," *New York Times Magazine*, May 9, 1982, pp. 22–28.

7. "Asian-Americans: The Drive to Excel," *Newsweek*, April 1984, pp. 4–8, 10–11, and 13.

8. Ibid, p. 13.

9. See Thomas Sowell, *The Economics and Politics of Race* (New York 1983), especially the chapters entitled "The Overseas Chinese" and "The American Experience," pp. 26–50 and 183–206.

10. Diane Mei Lin Mark and Ginger Chih, *A Place Called Chinese America* (Dubuque, Iowa, 1932), pp. 109–110.

11. Ibid., pp. 155–169. Also see Bok-Lim C. Kim, *The Asian Americans: Changing Patterns, Changing Needs* (Montclair, N.J., 1978).

12. Harry H. L. Kitano, *Japanese Americans*, 2nd ed. (Englewood Cliffs, N.J., 1976), pp. 204–205.

13. Ibid.

14. Petersen, "Chinese Americans and Japanese Americans," in *American Ethnic Groups*, p. 89.

15. George Stuart, *American Ways of Life* (Garden City, N.Y., 1954), pp. 11–12. See also Tricia Knoll, *Becoming American* (Portland, Ore., 1982).

16. See Herbert Hill, "Anti-Oriental Agitation and the Rise of Working Class Racism,"*Transaction/Society* 10(1973): 43–54; and Standford Lyman, *Chinese Americans* (New York, 1974), Chapter 4, "The Anti-Chinese Movement in America," pp. 54–85.

17. See Lyman, *Chinese Americans*, Chapter 3, "Chinese Community Organizations in the United States," pp. 29–53.

18. Norbert Wiley, "The Ethnic Mobility Trap and Stratification Theory," *Social Problems* 15(1967): 146–149.

19. Victor G. and Brett De Barry Nee, *Longtime, Californ'* (New York, 1973).

20. Melford S. Weiss, *Valley City: A Chinese Community in America* (Cambridge, Mass., 1974).

21. United States Bureau of the Census, *Race of the Population by States*, 1980 (PCBO–SI–3).

22. See Standford Lyman, *The Asian in the West*, Social Science and Humanities Publication No. 4 (Reno, 1970).

23. See Michi Weglyn, *Years of Infamy* (New York, 1976).

24. William Petersen, *Japanese Americans* (New York, 1971), p. 131.

25. See Sowell, *American Ethnic Groups*.

26. Milton M. Gordon, *Assimilation in American Life* (New York, 1964), see especially pp. 60–83.

27. Akemi Kikumura and Harry H.L. Kitano, "Interracial Marriage: A Picture of the Japanese-Americans," *Journal of Social Issues* 20(1973): 67–81.

28. See Harold H. Sunoo and Sonia S. Sunoo, "The Heritage of the First Korean Women Immigrants in the United States: 1903–1924," *Korean Christian Journal* 2 (1977): 144, 165.

29. Vincent N. Parrillo, *Strangers on These Shores* (Boston, 1980), p. 297. See also Lee Houchins and Chang-so Houchins, "The Korean Experience in America, 1903–1924," *Pacific Historical Review* 43(1974): 560.

30. See Illsoo Kim, *The Urban Immigrants: The Korean Community in New York* (Princeton, 1981).

31. Lisa Belkin, "For City's Korean Greengrocers, Culture Often Clashes with the Law," *New York Times*, August 11, 1984, pp. 25, 28.

32. Fred Cordova, *Filipinos: The Forgotten Asian Americans* (Seattle, 1983).

33. See Maxime P. Fisher, *The Indians of New York* (New York, 1980).

34. Ibid., p. 136. See also John Ness, "The South Asians: City's Mysterious Immigrants," The *New York Times*, October 7, 1972, p. 49; and Robert J. Fornaro, "Asian-Indians in America: Acculturation and Minority Status," *Migration Today* 12(1984): 28–32.

35. Lemuel Ignacio, *Asian Americans and Pacific Islanders: Is There Such an Ethnic Group?* (San Jose, Calif., 1976). For another view, see Paul Wong, "The Emergence of the Asian American Movement," *The Bridge* 2(1972): 32–39.

36. Fisher, *Indians of New York*, p. 137.

37. See *Pinoy Know Yourself: An Introduction to the Filipino American Experience* (Santa Cruz, Calif., 1976).

38. Of the relatively few publications dealing with the immigration of people

from the Philippines, there is no consistency regarding the spelling of the names of group members. Some, like Cordova, use "Filipino." Others use "Pilipino."

39. Harry H.L. Kitano, "Asian Americans: The Chinese, Japanese, Koreans, Pilipinos, and Southeast Asians," *The Annals of the American Academy of Political and Social Sciences* 454 (1981): 135.

40. H. Brett Melendy, "Filipinos," *Harvard Ethnic Encyclopedia of American Ethnic Groups*, ed. S. Thernstorm (Cambridge, Mass., 1980), p. 357.

41. *Statistical Abstract of the United States*, 1984 edition, p. 91 (Source: United States Immigration and Naturalization Service, Annual Report of 1980).

42. Lindsey, "New Asian Immigrants," pp. 22–28.

43. *The Bridge*, July (1984): 9.

44. Ibid.

45. W. Stanley Mooneyham, *Sea of Heartbreak* (South Plainfield, N.J., 1980).

46. Once established by precedent, heavy government aid has been used to assist in the resettlement of others fleeing from communist states, including Soviet Jews, Poles, "Marielitos," and some Ethiopians and Afghans. See Peter I. Rose, "The Harbor Masters: American Politics and Refugee Policy," in *Social Problems and Public Policy* (Greenwich, Conn., 1984). Also see Julia V. Thaft et al., *Refugee Resettlement in the United States: Time for a New Focus* (Washington, D.C., 1979).

47. Recent analyses include Bruce Grant, *The Boat People* (New York, 1980); Barry Wain, *The Refused* (New York: 1981); Peter I. Rose "Links in a Chain: Observations of the American Refugee Program in Southeast Asia," *Migration Today* 9, No. 3 (1981): 6–24; and Peter I. Rose, "From Southeast Asia to America," *Migration Today* 9, No 4 (1981): 22–28.

48. Peter I. Rose, "Some Reflections on Refugee Policy," *Dissent* (Fall 1984): 484–486.

49. John Finck, "The Indochinese in America: Progress Toward Self-Sufficiency," *World Refugee Survey*, 1983, pp. 56–59. There are negative reports, too, especially those that detail the activities of the Vietnamese—and other Asians—involved in organized crime in the United States. See, for example, "Triads and Yakuza," *Time*, November 5, 1984, p. 30.

50. See "Southeast Asian Refugees in the U.S.A.: Case Studies in Adjustment and Policy Implications," special issue of the *Anthropological Quarterly* 55(July 1982).

51. Han T. Doan, "Vietnamericans: Bending Law or Breaking in the Acculturation Process?," unpublished paper presented at the 92nd annual meeting of the American Sociological Association, 1979. See also Gail Paradise Kelly, *From Vietnam to America* (Boulder, Colo., 1977), and Darrel Montero, *Vietnamese Americans* (Boulder, Colo., 1979).

52. Nathan Glazer, *Ethnic Dilemmas: 1964–1982* (Cambridge, Mass.,1983), p. 315. Glazer is quoting from his and Moynihan's book, *Beyond the Melting Pot*, 2d ed. (Cambridge, Mass., 1971), p. xxiii.

53. *Ethnic Dilemmas*, pp. 319–323.

54. Ibid., p. 331.

55. See Ignacio, *Asian Americans and Pacific Islanders*.

56. Francis L. K. Hsu discusses the reality of marginality and the positive functions of double identity for Chinese Americans in *The Challenge of the American Dream* (Belmont, Calif., 1971), pp. 129–131. This remains a rather common view among those writing about the various Asian American communities from outside

as well as in. It is less well accepted by those concerned with the integration of Hispanics. See, for example, James Fallows's lengthy article, "The New Immigrants,"
The Atlantic, November 1983, p. 45.

The Reagan Years and Beyond

1. See Michael Lewis, *The Culture of Inequality* (Amherst, Mass., 1978).
2. William Julius Wilson, *The Declining Significance of Race*, 2d ed. (Chicago, 1980).
3. Ibid., p. 2.
4. William Julius Wilson, *The Truly Disadvantaged* (Chicago, 1987).
5. Anthony Gary Dworkin and Rosalind J. Dworkin, eds., *The Minority Report* 2d ed. (New York, 1982), p. 125.
6. Idem.
7. See, for example, Thomas Sowell, *The Economics and Politics of Race* (New York, 1983).
8. Nathan Glazer, *Affirmative Discrimination* (New York, 1975).
9. *The New York Times*, January 24, 1989.
10. Idem.
11. Shelby Steele, "The Recoloring of Campus Life," *The Atlantic*, February 1989, pp. 47–55.
12. Ibid., p. 47.
13. Ibid., p. 48.
14. Idem.
15. Henry Louis Gates, "Whose Canon Is It Anyway?" *The New York Times Magazine*, February 26, 1989, pp. 44–45.
16. *The Newest Americans*, report of the American Jewish Committee's Task Force on The Acculturation of Immigrants to American Life (New York, 1987).

Tempest-Tost

1. Thomas Keneally, *To Asmara* (New York, 1989), p. 118.
2. See Bill Frelick, *Yugoslavia Torn Asunder: Lessons for Protecting Refugees from Civil War* (Washington, D.C., 1992).
3. Roberta Cohen, *Human Rights for Displaced Persons* (Washington, D.C., 1992).
4. See Egon F. Kunz, "The Refugee in Flight: Kinetic Models and Forms of Displacement," *International Migration Review*, 7(1973): 125–146
5. Frelick, *Yugoslavia Torn Asunder*.
6. As quoted in Nathan Gardels, "Two Concepts of Nationalism: An Interview with Isaiah Berlin," *New York Review of Books*, November 21, 1991, 19–23.
7. Richard Shelton, "The Princes of Exile," *The New Yorker*, 45, October 22, 1973, p. 50.
8. Liisa Malki, "National Geographic: The Rooting of Peoples and the Terri-torialization of National Identity among Scholars and Refugees," *Cultural Anthropology* 7(1992): 25.
9. A. E. Houseman, "The Laws of God, The Laws of Man," in *Last Poems* (New York, 1922), pp. 28–29.

10. This is effectively shown in the recent documentary film *Rebuilding the Temple: Cambodians in America's Half Open Door, 1945–Present*, Claudia Levin and Lawrence Hott, producers, New York, 1991.

11. Paul Tabori, Frontispage, *The Anatomy of Exile* (London, 1972).

12. Diann Wong, "Asylum as a Relationship of Otherness: A Study of Asylum Holders in Nuremberg, Germany," *Journal of Refugee Studies* 4(1991): 159–163.

13. Robert E. Park, "Human Migration and the Marginal Man," *American Journal of Sociology* 33(1928): 891.

14. See, for example, Jeremy Hein, "Do 'New Immigrants' Become 'New Minorities'? The Meaning of Ethnicity for Indochinese Refugees in the United States," *Sociological Perspectives* 34(1991): 61–77.

15. Antranik Zuroukian, "Let There Be Light," in *Landscape and Exile*, ed. Marguerite Guzman Bouvard (Boston, 1985), p. 185.

16. See Lewis Coser, *Refugee Scholars in America: Their Impact and Their Experiences* (New Haven, 1984).

17. Peter I. Rose, "Toward a Sociology of Exile," *International Migration Review* 15(1986):768–773.

18. Elie Weisel, "The Refugee," in *Sanctuary*, ed. G. MacEoin (New York, 1985), p. 10.

19. M. Fletcher Davis, *Of Foxes and Birds and the Son of God: Ministry to Refugees and Other Strangers* (Cincinnati, 1982), p. 9.

20. Peter I. Rose, "Four Just Men," *Migration World*, 8:2(1989).

21. Sophocles, "Oedipus at Colonus," in *The Oedipus Plays of Sophocles*, tr. Paul Rouches (New York, 1958), p. 110.

22. Rudyard Kipling, "The Stranger," in *Rudyard Kipling's Verse* (Garden City, N.Y., 1945 ed.), p. 349.

23. See Aristide Zolberg, Astri Suhrke, and Serio Aguayo, *Escape from Violence: Conflict and the Refugee Crisis in the Developing World* (New York and Oxford, 1989), p. 7.

24. Bruce Grant, *The Boat People* (New York, 1980), p. 2.

25. Bill Frelick, "No Place to Go, Controlling Who Gets In," in *Forced Out: The Agony of the Refugee in Our Time*, ed. Carol Kismaric (New York, 1989), p. 164.

26. Emma Lazarus, "The New Colossus," in *Poems* (Boston, 1889), pp. 202–203.

27. Gil Loescher and John Scanlan, *Calculated Kindness: Refugees and America's Half Open Door, 1945–Present* (New York, 1986).

28. Felicia D. Hemans, "The Landing of the Pilgrim Fathers in New England," in *The Best Loved Poems of the American People*, ed. Hazel Felleman (Garden City, N.Y., 1936), pp. 217–218.

29. Israel Zangwill, *The Melting Pot* (New York, 1909), pp. 198–199.

30. Madison Grant, *The Passing of the Great Race* (New York, 1916, 3rd ed. 1944), pp. 88–92.

31. Kenneth Roberts, *Why Europe Leaves Home* (Indianapolis, 1922).

32. John Rowland, "A Connecticut Yankee Speaks His Mind," *Outlook* 136, October 22, 1924, pp. 478–480.

33. Julia Taft, David S. North, and David A. Ford, *Refugee Resettlement in the U.S.: Time for a New Focus* (Washington, D.C., 1979), p. 5.

34. Alejandro Portes and Rubén Rumbaut, *Immigrant America* (Berkeley, Calif., 1990), pp. 23–24.

35. See *New York Times*, February 17, 1992.

36. Eleanor M. Rogg, *The Assimilation of Cuban Exiles* (New York, 1974), p. 4.

37. Alejandro Portes, "Hispanic Minorities in the United States," in *Immigration Reconsidered*, ed. Virginia Yans-McLaughlin (New York, 1990), p. 171.

38. Charles Krauthammer, "Buchanan Explained," *The Washington Post National Weekly*, March 9–15, 1992.

"Of Every Hue and Caste"

1. Hutchins Hapgood, *The Spirit of the Ghetto* (New York, 1902), p. 5.

2. See Peter I. Rose, Introduction, *Through Different Eyes: Black and White Perspectives on American Race Relations*, ed. Peter I. Rose, Stanley Rothman, and William J. Wilson (New York, 1973), p. v.

3. Alexis de Tocqueville, *Democracy in America*, Henry Reeve text revised by Francis Bowen (New York, 1945), 2:391–92.

4. Quoted from "Talk with a 'Reasonable Man,'" by Milton Viorst. Originally appeared in the *New York Times Magazine*, April 19, 1970, p. 96. Copyright © 1970 by Milton Viorst. Reprinted by permission.

5. For recent assessments, see Ellis Cose, *A Nation of Strangers: Prejudice, Politics and the Populating of America* (New York, 1992); Lawrence H. Fuchs,*The American Kaleidoscope: Race, Ethnicity and the Civic Culture* (Hanover, N.H., 1990); Roger Daniels, *Coming to America* (New York, 1990); Walter Nugent, *Crossings: The Great Transatlantic Migrations, 1870–1941* (Bloomington, 1992).

6. See Ronald Takaki, *Iron Cages: Race and Culture in Nineteenth-Century America* (New York, 1979).

7. See, for example, Alejandro Portes and Rubén Rumbaut, *Immigrant America: A Portrait* (Berkeley 1990), pp. 94–140 passim.

8. See Stephen Steinberg, *The Ethnic Myth: Race, Ethnicity, and Class in America*, 2d ed. (Boston, 1989), esp. chap. 2, "The Ethnic Crisis in American Society," pp. 44–74.

9. A. M. Rosenthal, "The Lucky Americans," *New York Times*, December 8, 1992. Copyright © 1992 by The New York Times Company. Reprinted by permission.

10. From a speech delivered by Theodore Roosevelt in 1917, as quoted in *Roosevelt in the Kansas City Star*, ed. Ralph Stout (Boston, 1921), p. 137.

11. Ibid.

12. Horace Kallen, "Democracy versus the Melting Pot," *Nation*, February 18, 1915, pp. 190–94; ibid., February 25, 1915, pp. 217–20.

13. Kallen, "Democracy versus the Melting Pot," February 25, 1915, p. 220.

14. John Higham, *Send These to Me* (New York 1975), p. 208.

15. See John Roche, *In Quest for the Dream: The Development of Civil Rights and Human Relations in Modern America* (New York, 1963), pp. 86–87.

16. In Nicholas Appleton, *Cultural Pluralism in Education* (New York, 1983), p. 3.

17. See, for example, Ronald H. Bayor, *Neighbors in Conflict: The Irish, Germans, Jews, and Italians of New York City, 1929–1941* (Baltimore, 1978).

18. See Richard D. Alba, *Italian Americans: Into the Twilight of Ethnicity* (Englewood Cliffs, N.J., 1985).

19. Herbert M. Gans, "Symbolic Ethnicity: The Future of Ethnic Groups and

Cultures in America," *Ethnic and Racial Studies*, 2:1 (Jan. 1979). See also Steinberg, *The Ethnic Myth*, esp. pp. 44–74 *passim.*

20. Milton M. Gordon, *Assimilation in American Life* (New York, 1964), pp. 80–81.

21. See St. Clair Drake and Horace Cayton, *Black Metropolis: A Study of Negro Life in a Northern City* (New York 1945); Alan H. Speak, *Black Chicago: The Making of a Negro Ghetto, 1890–1920* (Chicago 1967); and the much more recent Nicholas Lemann, *The Promised Land: The Great Black Migration and How It Changed America* (New York, 1991). See also John H. Bracy, August Meier, and Elliot Rudwick, eds., *The Rise of the Ghetto* (Belmont, Calif., 1971).

22. See Pierre van den Berghe, *Race and Racism* (New York, 1967).

23. For a brief but pointed discussion of this phenomenon, see Gilbert Ofsofsky, *Harlem: The Making of a Ghetto, Negro New York, 1890–1930* (New York, 1964), esp. chap. 6 "The Other Harlem: Roots of Instability," pp. 81–91.

24. See Stanley Lieberson, *Ethnic Patterns in American Cities* (New York, 1963); and Karl E. Taeuber and Alma F. Taeuber, *Negroes in Cities: Residential Segregation and Neighborhood Change* (New York, 1965), esp. pp. 16–19.

25. James Baldwin, "The Harlem Ghetto," in *Notes of a Native Son*, ed. James Baldwin (Boston, 1955), pp. 57–72.

26. See Jim Sleeper, *The Closest of Strangers* (New York, 1990); Hillel Levine and Lawrence Harmon, *The Death of an American Jewish Community: A Tragedy of Good Intentions* (New York, 1992).

27. Raymond Mohl, "On the Edge: Blacks and Hispanics in Metropolitan Miami since 1959," *Florida Historical Quarterly* (July 1990): 69:1, 37–57.

28. K. Hugh Kim, "Blacks against Korean Merchants: An Interpretation of Contributory Factors," *Migration World*, 18(5):11–15 (1990); Susumu Awanohara and Shim Jae Hoon, "Melting Pot Boils Over" *Far Eastern Economic Review*, May 14, 1992, pp. 9–10.

29. Ralph Ellison, *Shadow and Act* (New York, 1953), p. 285.

30. Michael Harrington, *The Other America* (New York, 1962).

31. Kenneth B. Clark, *Dark Ghetto: Dilemmas of Social Power* (New York, 1965).

32. See, for example, Diana Ravitch, *The Great School Wars: New York City, 1805–1973: A History of the Public Schools as Battlefields of Social Change* (New York, 1974).

33. The Jules Feiffer Cartoon, from Robert Lantz, Candida Donadio Literary Agency, Inc., appears in Peter I. Rose, *They and We*, 2d ed. (New York, 1974), p. 79.

34. Martin Luther King, Jr., "I Have a Dream," *SCLC Newsletter*, 12:8 (September 1963).

35. See Jack Miles, "Blacks vs. Browns," *Atlantic*, 270(4):41–45, 48, 50–52, 54–68(Oct.1992).

36. Andrew Hacker, *Two Nations: Black, and White, Separate, Hostile, Unequal* (New York, 1992), p. 22.

37. See Martin Kilson, "Realism about the Black Experience," *Dissent* (Fall 1990), pp. 519–22, a response to Shelby Steele, "The Memory of Enemies: On the Black Experience in America," ibid. (Summer 1990), pp. 326–32.

38. Cose, *Nation of Strangers*, p. 219.

39. Glazer, "Politics of a Multiethnic Society," in his *Ethnic Dilemmas, 1964–1982* (Cambridge, Mass., 1971), p. 331.

40. Peter I. Rose, "Asian Americans: From Pariahs to Paragons," in *Clamor at the Gates: The New American Immigration*, ed. Nathan Glazer (San Francisco, 1985), pp. 181–212.

41. See David Rieff, *Los Angeles: Capital of the Third World* (New York, 1991).

42. Cose, *Nation of Strangers*, p. 219.

43. Seth Mydans, "Separateness Grows in a Scarred Los Angeles," *New York Times*, November 15, 1992. Copyright ©1992 by The New York Times Company. Reprinted by permission.

44. Milton M. Gordon, "Models of Pluralism: The New American Dilemma," in *America as a Multicultural Society*, ed. Milton M. Gordon, *The Annals of the American Academy of Political and Social Science*, 454 (March 1981): 187–88.

45. Ibid., p. 188. See also Bart Landry, "The Enduring Dilemma of Race in America," in *America at Century's End*, ed. Alan Wolfe (Berkeley, 1991), pp. 185–207 passim.

46. Arthur M. Schlesinger, Jr., *The Disuniting of America: Reflections on a Multicultural Society* (Knoxville, Tenn., 1991), p. 2.

47. W. E. B. Du Bois, *The Souls of Black Folk* (1903), as reprinted in *Three Negro Classics* (New York, 1965), p. 215.

48. Kallen, "Democracy versus the Melting Pot," p. 220.

49. Diane Ravitch, "Multiculturalism: E Pluribus Plures," *American Scholar*, 59 (3) (Summer 1990).

50. Ronald Takaki, "Multiculturalism: Battleground or Meeting Ground?" in *Interminority Relations in the U.S. Today: The Challenge of Pluralism*, ed. Peter I. Rose, *The Annals of the American Academy of Political and Social Science*, 530 (November 1993), pp. 109–121.

51. Schlesinger, *Disuniting of America*, p. 70. See also Dinesh D'Souza, *Illiberal Education: The Politics of Race and Sex on Campus* (New York, 1991).

52. Schlesinger, p. 76.

53. See, for example, Gunnar Myrdal, *An American Dilemma* (New York, 1944); E. Franklin Frazier, *The Negro in the United States* (New York, 1957), p. 680; Nathan Glazer and Daniel Patrick Moynihan, *Beyond the Melting Pot* (Cambridge, 1963), p. 53.

54. George M. Fredrickson, *The Arrogance of Race: Historical Perspectives on Slavery, Racism and Social Inequality* (Middletown, Conn., 1988).

Blaming the Jews

1. Seymour Martin Lipset and Earl Raab, *The Politics of Unreason* (New York, 1970).

2. Seymour Martin Lipset, "Jewish Fear, Black Sensitivity," *The New York Times*, March 9, 1990, A35.

3. As quoted in Paul Berman, "The Other and the Almost the Same," *The New Yorker*, February 28, 1994, p. 61.

4. Cecilia Stopnicka Heller and Alphonso Pinkney, "The Attitudes of Negroes toward Jews," *Social Forces* 43 (1965), 364–69; Peter I. Rose, "Blacks and Jews: The Strained Alliance," in *The Annals of the American Academy of Political and Social Science*, 454 (March, 1981), 55–69.

5. Tom Smith, *Jewish Attitudes Toward Blacks and Race* (New York, 1990); Mil-

ton D. Morris and Gary E. Rubin, "The Turbulent Friendship: Black-Jewish Relations in the 1990s," in *The Annals of the American Academy of Political and Social Science*, 530 (November 1993): 42–60.

6. Georg Simmel, *The Sociology of Georg Simmel*, ed. and trans. Kurt H. Wolff (Glencoe, Ill., 1950).

7. Ibid., p. 145.

8. Berman, "The Other and the Almost the Same," p. 62

9. Ibid., p. 64.

10. See Alice Kessler-Harris and Virginia Yans-McLaughlin, "European Immigrant Groups," in *Essays and Data on American Ethnic Groups*, ed. Thomas Sowell (Washington, D.C., 1978), pp. 107–137.

11. George M. Fredrickson, *The Arrogance of Race: Historical Perspectives on Slavery, Racism and Social Inequality* (Middletown, Conn., 1988).

12. See Andrew Hacker, *Two Nations: Black, White, Separate, Hostile, Unequal* (New York, 1992).

13. Philip S. Foner, "Black-Jewish Relations in the Opening Years of the Twentieth Century," *Phylon*, 36:4 (1975): 359.

14. James Baldwin, *Notes of a Native Son* (Boston, 1962), p. 125.

15. Norman Podhoretz, "My Negro Problem—and Ours," *Commentary*, February 1963, pp. 93–101.

16. Martin Luther King, *Where Do We Go From Here?* (New York, 1967), p. 92.

17. As quoted in Michael Berube, "Public Academy," *The New Yorker*, January 9, 1995, pp. 72–80.

18. Julius Lester, "A Response," in *Black Anti-Semitism and Jewish Racism*, ed. Nat Hentoff (New York, 1970), p. 232.

Caretakers, Gatekeepers, Guides, and Go-Betweens

1. Peter I. Rose,"Some Thoughts about Refugees and the Descendants of Theseus," *International Migration Review*, XV, 1–2, Spring-Summer 1981, 8–15.

In Whom They Trust

1. See G. L. Durlacher, *Strepen aan de hemel* (Amsterdam, 1985); and G. L. Durlacher, *Drenkeling: Kinderjaren in her Derde Rijk* (Amsterdam, 1987).

2. Samuel P. Oliner and Pearl M. Oliner, *The Altruistic Personality: Rescuers of Jews in Nazi Europe* (New York, 1989).

3. In a review essay on Avarham Tory's "Surviving the Holocaust: The Kovno Ghetto Diary," in which he discusses Tory's descriptions of Germans and Lithuanians and their treatment of Jews, and describes those Gentiles who tried to rescue Jews and were routinely executed, often along with their familes, Istvan Deak raises several important questions. Not least: "How many Americans [or others] could conceive of risking and even sacrificing their lives and those of their families for the sake of a stranger?" See Istvan Deak, "Heroism in Hell," *New York Review of Books*, November 8, 1990, 52–58.

4. Recently there has been a renewed interest not only in the rescuers but in the people they saved. A number of conferences by organizations such as the Anti-Defamation League's Jewish Foundation for Christian Rescuers have been held.

They had tended to focus on "The Hidden Child" stimulated, at least in part, by the late Louis Malle's feature film *Au Revoir Les Enfants* and Myriam Abramowicz's documentary *Comme Si C'etait Hier* ("As If It Were Yesterday"). For a discussion, see Jane Marks, "The Hidden Children," *New York Magazine*, February 25, 1991, pp. 39–46.

5. Some may have accepted payment as a means of defraying anticipated costs for food, bribes, etc., while others, probably very few, saw this as a way to benefit from the misery of others.

6. In the course of my research I was to meet several social scientists whose research, especially that aspect that deals with the politics of rescue in the U.S., paralleled my own. Most notable are the studies of Gilburt Loescher and John Scanlan, Norman and Naomi Zucker, and J. Bruce Nichols.

7. For a discussion of this general "type," see Roy Lubove, *The Professional Altruist: The Emergence of Social Work as a Career* (New York, 1983).

8. See Lubove, *The Professional Altruist.*

9. Teresa Hayter and Catherine Wilson, *Aid: Rhetoric and Reality* (London, 1985).

10. Barbara Harrell-Bond, *Imposing Aid: Emergency Assistance to Refugees* (Oxford, 1986).

11. Myles F. Harris, *Breakfast in Hell* (New York, 1987).

12. Gil Loescher and John Scanlan, *Calculated Kindness* (New York, 1986).

13. See Robert G. Wright, "Voluntary Agencies and the Resettlement of Refugees," *International Migration Review*, 53/54, 1981, 157–174; David S. North et al., *Kaleidoscope: The Resettlement of Refugees in the United States by Voluntary Agencies* (Washington, D.C., 1982); and Robert Gorman, "Private Voluntary Organizations in Refugee Relief," in *Refugees and World Politics*, ed. Elizabeth G. Ferris (New York, 1985).

14. A report of the excursions to Southeast Asia appears in this volume in Part II as "Caretakers, Gatekeepers, Guides and Go-Betweens" and "Long Night's Journey."

15. According to one researcher, Jeremy Hein, among those who were "refugee-refugee workers," a disproportionate number are those who had been members of "middleman minorities" prior to their own exodus. See Jeremy Hein, "State Incorporation of Migrants and the Reproduction of a Middleman Minority among Indochinese Refugees," *The Sociological Quarterly*, 29:3, 1992, 463–468.

16. The largest number returned were from those in the largest agency, the Migration and Refugee Service of the U.S. Catholic Conference, 169. This was 38 percent of the total number of initial returns. Fifty-two persons from the World Relief Refugee Service also responded as did 50 from the International Rescue Committee. There were 38 responses from the Hebrew Immigrant Aid Society; 29 from the Lutheran Immigration and Refugee Service; 17 from Church World Service; 16 from the American Council for Nationalities Services; 13 from the New York Association for New Americans; 8 from the YWCA and 7 from the Presiding Bishop's Fund for World Relief of the Episcopal Church. Fewer than 5 responses were received from those working for the other volags.

17. Many years ago, the same choices were offered to nursing students and licensed nurses in a study of nursing education. There, too, the checked responses turned out to be crucial indicators of self-perceptions and were good predictors of responses to a host of other questions. See Anne Hansen, Rodney F. White, and Peter

I. Rose, "Can More Nurses be Recruited?" *New York State Nurse*, 20, 1958, 5–9.

18. See discussion of the research of Samuel and Pearl Oliner on *The Altruistic Personality*, note 2.

19. See Morton Hunt, *The Compassionate Beast* (New York, 1989); also Alfie Kohn, *The Brighter Side of Human Nature: Altruism and Empathy in Everyday Life* (New York, 1990); and Leonard Berkowitz, "Helpfulness and Altruism," in *A Survey of Social Psychology*, ed. L. Berkowitz (New York, 1986).

20. A full report of the proceedings of the meeting and a summary of the discussions are published in Peter I. Rose, ed., *Working with Refugees* (Staten Island, N.Y., 1986).

The Vicars of the Volags

1. Aaron Levenstein, *Escape to Freedom* (New York, 1983).

2. James Carlin, *The Refugee Connection: A Lifetime of Running a Lifeline* (New York, 1989)